The Egalitarian Sublime

A Process Philosophy

JAMES WILLIAMS

EDINBURGH
University Press

Edinburgh University Press is one of the leading university presses in the UK. We publish academic books and journals in our selected subject areas across the humanities and social sciences, combining cutting-edge scholarship with high editorial and production values to produce academic works of lasting importance. For more information visit our website: edinburghuniversitypress.com

© James Williams, 2019, 2021

Edinburgh University Press Ltd
The Tun – Holyrood Road, 12(2f) Jackson's Entry, Edinburgh EH8 8PJ

First published in hardback by Edinburgh University Press 2019

Typeset in Garamond by Biblichor Ltd, Edinburgh

ISBN 978 1 4744 3911 4 (hardback)
ISBN 978 1 4744 3912 1 (Paperback)
ISBN 978 1 4744 3913 8 (webready PDF)
ISBN 978 1 4744 3914 5 (epub)

The right of James Williams to be identified as the author of this work has been asserted in accordance with the Copyright, Designs and Patents Act 1988, and the Copyright and Related Rights Regulations 2003 (SI No. 2498).

Contents

Acknowledgements	v
1 Introduction	1
2 Microcritique and the Sublime	8
Between historical objectivity and radical innovation	8
Microhistory	15
Method and the problem of exclusion	26
Patterns of fragments	32
3 Nietzsche Against the Egalitarian Sublime	36
Only for the few	36
The sublime as effect	40
Untimely, sublime	46
Sublime individuals against cohesive communities	52
Through the few, but for the many?	62
Individuals and masses	73
4 The Return to the Sublime	76
The search for value	76
Nostalgic social sublime	85
Diagrams of the technological sublime	90
The environmental sublime	98
5 Sublime Miseries	108
From high to low	108
Kant: equality in universality	115

	Schopenhauer's sublime consolations	121
	Žižek: a depressing lesson about horror and suffering	133
	The abject and egalitarian sublime	149
6	Defining the Egalitarian Sublime	155
	The sublime and egalitarian politics	155
	Unequal by definition	161
	Not after the sublime	173
7	Conclusion: The Sublime as Crisis	177
	Notes	181
	Bibliography	191
	Index	197

Acknowledgements

This research began with a conference on the sublime and music, run by Eddie Campbell at the University of Aberdeen in 2015. I am grateful to him for his encouragement and helpful suggestions. Over the next few years, I benefited from conversations with many friends and colleagues. I will single out Brian Smith, Tina Röck, Keith Ansell Pearson and Michael Wheeler, for an intellectual generosity that took me far beyond the areas I was most familiar with. Deakin University has provided me with an academic home, and my investigation into the sublime has been supported by colleagues at Deakin, Jack Reynolds, Sean Bowden and Jon Roffe, and their fellow Melburnians Maria Nichterlein and John Morss. The research continued with a series of seminars at Cologne University, in the summer term of 2016. Many of the ideas developed here can be traced back to debates with students and colleagues in Cologne. The book is dedicated to them as unwitting, perhaps unwilling, co-authors. The idea of *the* author persists and perhaps grows stronger in this age of name-driven and lightning-quick, if ephemeral, digital celebrity. One of the main ideas of my essay lies in the deception intrinsic to any definition of the sublime. The sublime obscures its own construction and the imposition of values it leads to. There is a similar deception in the author's name. It hides essential contributions by editors and copy-editors – my thanks go to Carol Macdonald and Tim Clark for their expertise and patience. The name also conceals a deep debt to the precious support system offered by libraries. Without the National Library of Scotland and its dedicated staff, this book could not have been written. The heart of my support systems is also the source of my deepest thoughts and feelings: Claire, Rebecca, Nathan and Al.

Chapter 1

Introduction

We call sublime all that is supposed to be the very best. What if the best is the worst? What if the best leads to inequality and exploitation? This book criticises the sublime, in its long history and recent turn back to sublime art and emotions. Demonstrating that the sublime has always led to inequality, through critical interpretations of Burke, Kant, Nietzsche, Schopenhauer and Žižek, and repudiations of recent environmental and technological sublimes, the book argues for an anarchist sublime: multiple, self-destructive and temporary, opposed to any idea of a highest value to be shared by all, but imposed on the powerless.

The sublime has always been a sign for the highest values, yet definitions of the sublime have also had social, cultural and political effects resulting in harsh and persistent inequalities. This is because, in historical cases, the way sublimity leads to superior values also implies a wide variety of distinctions around them. These distinctions entrench inequality in arriving at the highest. So a manner of searching for the most elevated values turns out to arrive at some of the worst political consequences.

Historically, and in recent thought, there is always the hope that superior values associated with the sublime will be long lasting. This is a dangerous wish, when the values and ways to them turn out to be divisive and damaging. Yet there have been no instances of the sublime free of this damage. Even when the aim is to share the highest values universally, the definitions of universal and of the sublime still retain their unequal effects. Even when guided by the purest of intentions, the process going from the production of the sublime by a few, to its imposition on the many, makes the aim of universal access to the best impossible.

In response, I will claim that if there is to be an egalitarian sublime, it will have to be anarchic: multiple, creative, self-critical and self-destructive.

It will have to work against systems giving rise to inequality, including those versions of the sublime implicated in unequal values. The sublime should also be subservient to a politics of equality, rather than a foundation for them. This is a sceptical version of the sublime. Since the sublime and values have always turned out badly, we should only follow the sublime and adopt values warily, looking to the decay and violence in them, and discarding them for others as they fail us. The sublime is only truly equal when it knows itself to be unequal.

For this sceptical sublime, value emerges in many different ways. This multiplicity is also a value: not one sublime but many. Does this mean the sublime is about individuals with different values competing with one another? This question misses the ideas of collective emergence and creation in the sublime. It also misses the point that value only makes sense when shared in some way. Though inequality and how to avoid it are deep challenges for any definition of the sublime, they are concerns because the highest values emerge and matter communally, across multiple, interconnected and shifting groups. Only thereafter do they serve to divide communities and individuals.

Why describe the sublime as production and creation? Historically, it has more often been defined as a kind of receptivity and passivity. The sublime happens to us. When it happens, the highest values are expressed and received, their certainty underwritten by the power of emotion. This line of thought misses three roles for production and creativity. First, if the sublime is simply received during the communication of value, why has it been necessary for writers to define and redefine it, in order to promote it? As an idea, the sublime has always been invented as well as experienced. Second, while the sublime is supposed to strike at passivity, it is also taken to be something we need to be readied for, in order to experience it. As such, it only stands out for active and educated forms of attention. Third, taken not from the side of the reception but from that of the sending, the sublime message or event emerges over time; it is crafted, or occurs in settings that have been shaped or manufactured. Even at its most natural, it is preserved, or reinstated, or designed. The sublime object is constructed over time.

This essay is therefore about how the sublime is made as unequal. It will be claimed that the sublime is fabricated when it is defined, as it has been from its very beginnings in classical rhetoric, right up to its modern and post-modern definitions. It will also be claimed that it is partly made when it is experienced. How it comes to hit us is prepared for and followed in creative ways. Finally, the sublime is made whenever the world is imagined differently and changed.

There is a feedback loop from definitions of the sublime, to ideas and values about how the world should be transformed and experienced, to unequal outcomes for those who inhabit that world – whether they be humans, other animals, plants or objects – and finally back to new attempts to get the sublime right. Value begets value, but not necessarily the value it wants, or pretends to want.

References to history are repeated here because work on the sublime is necessarily historical. It doesn't matter how much you believe you have defined a new sublime, your novelty is but a figure in a very long historical series. It is a daunting line to belong to, haunted by some of the most influential thinkers, where they often come closest to wretched and shameful conclusions, ending in racism, sexism, division between animals, belief in superiors among equals, and world-ending despair.

Even the most knowing recent moments in this history touch this baseness, when they reject the sublime, but leave the place of value vacant and ready for charlatans, cynics and nihilists. That's why this essay has a subplot tending towards the multiple, pessimistic, critical and self-destructive sublime, rather than concluding with its mere dismissal. We can't have done with value without inviting a return to discredited ideals that all wisdom should fear. This is one of the reasons the sublime is persistent. New thinkers keep returning to it, because getting our highest values wrong has such terrible consequences.

Behind the problem of the sublime, there is hence also a problem of history. What is the right way of telling, or collating, or recreating the history of an old and yet tenacious concept like the sublime? The essay begins with a chapter on historiography and method. In following ideas of microhistory, a relatively recent historical practice, it develops an approach called microcritique. This method alternates between close-up views of precise historical evidence, taken from many influential texts on the sublime, and wide spans of more speculative and suggestive vision, where the two perspectives inform, correct and transform each other, allowing no reduction to a single picture.

This is risky work, as shown by the contradictions latent in ideas of transformation of evidence, or in the redundancy implied by the correction of a vision. If evidence is fact or truth, why would we need speculation at all? The study of the methods of microhistory is designed to address this question, but that's not enough, because even if it can be answered satisfactorily, another more difficult problem remains. What is the right form of speculation? Is it story-making, the weaving of a narrative thread through history? Or is it a more scientific type of hypothesis, to be verified by the evidence, or a moral and legal judgement of history? Or perhaps it is a creative and artistic presentation, or maybe a debate within the confines of a carefully defined subject, with scholarly rules of engagement and representation?

The answer suggested here combines the analysis of definitions on the basis of historical interpretation, with the division and organisation of those definitions in terms of sets of concepts, and more speculative diagrams aiming to map the effects of those definitions, not only around those concepts, but much more widely on societies viewed in terms of equality. The method is to read, define, organise and map. It is necessarily a selective method. Not everything can be read. The definition will have to be reductive, as will the maps or diagrams. Many maps will be omitted. It's an essay.

Using ideas reflecting division and distinction, I will analyse the sublime through the effect of definitions. The complications of the concept are mirrored by the number and range of these ideas. They are: 'inside', 'outside', 'active', 'passive', 'individual', 'collective', 'multiplicity', 'classification', 'wild nature', 'tamed nature', 'urban spaces', 'catastrophe', 'spontaneous', 'inviting critique', 'repressing critique' and 'manufactured'. They appear in groups of four throughout the book, in simple diagrams mapping different versions of the sublime. The diagrams work together and they are followed by different interpretations. The variety of readings stems from the problem of value in the sublime. Since there are many different values there are also different views reflecting them.

A concept such as 'wild' occurs within a value system, sometimes invoking negative threats, at other times excitement and vivid existence. Even if we can draw a map of how a definition of the sublime pulls the world towards or away from wild nature, this is only a beginning, since we still need to decide on the value of wildness. Similarly, 'spontaneous' and 'manufactured' can stand for negative or positive values for the sublime, depending on whether we think something occurring naturally, as an immediate truth, is superior to a work of art, as a truth shaped by techniques and imagination.

In response to this uncertainty, the direction of the essay is set by the problem of egalitarianism. Is it possible to devise a theory of the sublime that does not lead to inequalities? The ideas of collective, individual, multiplicity and classification are important in deciding how the effects of the sublime include new classifications and boundaries between people, how they split us into individuals, or shape a new universal collective, or encourage multiple and unstable accounts of the sublime. Less directly, so are the ideas of critique, manufactured, catastrophe and active. They determine how the sublime is open to challenge, how it might be made to deceive, whether it builds on, responds to, or even leads to catastrophe, and how it implies activity or passivity.

The selection of egalitarianism brings order and priorities to the interpretations, but also weakness and prejudice to the reading. At no point will I question the value of egalitarianism itself. This is not because it is an unimportant and open question, but rather because I have chosen to take this premise as a way to approach the sublime. The relation between the sublime and equality is at once a central aspect of modern ideas of the sublime since Kant, and a little studied aspect of the historical sublime.

It is well understood how Kant's sublime leads to ideas of universal moral laws, yet a feature of recent work on the sublime concerns the extent to which his philosophy has a legacy of inequality and corrosive values. I will expand on these ideas to show how all philosophies of the sublime suffer from problems of inequality. Their definitions connect objects, nature, art, science, technology, emotions, ideas, actions and morals to our highest values, but they also imply deep and damaging distinctions. I will map out these links, while acknowledging that there are two more pressing demands beyond the scope of this study. How can we be equal politically? When will we be equal?

After these reflections on method, the close study turns to Nietzsche, in Chapter 3. His philosophy seems to be the least promising for egalitarianism, yet it puts forward a sophisticated and original definition of the sublime. Despite its statements of deep inequality between masses and superior sublime creators, his writing promises a future for humanity in the sublime. This contradiction will be approached through the idea of the untimely, another historical term closely matched to the sublime in his work.

As untimely, Nietzsche's sublime is predictive rather than descriptive. It foresees a different future thanks to the sublime. All definitions of the sublime have effects on their environments through their defence of different senses of value, but only some are explicit in departing from the temptation to use the sublime as a label, as a way of picking out some objects, natural features, individuals or artefacts in the world. Nietzsche is the strongest defender of the sublime as created rather than experienced.

In Chapter 4 the essay turns to two recent philosophies of the sublime that take the historical sublime and do something different and ambitious with it. In *American Technological Sublime*, David E. Nye defends a technological sublime allied to democracy. This sublime is experienced collectively and without recourse to high culture or theory. It promotes progressive values of social integration and improvement; for instance, in the joint experience of technological progress as presented in world fairs or national celebrations.

Responding to some of the most urgent ethical and political challenges of our age, in *The Sublime in Modern Philosophy: Aesthetics, Ethics and Nature*, Emily Brady advocates an ecological sublime. She argues that, timely rather than untimely in the Anthropocene, sublime experiences of nature and responses to them lead to moral attitudes where nature is respected and esteemed. Far from Nye's belief in the progressive potential of sublime technology – though he tempers this belief as technology gains in power – Brady nonetheless shares his commitment to the moral value of the sublime.

Among recent works on the sublime, Brady and Nye stand out for their renewal of the sublime in a social setting where we are brought together by sublimity, the values it instils in us, the energy it conveys, and its paths to a better world. The essay examines both philosophies closely, not only testing them as opportunities for equality, but also drawing out new concepts and maps of directions for understanding the effects of the sublime.

These positive and progressive recent approaches to the sublime are unusual. Though there has been a return to the sublime over the last four decades, the return is more in mourning and mistrust than full acceptance of the historical legacy of the sublime. After the environmental and technological sublimes, the essay turns to this more sceptical vein. Chapter 5 is on sublime miseries, or definitions of the sublime focusing on its negative consequences, as well as its unconscious basis. They are many, ranging from individual despair to collective disempowerment.

To understand the reaction against progressive ideas of the sublime, the chapter begins with Kant, a figure all turn to, and then turn against, in seeking to uncover how sublime enlightenment ideals were followed by centuries of horror, despite the application of those ideals to international moral and legal institutions and to individual morality. The rejection of Kant began in the nineteenth century, with Schopenhauer's exceptionally subtle, but ultimately doomed, definition of the sublime as an elevation away from the will.

Having by-passed Hegel, discussed briefly in the earlier chapter on technology and the environment, the chapter on misery turns back to him through his heir, Žižek. Žižek's philosophy can be seen as a relentless attack on the association of the sublime with the highest values. His critical view of the sublime is the culmination and closing moment for the sublime defined as universal. However, it is not the end of the road for the sublime. To show the potential for a multiple and internally conflicted definition of the sublime, the chapter closes with Kristeva's abject sublime, a refined and literary approach showing the way to new ways of thinking about the sublime after rejection of the universal and idealist traditions.

The final main chapter of the essay returns to the problem of equality. This time, the topic is the secondary position the sublime should take in relation to egalitarian political and economic aims and systems. Even when it is at its most egalitarian, the sublime must not be taken as the basis for an egalitarian society. Instead, its role is much more limited, involving criticism of the unequal tendencies of the sublime and a position within debates about values within wider egalitarian political systems.

Through the example of the exclusion of animals from the sublime, a return to the idea that the sublime is unequal by definition leads to greater scrutiny of how the manufacture of the sublime has direct and violent consequences, where its closeness to propaganda comes out most strongly. This appears not only in extreme examples but also in paradigmatic cases, such as Addison's praise for the natural sublime, where the sublime divides the world into leisured experience and hard toil.

Beyond brute propaganda and manipulation, the modern sublime is ideological and complicit in the most violent inequalities of modern thought. This occurs in Kant, not only in his racism, expressed in his early writing on the sublime, but also through the universality meant to guarantee equality, but instead promoting a particular ideology. The mechanics of this self-contradiction are studied through Adorno and his critique of negativity in the sublime.

If the sublime is to survive its own negative legacies, it must lose its claims to universality. There are no justified and universal superior values communicated by the sublime. Intense experience, driving existence beyond its limits according to new values, must be part of an anarchic and chaotic multiplicity, constantly reminded of the dangerous temptation to impose false distinctions and inequality on others.

Chapter 2

Microcritique and the Sublime

Between historical objectivity and radical innovation

The practice of calling certain things sublime and others not has a history of around two thousand years. Over the centuries, there have been grammatical definitions of the sublime, literary and religious reflections, empirical observations, rational deductions and historical summaries. Influential writers on rhetoric, poetry, literature, science, nature, philosophy, politics, religion, history, technology, architecture and art have turned to the sublime in order to express ideas they believe to be important.

Very few grand events or objects haven't been called sublime. The word covers natural phenomena such as avalanches as well as technological feats such as nuclear blasts. It is associated with internal experiences but also their external triggers, with inner turmoil and outer grandeur. When we have sought to describe impressive, troubling or awe-inspiring experiences, we have repeatedly turned to the idea, in contrast to lesser and tamer categories of value such as the beautiful, the pretty, the decorative or the pleasing. The sublime is therefore a well-worn, perhaps even tired concept, imprecise and general due to its long history and wide application, yet still often used when we need to indicate great significance.

Emily Brady describes this vagueness of the idea of the sublime as a loss of core meaning: 'But it also reveals a notion that, like other "big" ideas, has perhaps become too broad for its own good, losing its central meaning through its various transformations over the centuries and from treatment by so many different perspectives.'[1] The sublime has certainly become vague, but this is the fate of any ageing concept. They become mired in their own history. The deeper problem for a concept such as the sublime, for value, or for truth as anchor on reality, is that despite its vagueness it still matters and is taken to matter.

To new writers on the sublime, this combination of many different uses and yet similar claims to importance raises two persistent challenges, one constructive and the other critical. First, how can we be true to the history of the sublime while adapting the concept to new situations? Second, how can we be critical of different past uses of the sublime, yet remain faithful to their specific understanding of the idea?

For example, the earliest references to the sublime are about rhetoric, or how to compel an audience through excellence in discourse.[2] If we take definitions and distinctions from those classical writers to develop a modern line of thought, aren't we building with the wrong kind of blocks, ill-adapted to their new setting? If we critically apply definitions and values derived from later philosophy of art to those classical disputes, haven't we merely deployed a different frame of reference, rather than criticised the original term, or intervened cautiously in those already intricate debates?

The sublime also has a long history at the centre of debates between classical and modern values. Boileau, an influential seventeenth-century translator of Longinus into French, was, with Perrault and Fénelon, one of the main protagonists of the quarrel between ancients and moderns. Through his translation, and then in other works, Boileau sides with the ancients. Tracking the enduring importance of rhetoric, as anchor to an ancient and better world, Barbara Warnick describes how 'Boileau sought to criticise his contemporaries and to show how far French poetical production had departed from ancient poetry.'[3] This places the sublime at the heart of conflicts between ancient, proven and established values, and those of the new, with all the political implications of these struggles.

Contradicting his claims to the highest values, but confirming the social and political implications of claims to superiority, Boileau's style can be mean-spirited and lowly; as for instance in his satire on women, *Satire X, sur les femmes*. By attacking the shallow wiles and fleeting virtues of women, he criticises the moderns and their patrons, the *salonnières* holding Parisian intellectual *salons*, where new works and ideas were exchanged and discussed: 'There, fake wits take office: there, all verses are good, so long as they are new.'[4] This denigration of women, especially if they make claims to higher values or positions, is a constant in the history of the sublime. Quarrels between ancients and moderns continued beyond France, still with the sublime at their centre; for example in Wren's church architecture, where sublime Baroque spaces are influenced by the desire to 'combine rational inference with the testimony of the ancients'.[5]

Two responses to these challenges give us opposed poles with which to judge other instances of the sublime. We can think of these extremes as ideal tendencies. They are at different ends of a scale, where no actual work goes right to those excesses, but where each contribution to the sublime can be situated in relation to them. On the one hand, we can aim for total historical comprehensiveness and accuracy, detailing the many different positions covered over two millennia, but refusing to conflate any of them for fear of incorrectness or reduction. I'll call this pole 'historical objectivity'. On the other hand, we can discard past reflections on the sublime and aim for something completely new, perhaps by appending a novel epithet such as 'digital' to refer to the sublime afforded by new digital simulations in film and games with their imaginary landscapes and terrors. I'll name this 'radical innovation'.

Peter Adamson's podcast and book project *A History of Philosophy Without Any Gaps* is a good example of historical objectivity in operation. It also explains why I am using the idea of tendencies somewhere between objectivity and innovation to describe the challenges of writing about the complete history of the sublime and why I am eschewing simple judgements about these tendencies. One of Adamson's goals is to show the historical importance of philosophers often judged to be minor or simply ignored. Given this important aim, his approach of relative completeness and wish to 'avoid skipping from highlight to highlight' makes sense.[6] However, this explicit aim is also part of his approach and of our understanding of it. This means Adamson's work is not meant to replace new and more general interpretations, but instead to inform them and help to avoid damaging omissions when a broader line of argument is made.

When not taken strictly on its own terms, each of the extremes has weaknesses. In trying to be as respectful as possible to differences, historical objectivity is at risk of settling on a definition of the sublime too encompassing to allow for precise analysis. The sublime becomes another name for great, grand or powerful. As a consequence it is no longer possible to use the term in a constructive and novel manner. A comprehensive survey of the history of the sublime can be given, but the survey leads to no further use.

The danger for radical innovation, in its desire to break with the past, is to cut away from an essential aspect of the sublime. The new theory makes a claim for a different and important idea, but in fact loses sight of what mattered about the sublime in the first place. For instance, after Burke, the sublime has frequently been defined through an oscillation or tension between opposites: delight and terror, pleasure and pain. If we now manufacture a concept where these difficult oppositions are missing, we are in danger of losing one of the most important modern intuitions about the sublime, its propensity to cause attraction and repulsion at the same time and thereby to introduce a split state into experience.

Like makers of shoddy revivals, we might think we have done something new and interesting through innovation, when we have in fact simply impoverished a valuable line of thought. For the digital sublime this error could be to confuse the amazement provoked by computer-generated imagery with the much more powerful emotions of Romantic experience, mistaking the pleasure at a well-filled screen with the joy and fear of crossing mountain ranges at real physical risk. To the Romantics our digital sublime would be merely beautiful, since it is lacking in awe-inspiring bodily effects – at least until films and games directly threaten real lives through artificial simulations, where the watcher is put at risk, rather than the protagonists.

In addition to the flaws under inspection from external viewpoints, the tendencies of historical objectivity and radical innovation could be seen to fail on their own terms. Given the range and differences of historical appeals to the sublime, objectivity can rapidly fall into nominalism, a description of many types of the sublime, descending into ever more fine-grained distinctions but with no valid appeal to the general concept of the sublime to bring them under.

In a literary setting, the most thorough and illuminating recent historical study of the sublime is by Robert Doran. His work on Longinus, Boileau and Kant (among many others) is a cautious response to the problem of tracking the origins of the sublime and assessing whether a firm meaning can be ascribed to the idea even at its beginnings. For example, in searching for antecedents to Longinus (or pseudo-Longinus, given the uncertainties of authorship), Doran shows its Greek roots and demonstrates how these also contain the emotion of terror that will come in and out of favour in defining the sublime from thereon: 'Thus the idea of the "sublime" as an aestheticized terror at the limit of the sacred has its roots in the Greek terms Longinus uses to describe the experience of sublime intensity.'[7]

Doran's philological and literary critical approaches are highly effective responses to the problem of the variety of the sublime. Over the course of this chapter, I will argue for a different historical approach counter to the critical unity Doran finds in the sublime in contending that 'the sublime possesses an intrinsic critical function, and that an argument for its unity can be launched from the perspective of the theory of sublimity itself'.[8] The difference is about the effects of the sublime on wider conceptions of value and the political implications of those effects. Doran's study is an outstanding resource, but the consistency it finds in the sublime is one of critical and literary lines, internal debates, legacies, borrowings, responses and variations on a critical term. I am interested in the ways in which the different definitions of the sublime lead to different ideas of value and to contrasting political implications, in particular around the possibility of an egalitarian sublime.

This is not to deny the importance of an intrinsic critical approach, but rather to reflect on how intrinsic differences and definitions lead to differences in extrinsic implications and in how a term should be taken and judged extrinsically. It is important to understand how the idea of the sublime grew and evolved in a critical context, but it is more important to follow how this evolution changed the world around it and how it continues to do so. Even if the latter depends in part on the former, the unity found in the first can shatter into disunity when studied through the external effects of the definitions and approaches it unifies. Furthermore, intrinsic critical lines have a portent and scope that turn them from literary refinements into social and cultural forces, often at odds with one another and presenting new challenges for the question of what we should do with the sublime now. That question is behind my search for a method quite distant from Doran's.

As an example of this divisive profusion of sublimes, in a survey restricted to religion and the sublime, Andrew Chignell and Matthew Halteman list four main types of the religious sublime, with many subdivisions: the theistic sublime, with conversion, or corroboration, or transformation; the spiritualistic sublime; the dymythologistic sublime; and the nontheistic sublime, with abandonment of belief, or rejection of a doctrine, or evil as abjection.[9] Chignell and Halteman go on to note the conflicts this profusion gives rise to: 'Given the various ways in which the sublime relates to the religious, it is no surprise that some people will regard one or more of these models as having exciting theoretical and practical consequences, whereas others will view that same model with scepticism, suspicion, or even alarm.'[10] Writing about the Romantic sublime, Samuel H. Monk summarises the problem: 'No single definition of the term would serve in any single decade for all writers, for such unanimity was never attained; but the word naturally expressed high admiration, and usually implied a strong emotional effect, which, in the latter years of the century, frequently turned on terror.'[11]

Endless descriptions lacking a critical and creative overview are the main weakness of nominalism. Even when it hazards a general definition, it turns out to be vague, lacking in critical discernment and invention. A particular school of the sublime, such as that of the British empiricists, would then be subdivided not only between different thinkers, but among periods for each thinker, then works, then sublime objects, then types of subject, and their subtly different experiences. As the historical description gains in accuracy, it loses itself in endless subdivisions. A truth that might serve some purpose disappears into a chaos of names, with a blunt general definition covering them.

Conversely, radical innovation is in danger of making an absolute break with historical versions of the sublime, to the point where it leads to a misnomer. At worst, this would mean that the name 'sublime' is used parasitically and illegitimately, its historical resonances operating in the background of a new and in fact unrelated idea. The new term draws strength from the old one, but in fact has no right to it.

Santayana's adage on the necessity of continuity for progress, from his *The Life of Reason*, warns of the risks of radical breaks: 'Progress, far from consisting in change, depends on retentiveness. When change is absolute there remains no being to improve and no direction is set for possible improvement: and when experience is not retained, as among savages, infancy is perpetual. Those who cannot remember the past are condemned to repeat it.'[12] A complete cut with the past is always self-defeating, since the clean break dooms any possibility of wise judgement. In relation to the sublime, this logic underestimates the value of chance encounters and inflates the power of wisdom. The experience of the sublime can be a chance for a new life and for new ideas when past wisdom has failed us. This is also true for new definitions of the sublime, with their potential for indicating new values and dispensing with old ones.

There is also a contradiction in Santayana's example, where he fails to learn from his own argument by describing 'savages' as failing to retain experience. Historical evidence points to the experience of hunter-gatherers and their deep learning about how to live on the land, in close-knit and interdependent groups, often in violently inhospitable climatic and natural conditions, where the unreliability of any single food supply is the norm.

Robert Suzman describes the success of hunter-gatherers through an egalitarianism based on avoiding jealously thanks to the redistribution of plentiful food from the few to the many:

> Ju/'hoansi are not alone in their aggressive rejection of hierarchy. This deep sense of egalitarianism is so widespread among hunter-gatherers that it cannot be simply dismissed as an arbitrary cultural trait. Egalitarianism played a role in ensuring that the Khoisan became the most stable population group in human history just as it must have played a role in enabling Homo Sapiens to expand so rapidly and easily at the expense of other hominids everywhere.[13]

If we take account of this later research, Santayana's remark is doubly wrong. It is false to claim that 'savages' are unsuccessful and it is false to claim that they lack common memory. To take account of this, we need to change both what we count as success and what we count as memory.

Earlier communities did not and could not easily forget their past. Former experiences – woven into oral tradition – were a condition for survival. Nineteenth-century Arctic explorers died close to peoples living successfully on the same ice that was killing the more technologically advanced outsiders. The remains and fate of Sir John Franklin's third 'finely outfitted and trained' expedition that ended in starvation in 1848 are partly known through Inuit accounts.[14] The Inuit survived where Franklin and his men perished: '[The Canadian Arctic explorer] Stefansson concluded that the chief failure of the Franklin expedition, and other nineteenth-century British explorers of the Arctic, was in their refusal to respond to the harsh environment by adopting the survival techniques employed by the Inuit.'[15] Forgetting without carefully reflecting on why you would want to forget is a modern failing, caused by our overconfidence in the future and our doomed power over it. We now know that Santayana's lesson can be reversed. We moderns have much to learn about sustainable living based on the experience of so-called primitive communities. They could have taught us about life, but we often brought new ways of dying to them (and to ourselves).

I am drawing attention to these dangers and risks as a lesson for method. My aim of arguing for an egalitarian sublime seems to fall foul of all the mistakes I have warned of when defining historical objectivity and radical invention. The idea of an egalitarian sublime appears to be at odds with most, if not all, of the past definitions of the sublime. It is also out of step with both earlier and new definitions of the egalitarian, such as Suzman's description of an egalitarianism based on give and take around unpredictable and irregular rhythms of plenty and need.[16]

The difference between the egalitarian sublime and earlier definitions of the sublime is one of my main claims. This means both flaws that affect theories of the sublime are likely to apply to the idea of an egalitarian sublime: it might well fail as a critical approach to historical positions; it might also fail to count as a theory of the sublime and of egalitarianism at all. How can an egalitarian sublime claim to have any critical validity for earlier ideas of the sublime? Why embark on the project to define an egalitarian sublime, if this means breaking with past uses?

The deep problem here is not about definitions, but about methods. I have defined historical objectivity and radical innovation as responses to the challenge of constructive and critical approaches to a longstanding and broad concept of the sublime, but these definitions are in effect descriptions of methods. Objectivity and innovation are methodical ways of reacting to and building on the past. They are not positions; they are interventions.

It is easy to think of method as the dull part of study, something we have to do to get things right. Once we have them right, bury the method and never speak of it again. It is wrong to do so, though, since method is the connection between the problems of enquiry and its outcomes. When we forget or conceal method, we turn away from the very reason research matters: to allow us to continue to work through shared problems in new and better ways.

I began by defining theories of the sublime as practices, because they are experimental methods. The failings described above are weaknesses of the methods supporting definitions of the sublime, where objectivity gets caught in overly intricate and disparate analyses of different cases and where innovation falls into the trap of assuming continuity in absolute difference. The difficult problem for a philosophy of the egalitarian sublime is therefore whether there is a method suitable for working on it, and whether this method can be free of the flaws of extreme objectivity or innovation. How can an egalitarian philosophy approach the sublime?

Microhistory

The problem of method in the search for an egalitarian sublime is a problem of historiography, or of the 'writing of history'.[17] George Iggers extends this dictionary definition of the term in two ways: '(1) to refer to the study of the history of historical writing as distinct from the writing of history; and (2) to refer to the concern with theoretical and methodological questions that relate to historical writing'.[18] The second definition matters most for the problem of the sublime, where historiography is about problems of method and theory.

Even after this narrowing down of definitions, historiography remains a vast field. Iggers' remarks come from his Foreword to Susan Kinnell's annotated bibliography of the term; her research stretches to 8,772 entries across two volumes (in 1987). I don't propose to cover this daunting topic in full. Instead, I will follow one group of historians, mainly through a single member, Carlo Ginzburg, well known for his book on heresy, *The Cheese and the Worms*. It will become apparent, over the course of this essay, that this close focus reflects what I have adopted from Ginzburg. The plan is not to judge his work as history, but to learn from it as a model for philosophical method as it applies to the sublime.

I admire Ernst Breisach's view on clear-cut judgements about historiography: 'once the link between history writing and the human condition is grasped in all its complexity, simple solutions vanish'.[19] Like philosophy, historiography is the product of deeply felt consideration of the human condition, whereas definite judgements are a trade-off between the desire to have settled decisions, preferably ones that benefit ourselves, and the resistance of subjects and conditions to distinct categories, such as 'responsible' and 'innocent'. Who is fully innocent and who is guilty without mitigation, if our worlds are complex products of communal activity and shared evolution?

For my work on the sublime, the primary task of method is not judgement but learning as a ground for action; where to learn without judgement is the best way to maintain a cautious relation to the past. It is about reflection on the disputes of historiography, as debates connecting problems of method to ethical and political engagement. An example of this interaction of method and practice can be taken from the German *Historikerstreit*. Beginning in the mid-1980s, this was a series of historical, political and philosophical arguments about whether the Nazi past should be maintained as part of German identity in the present and, if so, how best to remember that past for Germany's future.

The *Historikerstreit* was a problem of method as well as a moral debate, since if history detects an entanglement of culture and politics, rather than simply recording the acts of a particular set of politicians and soldiers, then Nazi violence could be seen to remain latent in contemporary and future thought. Forms of cultural memory could then be as important as historical records for future remembrance.[20] There are many examples of such cultural testimony in post-war German art and literature; for instance, in Anselm Kiefer's re-inscriptions of Germany's Jewish past and memories of the Holocaust:

> A Jewish mystical and intellectual past and tradition emerge out of the shadowy chambers of the cellar space, introducing into the visual, linguistic and acoustic landscape of postwar Germany the absent other, the Jew, signified in the foreign sounds of the Hebrew language – the word *Merkaba* – and in the remote and esoteric traditions of Jewish mysticism – Kabbalah.[21]

In a penetrating discussion, dedicated to Kiefer, Peter Sloterdijk studies the tension between historical redundancy and the duty of memory through different definitions of the sublime. For Sloterdijk, the classical sublime 'has no future and will only survive in those omnipresent famous caricatures fit for mass culture as horror, tension and distortion'.[22] The classical sublime of awe, immensity and grandeur, often associated with gods, has no place in modernity, other than in the cultural simplifications of horrifying events such as war, violence and ecological disaster rendered as forms of mysterious power worthy of awe and terror. This recent mock-classical sublime is a twofold distortion, hiding the complex nature of events and turning us away from their sources in human actions, ideas and natural causes. When simplified and half-forgotten in this way, the classical sublime becomes politically repressive.

There is an intriguing resonance between the works in the collection Sloterdijk is contributing to and the themes of the invisibility of battles and of the contradictory aims of founding and warning against nations. Both turn out to be important for Ginzburg's argument. In his series of woodcuts about the Battle of Hermann, Kiefer connects the defeat of Roman legions in the Teutoburg forest in 9 CE to Nazi propaganda around German myths and historical figures. The Battle of Hermann only becomes visible, and only partly, when its mythical effects are brought into modern culture and violence.[23] Not only are great battles impossible to see in full, they also only come into view when serving new conflicts and interests, above all those of propaganda.

For Sloterdijk, there is another sublime retaining contemporary significance: 'the second residue of the sublime, the sense of the Higher per se that should remain as indefinite as long as possible in order to avoid the instantly religious never gets completely submerged for all the profanities and de-sublimations'.[24] Independent of any given sublime power or object, there is also a feel for higher values as ways beyond a world devoid of superior causes or reasons, left with only base interests and neutral forces. This sublime must resist religious and natural representations, while preserving a sense for higher purpose and value.

In the search for an egalitarian sublime, Sloterdijk is taking risks in attaching the new sublime to 'the Higher'. Ideas of height, exceptional standing and collective assent, indicated by the capital letter and definite article, are already on the way to divisiveness, exclusivity and hierarchy, and hence also to their mundane distortions. Against *the* Higher, the egalitarian sublime seeks difference rather than division, democracy rather than exclusivity, and multiplicity rather than hierarchy. Nevertheless, Sloterdijk's analysis touches on a methodological problem that is persistent for the sublime. How can we be both against and for the sublime? It also identifies the critique required for ideas borrowed from a tainted past. How can we carry the past forward guardedly?

In answering these questions, my aim is to learn from the method Ginzburg and others have described as microhistory. Despite its name, the method should not be understood as simply working on limited objects, details or minutiae. On the contrary, as defined and practised by Ginzburg, through techniques contrasting micro and macro views, microhistory responds to the difficulty of writing about periods and topics defying a single overview. The object of study is resistant to homogeneous representation because it is constituted by heterogeneous elements. This heterogeneity is a challenge to microhistory, as an attempt to encompass fragments and their sum, a problem inherited from the old but persistent philosophical puzzles of mereology.[25] The challenge corresponds to the problem facing an account of the full sweep of works on the sublime, since a general theory fails to do justice to the components making up the complete topic. A different approach is required, and that's what microhistory can help us with.

In his essay 'Microhistory: Two or Three Things that I Know about It', Ginzburg gives an astute description of the difficulties calling for microhistory.[26] He begins with a remark about the impossibility of gaining a single view of a battle. The whole conflict remains invisible, except in great visionary works, such as Altdorfer's Renaissance painting *The Battle of Alexander at Issus*.[27] Altdorfer combines highly detailed fractions of the battle, painterly qualities such as the symbolic use of colour, focus and texture, overstated contrasts between scales and topics, mythical and religious themes, and natural and imaginary landscapes into an overall vision. Visibility emerges through the artistic composition of heterogeneous local and large-scale fragments.

Describing the painting, Christopher Wood follows the complexity and originality of Altdorfer's techniques for rendering the battle: 'The upper half of the *Battle of Alexander* expands with unreal rapidity into an arcing panorama comprehending vast coiling tracts of globe and sky.'[28] The panorama is the large-scale battle, but it is only captured through interactions between different dimensions: 'It is as if the momentous collision of armies exploded outwards into three dimensions, and was only then projected back onto the planar surface.'[29] This to-and-fro between different scales, dimensions and realms is the narrative basis for microhistory.

The past is retold through difficult compositions, rather than single images. These compositions cohere thanks to abstract diagrams and imagination: 'Only an abstract diagram or a visionary imagination such as Altdorfer's can convey a global image of [the battle].'[30] The most important point is that, without settling on a single dimension, the diagrams work dynamically, that is, through unresolved backward and forward, and inwards and outwards, movements: 'A close-up look permits us to grasp what eludes a comprehensive viewing, and vice versa.'[31] Though Ginzburg contrasts the abstraction of the diagram with the visionary quality of the artist's imagination, both compositions must be seen as artistic, in the sense of creative and experimental. They are series of different and incomplete essays at history, instead of increasingly accurate versions on the way to an ideal representation. The aim is to communicate with the past rather than reproduce it.

Wood's remark on the unreality of movement in Altdorfer's painting is challenging for Ginzburg's adoption of it as a model for history. If the painting makes a real battle unreal, how can it stand as a model for a discipline that ought to come as close to past reality as possible? There is a clue in the idea of possibility. If it isn't possible to bring back the real past, except by appealing to techniques departing from reality, then the problem isn't about mimicking any supposed form of the real, but rather about how best to work with the past in creative ways. If that's the case, then retaining a supposedly homogeneous and well-ordered form for reality might be exactly the wrong way to return to the past. Copying according to a strict formal representation of the real might in fact introduce greater distortions than diagrammatic narratives and painterly techniques.

Altdorfer's art and Ginzburg's microhistory break with linear time and regular space to achieve a better retelling of the relation between the whole and its heterogeneous parts. For Wood, the painting of the battle expresses much more than a set of objective facts understood as changes in the occupation of space-time locations such as 'Alexander was here' and 'Darius was there'. It narrates historical turning points, forces, clashes and changes in direction: 'For the picture represents an historical pivot, the expulsion of a force from the East, a muscular resistance to the left-to-right flow of history.'[32] These effects are a translation of the battle's complex unfolding and many-layered quality; not only a meeting of two armies, but the wider destiny of empires and the narrower fate of particular actors: *the movement from East to West turned on these clashing events around these individuals.*

The motivations of Altdorfer's narrative are contemporary as well as historical. In referring back to the earlier defeat of Persian forces, during the later Siege of Vienna in 1529, Altdorfer is providing hope to his contemporaries for relief from the threat of Suleiman the Magnificent's Ottoman rule. This interdependence of narration, contemporary relevance, evidence and truth is a constant concern in Ginzburg's work. When making his initial remark about the invisibility of battles, he alludes to two themes important for his research and for the problem of history, yet always treated in a discrete and often tangential manner in his books and essays. This obliqueness should not be confused with disinterest. The subject matter is at the heart of his historical commitments, but it must be studied through secondary manifestations.

The first theme is propaganda and its relation to evidence. The invisibility of battles allows for deceitful manipulation. Ginzburg gives the First Gulf War as an example of the creation of the battle through propaganda and media control: 'A battle, strictly speaking, is invisible, as we have been reminded (and not only thanks to military censorship) by the images televised during the Gulf War.'[33] The war was presented through live video images from US bombers and virtual reconstructions that gave the impression of conflict without ever showing the full ground battle or wider aspects of the war, such as the sabotaging of control systems and the grounding of Iraqi planes, or the earlier US military and financial support for Iraq in its war with Iran, which had helped Iraq become a dangerous regional power.[34]

Ginzburg has a distinctive reading of the potential for propaganda in the invisibility of battles and history more widely. He turns down familiar but caricatured responses to the invisibility of history and its potential for falsification. He is a critic of the postmodern abandonment of truth and reality, but he also rejects the positivist insistence on objective reality, exclusively accessible through scientific methods. These positions are caricatures because, on both sides, every sophisticated reflection on the problem involves recognition of some role for objectivity and some risk of distortion in any narrative or presentation of facts. This means opponents tend towards a middle ground, when we cut away from the posturing of general debates and look at practice. Pure absence of truth and pure objectivity are abstractions, substituting misleading problems about absolutes for the pragmatic problem of how best to blend truthfulness and invention in order to connect past, present and future.

However, the surprising aspect of Ginzburg's position is his resistance to the middle ground between strong relativism and positivism. He searches for an apparently contradictory combination of strong obligations to evidence and to narrative invention. Instead of drifting towards the middle ground, microhistory connects rigorous commitment to the extremes. This merger of deep obligation to evidential proof and yet abandonment of brute objective reality in favour of speculation makes microhistory different and notable, since it involves a joint transformation and intensification of what other approaches view as incompatible approaches.

Narrative has as an ambiguous relation to propaganda and to its violent consequences. For Ginzburg, narrative is necessary, because it is the way to relate the whole and its fragments. It is also a tool of propaganda since it allows events to be manipulated. The solution to this contradiction can be found in how the historian employs evidence. Ginzburg reflects on this in his meditation on proof and rhetoric, *History, Rhetoric and Proof: The Menahem Stern Jerusalem Lectures*. His central point is that sources are neither simple positive facts nor hopelessly opaque misrepresentations: 'Sources are neither open windows, as the positivists believe, nor fences obstructing vision, as the skeptics hold: if anything we could compare them to distorting mirrors.'[35] These mirrors call for a constructive combination of narrative and evidence: 'The analysis of the specific distortion of every specific source already implies a constructive element.'[36]

In Ginzburg's histories, there are many examples of how to achieve this combination of evidence and constructive narration in critical work against propaganda. His analysis of the role of the arrival of the relics of St Stephen on Minorca demonstrates how the passage from the veneration of the Maccabees to the veneration of Stephen was the condition for religious violence against the Jews.[37] The careful disentanglement of Maurice Joly from guilt in the writing of the *Protocols of the Elders of Zion* shows how a modest and speculative tracing of textual connections can still arrive at significant conclusions: 'Imagining an omnipotent individual who models society in accordance with his own wishes, Joly involuntarily made possible the deplorable, posthumous fortune of the *Dialogue aux Enfers*. The compilers of the *Protocols* poured the materials from Joly's work into a pre-existing mould, the delusional Jewish conspiracy.'[38] The mark of Ginzburg's narrative is in the idea of 'making possible'. It is a speculative connection required for the telling of uncertain connections among many texts and authors. The effect of evidence in Ginzburg's critical analysis is in the judgement on Joly ('involuntarily') that counters accusations making him an author of the *Protocols*. This is the kind of judgement we learn from, rather than rest with.

Ginzburg turns down the attraction of positivist and relativist extremes in his study of Natalie Zemon Davis's *The Return of Martin Guerre*. Reviewing this influential work of microhistory, he draws attention to the compatibility of narration and evidence-based knowledge: 'a greater awareness of the narrative dimension does not imply a weakening of the cognitive possibilities of historiography, but rather, to the contrary, their intensification'.[39] His argument depends on a sense of narrative invention as a careful threading of evidence and speculation based on possibility, where to invent does not mean to create freely: 'The term "invention" is deliberately provocative, but somewhat deceiving.'[40] To invent is to speculate on the possible on the basis of evidence.

Davis acknowledges Ginzburg and another important microhistorian, Emmanuel Le Roy Ladurie, at the beginning of her book.[41] In an evocative metaphor, she goes on to explain how her research combines creative narration and evidence from the past: 'What I offer you here is in part my invention, but held tightly in check by the voices of the past.'[42] According to Ginzburg, Davis's history 'is not based on the juxtaposition between "true" and "invented," but on the integration, always scrupulously noted, of "reality" and "possibility"'.[43] This appeal to possibility alongside certainty puts Ginzburg's interpretation of Davis at odds with the thesis set out by Sigurður Gylfi Magnússon and István M. Szijártó that 'Microhistory is therefore, according to Levi or Davis, first and foremost a tool to discard deterministic history.'[44] This principled negation is contrary to microhistory, if it is understood as tentative speculation shaped by evidence, including evidence for causal relations.

For Ginzburg, the point is to combine determination and potential difference, rather than oppose individual or micro indeterminacy to large-scale determinism. Here, reality should be understood as historical evidence and speculation about possibilities. Narration connects threads in ways that are consistent with each piece of evidence, yet also dependent on surmising what might have happened. The challenge for a philosophy of the sublime, inspired by this version of microhistory, is how to interpret evidence and possibility for a concept-based study, rather than a history of acts and events.

The reference to the invisibility of the First Gulf War calls to mind a notorious instance of so-called postmodern excess from Jean Baudrillard's newspaper articles and essays collected as *The Gulf War Did Not Take Place*. In his introduction to the collection, Paul Patton refutes the easy conclusion that Baudrillard is absurdly denying the reality of the war. On the contrary, he is arguing for an augmented kind of reality that takes account of the role of manufactured images and virtual realities in constituting our experiences of events: 'we live in a hyperreality which results from the fusion of the virtual and the real into a third order of reality'.[45] Patton is arguing against

Christopher Norris and his failure to distinguish between arguing for the role of virtual images in the constitution of reality and arguing for the negation of 'all distinctions between truth and falsehood'.[46] One does not follow from the other and there is plenty of evidence that Baudrillard makes truth claims, including when he is arguing for hyperreality.

The idea of the hyperreal is a challenge to theories based on a concrete and material reality, since it adds a virtual component to it. Definitions of the sublime are also challenged by the hyperreal. The sublime has often been defined in relation to natural events and landscapes, but in the hyperreal it is associated with virtual techniques and effects. The shock and awe warfare of the First Gulf War is described as sublime and as inducing a sublime experience for the television viewer, because it combines terror and attraction at a safe distance from causes. This is at odds with claims that the sublime should involve real threat, but consistent with Kant's definition, where terror is not fear but rather an imaginary projection – a 'What-if?' reflection rather than an overwhelming and direct 'Run away!' In following Ginzburg's method, the aim of my study of the sublime is to combine evidence from different theories of the sublime with new diagrams of their relations and the potential for an egalitarian sublime.

It is important to separate the idea of a sublime safe distance from destruction from the notion that there is no destruction. Baudrillard is not claiming the latter and should not be taken as supporting the idea of a clean or surgical war. When Tanine Allison says that Baudrillard's 'description neglects the massive destruction on the ground' it is a misrepresentation of his argument.[47] Baudrillard is describing the television images and the armchair experience of modern warfare, not the horror on the ground. In fact, when Baudrillard claims the war did not take place he is supporting Allison's critique of the dangerously detached sublime of Second World War video games and films. The points he is drawing our attention to are: who it did not take place for, how it did not take place, and why.

In discussing Baudrillard, Norris speaks of an 'out-and-out sceptical mistrust of truth claims' but then contradicts this claim in admitting that Baudrillard frequently uses the constative register, dependent on truth claims.[48] It is perfectly consistent to make truth claims while criticising other false claims to truth and speculating about what kind of reality these commit us to. Scepticism is not a denial of truth. It is a means to investigate how truth can be manipulated. This is important for the search for an egalitarian sublime, since the control and manufacture of sublime falsehoods has been and will continue to be a way of maintaining power thanks to the opportunities of war and conflict.

Once we dismiss one-dimensional readings of Baudrillard, it is possible to see points of contact with Ginzburg. Baudrillard's concluding remarks about the war are theories about its real aims: 'The crucial stake, the decisive stake in this whole affair is the consensual reduction of Islam to the global order.'[49] There is a wider plan underlying the stated aims of defeating Saddam Hussein after his invasion of Kuwait: to create a general consensus around the reduction of Islam within the Western democratic and economic order. Whether we think this is true or not, the idea of an ultimate stake of the war, to be connected to the evidence of how it was prosecuted and presented, is in the realm of matters of possibility that Ginzburg adds to matters of evidence.

The kind of speculative argument put forward by Baudrillard is a thesis that could be examined and perhaps strengthened, if we adopt interactions between large and small-scale perspectives, allied to careful evidence gathering. The deeper lesson I want to retain isn't in the exact correspondence between the two thinkers. It lies in the potential of methods from microhistory to bridge between evidence and speculation using narrative and diagrammatical techniques, dynamic mappings of the effects of definitions of the sublime.

The reference to the Gulf War is also a clue to the second background theme to Ginzburg's microhistory: historiography cannot and should not seek to escape engagement with contemporary problems. This can be understood as a concern to learn the lessons of history, but also to be aware of the contemporary commitments carried by any historical study. Consciously and unconsciously, history struggles with contemporary aims and presuppositions. In that sense, we should value, but also remain wary of, history as political, both in its conduct towards the past and in its efforts to change the present.

This critical awareness goes in two directions: outwards to the historical object and inwards to the writing of history. In relation to historical analysis, every study inevitably brings a series of concerns and commitments that must be minimised for a true representation to emerge. Yet these presuppositions can never be fully avoided and the object will remain shrouded in them. Objectivity is the aim; it is also impossible. This paradox means that history is caught in a conflict due to its motivations and techniques. How can they be made to disappear to allow the object to come forth as untouched as possible?

In relation to the writing of history, every study has overt and hidden motivations about contemporary aims. These explain why the study matters and how it can contribute to its world. They answer the question 'Why have we bothered?' These motivations can be as personal as a search for individual meaning, or as universal as the quest for eternal truths. They can be as apparently insignificant as the justification of a matter of taste, or as important as lessons for or against revolution. By definition, the effect of the historical writing on these aims should be maximised, while staying true to the evidence. Enquiry is in part justified by attaining political aims. It would be perverse not to seek to satisfy them. When writing about an egalitarian sublime this problem of commitment is intensified; first, because the sublime is a vehicle for our highest values, or their collapse; second, since egalitarianism and opposition to it are among our most persistent political problems, from the earliest debates about democracy to the cycles of extreme inequality and resistance to it characterising the capitalist age.

This means that there is tension between the principle of objectivity and the aims of history. It implies that neither can be taken alone and hence fully obeyed. A first stab at summarising this socially engaged aspect of Ginzburg's work is that history must balance ethical and political responsibilities: accuracy about the past and commitment to the future. Yet, shouldn't the aim of history be strict objectivity, not in the sense of objectivity as an aim in itself, but where truth becomes the proper aim and purpose for history in its role of having positive effects on the present?

To understand why there can be no perfect balance between accuracy and political commitment, especially in pure objectivity, we have to return to Ginzburg's account of historical vision and its dependence on movement between the micro and macro. The dialectic between close-in history and overall vision is a response to heterogeneity. There is 'a constant back and forth between micro- and macro-history, between close-ups and extreme long-shots, so as to continually thrust back into discussion the comprehensive vision of the historical process through apparent exceptions and cases of brief duration'.[50] The key terms here are 'continually thrust back' and 'exception'. They indicate how the overall vision, including any supposedly objective large-scale representation, should be continually brought into question. However, this does not prove those visions are necessarily insufficient.

Ginzburg's arguments for that insufficiency stem from the failures of three assumptions: about the kind of onlooker, about the nature of historical vision, and about the form of the field of enquiry. In common sense, as shown for example in popular imagery, an event is viewed from the perspective of a single person or point of view: a general overlooking the battlefield, a detective considering all the clues. There may be many people seeing the event, but they either see it as one, or one vision is the only true one, or we flit from single vision to single vision. Furthermore, each viewing involves a passive set of eyes or mind, receptively absorbing a unified field, like the view of a mountain range as we stare tiredly out of the window of a plane. If we follow Ginzburg, three features of this representation are false, and this explains why battles must remain invisible: the field is not unified, the vision is not passive, and there is never a single set of eyes.

To explain why the field is not unified, Ginzburg appeals to an ontological claim according to which 'reality is fundamentally discontinuous and heterogeneous'.[51] Borrowing from the film theorist Siegfried Kracauer's law of levels, he concludes that discontinuity implies that 'no conclusion attained apropos a determinate sphere can be transferred automatically to a more general sphere'.[52] This is because the general vision and the thing viewed close-up are of different kinds. The close-up is complex, detailed and fragmentary in ways contradicting the homogeneity of the overall view. It is like the track of our vision as we move from feature to feature across a lover's body. Against this, the overview is a general definition, functioning like a text-book illustration as it reduces differences to a simplified image. It always fails to capture the fragmentary detail of the individuals it should apply to.

The problem can be explained through the difference between your concerned gaze and the cursory glance of a guard – or the equivalent checks of a machine over a closed-circuit television image. Where one is sensitive to minute and individual variations, the other only recognises generic contrasts. The level of your individual look, the close-up of microhistory, and the level of the guard's inspection or the machine's algorithms cannot be reconciled without doing violence to intricate and yet fragmentary events at the micro level. You are sensitive to the multiple aspects of eyes, creases around the mouth, texture and shades of skin, twitches and tiny inflections, in ways the skimming overview or machine-learned tests never reach. The guard might well pronounce an image healthy according to brute features, where you feel the oncoming of distress and collapse.

The difference between levels is based on the anomalous status of the micro. Once the historian turns to the detail of a small portion of history, it is seen to depart from the normal and normative assumptions of any overview. Ginzburg discovered exactly that when he studied legal documents in Venice at the start of his career. The close-up view uncovers unexpected richness in 'the more improbable sort of documents' such as testimonies before ecclesiastical and lay courts.[53] Furthermore, the social fabric observed by microhistory turns out to be composed of many different actions and individuals rather than the repetition of similar acts by interchangeable agents: 'any social structure is the result of interaction and of numerous individual strategies, a fabric that can only be reconstituted from close observation'.[54] Taken as a whole a fabric might seem to be uniform and fit normal assumptions, but this evenness emerges from multiple differences.

In his essay on microhistory, Ginzburg touches only briefly on the consequences of this mismatch between macro and micro, but his remarks are far-reaching. Firstly, the problem of how to reconnect heterogeneous scales generates the need for narrative and connecting diagrams. The speculative hypothesis seeks to reconcile the richness and diversity of different micro observations with a more tentative and experimental consideration of shared possibilities: 'the relationship between this microscopic dimension and the larger contextual dimension became in both cases (though so diverse) the organizing principle in the narration'.[55] Secondly, since this accommodation of micro and macro must not eliminate their heterogeneity, while still putting them in contact with one another, new techniques are drawn into the writing of history to maintain a difficult rather than smooth relation.

Here, we can see Ginzburg's determination to keep two extremes together, rather than fall into endless subdivision – the nominalism I spoke about earlier – or return to reductive overviews that amount to distortions from the point of view of a vision sensitive to complex details and fabrics, or seek some impossible fusion in the middle ground. His fundamental lesson is that 'the results obtained in a microscopic sphere cannot be automatically transferred to a macroscopic sphere (and vice versa)'.[56] His critical claim is that 'this heterogeneity, the implications of which we are just beginning to perceive, constitutes both the greatest difficulty and the greatest potential benefit of microhistory'.[57] We must create methods preserving heterogeneity yet also speculating about the whole.

Method and the problem of exclusion

The split in the historical field between micro observation and macro generalisation calls for a new method where differences between levels are not obliterated. This means no general thesis or speculative claim should ever be left as a satisfactory account, unchallenged by complex and anomalous evidence. There are two main reasons why this is particularly hard. First, methods are in danger of reintroducing homogeneity through their own presuppositions and techniques, irrespective of particular theories about specific topics. There is a general and pernicious gravitation back to homogeneity when a vision is unified in its subject or object. For instance, if a narrative is from a single perspective, or if a set of different objects is assessed according to a single frame of reference, or if the same vocabulary is applied to different entities, then fragments are in danger of omission or distortion.

Second, it is difficult for methodology to acquire the techniques necessary for fragmentary vision, because the history of method has been dominated by procedures designed to achieve synthesis, unity and simplification. Synthesis draws individuals together. Unity makes them as one. Simplification refines this unity, so it can be easily reproduced and maintained. Where are we to find techniques that don't rely on generalisation, overall theories, elimination of anomalies, smoothing out of statistical outliers, tendency towards a mean, and the search for essential features and shared qualities?

The answer is already present in Ginzburg's terminology, whether it is taken from painting, film, literature or technical models. Painting gives him the idea of the fragmentary or difficult whole. The motif of close-ups and long-shots is taken from film. Literature provides the examples of dialectics between careful appeals to evidence and speculative narrative. Technical models, from history and other subjects, suggest the importance of diagrams. This range of sources is striking and testament to the breadth of Ginzburg's interests. However, the number of forms of inspiration is less important than the fact that they are brought together to complement and contrast with each other.

The list of methods sensitive to difference and fragmentation suggests another problem for microhistory. Methodology is not alone in favouring homogeneity and simplification over obtuseness and complexity. General communication and popular narratives avoid difficult forms such as space-time dislocation and lack of human figures, representations and scale. These are often reserved for high, rare and elite art forms. Narratives lacking a beginning, middle and end are frustrating. Arguments without clear premises and conclusions seem pointless. Images and works free of recognisable human characters can be too demanding. They often require training and habituation before they become accessible. Irrespective of aesthetic criteria, this problem is about practical exclusion. Should a new methodology and philosophy be exclusive, out of reach for large numbers of willing readers?

Though the question of exclusion might present a persistent challenge to many art forms, microhistory has a good answer to it. This is because dislocation in microhistorical narratives takes place between micro and macro levels rather than in them. Within micro observations, we are given intricate accounts of individuals. Sources are used to recount actions, beliefs and events around particular lives in an easily understandable form. The human comes out more distinctly rather than disappearing. This method can be described as humanist, because it collects recognisably human pieces.

Communication on this micro level invites sympathy and empathy; it helps us to learn from others as different. This is the reason Ginzburg is frequently inspired by nineteenth-century novels and why he believes history has much to learn from them, even in questions of documentary evidence: 'narrative processes act like magnetic fields: they provoke questions and potentially attract documents . . . a procedure such as free direct discourse, which came into being to respond, on the terrain of fiction, to a number of historical questions, may be considered as an indirect challenge to historians'.[58] Importantly, sympathy through the novel should not be seen as communication with closed and unified individuals, a kind of recognition between closed selves. It is rather a sensation and understanding of diversity even within the self: 'For Stendhal, the "I" is synonymous with multiplicity.'[59]

At a more general level, the speculations of microhistory can be put in accessible ways as hypotheses about connections between individual lives and broader historical causes, effects, events and outcomes. The more difficult breakdown of common sense occurs after this scene setting and speculation, in two cautious ways. First, in speculation itself, confidence and theoretical solidity are replaced by more tentative and multiple suppositions. Second, a gap is opened between these suppositions and the micro-level evidence by the resistance of individual lives to general overviews.

Instead of a difficult initial perception, as caused by an abstract or fragmentary work of art, in microhistory we encounter absorbable observations and hypotheses, mediated by a more difficult tension between individual detail and general narrative. It doesn't become harder to see and understand. It becomes harder to connect what we see to what we understand. Individually, the pieces make sense. As suppositions, the hypotheses make sense. Yet the whole doesn't cohere, because it isn't allowed to settle due to the mismatch between evidence and speculation.

This resistance of individual lives to historical generalisation and to attempts to bend them to abstract and often cruel rules is the mark of Ginzburg's humanism, whether it applies to his sympathetic portrayal of the heretic miller Menocchio, or to the unfortunate Venetian Bertuccio Isarello. In tracing back to Isarello from Stendhal and Byron, Ginzburg gives his trademark caution about the difficult relation between narration and evidence: 'Our journey backward from library to archives, from Julien Sorel to the conspiracy of Marin Falier, has been highly discontinuous. Between Israël Bertuccio and Bertuccio Isarello there is more than the divide separating fiction from historical reality. In the continuous variation of the contexts, everything – from names to social status – dissolves.'[60] The lesson is also familiar in the care taken to explain this discontinuity through individuals, both those writing and those written about. We might have expected an elite form, but we find a popular one: 'Ginzburg arrived at Menocchio's case from the study of popular culture, and his own implicit preferences prompted him to point to a pre-Christian, oral, popular culture as the inspirer of the miller's ideas, instead of understanding these from Menocchio's life.'[61]

Where others might worry about the difficulty of clashes of levels and perspectives, Ginzburg finds humane and humbling lessons. Once again, there is a combination of historical evidence and narrative invention: 'with a sudden shift in perspective [Montaigne] looked at us, through the eyes of the Brazilian natives who had been brought to Rouen, where they stood before the king of France'.[62] This blend of the literary and historical creates a shock in one world with a delayed warning for another: 'What they saw, and what he saw through their eyes, made no sense at all . . . his words are still painful to read: "They found it strange that these poverty-stricken halves should suffer such injustice, and that they did not take the others by the throat or set fire to their houses."' For Ginzburg, multiple perspectives foster sympathy for others and understanding of their reasons, environment, feelings and thoughts. The lessons can be described as egalitarian, if we take this as an equality of individuality: all humans are complex and different in ways deserving of sympathy, care and protection.

Though Ginzburg's humanism avoids the problem of exclusivity and leads to a version of egalitarianism, I do not intend to follow its lead. There is a downside to its attention to the human individual and to its accessible historical accounts of a life. It limits the kind of speculation and possibilities we can draw around existence, since these must start with something widely recognisable as an individual human life. It also limits the type of challenge those speculations can mount against generalisations and against the erasure of differences, because these are limited to the opposition drawn between violent oppression and individuality. Finally, against his trust in the humanistic arts to approach evidence as proof, his humanism might also give a false representation of that evidence, tainting it with the expectation of finding the human individual. In developing a critical distance from Ginzburg, it will be important to be aware of how this rejection allows for a return of the negative point about exclusivity and, perhaps more importantly, a questioning of the wisdom of a potential departure from humanist principles.

Towards the end of his reflections on microhistory, in opposition to the idea of a single perspective, Ginzburg returns to painting and to the work of Boccioni for a succinct but evocative description of the thesis that the historian or onlooker is always many. There is no historian with a settled and unique identity. Instead, the fragments and different levels of the outside world lead into and give rise to the self: 'If this is a self-portrait, then its model is Boccioni's paintings in which the street leads into the house, the landscape into the face, and the exterior invades the interior, the "I" is porous.'[63]

This concern for the multiplicity and connectivity of identities is important for the idea of the sublime as multiple, as we'll see later in the work of Julia Kristeva on the abject sublime. The sublime has many ways to affect us and, when it does so, it is not as individuals but rather as fragile and manifold processes connected through shared histories taken differently. An Italian futurist painter and sculptor, Boccioni (1882–1916), painted *The Street Enters the House* in 1911, in the same year that he painted *Simultaneous Visions*, where house, streets, trees and materials enter into two mirrored and connected faces. This creates a cohering yet also clashing series of influences and visions.

A year later he painted his greatest work, *Materia*, where his mother's portrait dissolves into shards of matter, cityscapes and objects, only then to be reconstituted with them: 'urban background, home interior, and especially the potential eclipse of the distinction between inside and outside, a fusional movement achieved simultaneously with irradiation'.[64] Boccioni's art is one of multiple flows, leading from many different and separate sources, often depicted expressively and at speed, into more settled and familiar settings. The boundaries of the self or the house are broken by impulses from the outside such that everything interior is generated by obscure and manifold external influences: 'Every verification with the outside world must end up in the created work.'[65]

There is a dissonant aspect to Ginzburg's admiration for Boccioni to consider. After Boccioni's death, falling from a horse while serving in the Italian army in the First World War, futurism was to become one of the main sources of official fascist imagery. As Jews and left-wing anti-fascists, Ginzburg's parents, Leone and Natalia Ginzburg, were persecuted by the fascists. His father was tortured and murdered by Nazis after his arrest by the Italian police in 1944. Ginzburg's history is resolutely on the side of victims of persecution and discrimination.

Part of the answer to this shocking juxtaposition is that the connection of futurism to fascism is incomplete and uncertain. Commenting on Boccioni's masterpiece of futurist sculpture, John Golding reminds us that it is 'a revolutionary work which carries within it the seeds of a reaction'.[66] So the link should not be taken straightforwardly as grounds for dismissal of futurism and of the idea that it could be progressive. It is certainly reason to be wary. Ginzburg conveys this caution through his commitment to evidence against falsehoods and propaganda.

For Ginzburg, when interpreting Boccioni, the porosity of the self is of a special kind. We could think of it as conscious, in the sense of an awareness of our roots and influences. As such, the subject of that awareness could be a more deeply unified and reflective self-identity, providing a single intellectual perspective. Contradicting this supposition, Ginzburg describes it as a necessarily unconscious invasion from the outside. This unconscious aspect to the self will be a central theme for the later sublime. Perhaps the sense of an external disruption explains his enthusiasm for Boccioni's paintings. With a debt to cubism, they spin from the outside to a churned and shattered inside.

Ginzburg's explanation of an absence of consciousness rests on two justifications, one apparently more plausible than the other, though both rely on hindsight, experienced not as some kind of serene awareness but rather as a shocking revelation. When reviewing the pattern of his work and life, he reports how 'both the boundaries of the group to which I belonged and my own boundaries of self seemed retrospectively shifting and uncertain'.[67] In the middle of plans and activities, we might well think that there is a clear line and identity for the self: who we are, what we want, where we are going. However, looking back at the most significant aspect of his vocation as a historian, the pattern of Ginzburg's research and the writing of his books unfold in uncommon and surprising ways: 'To my surprise I discovered how important to me were, unknowingly, books I had never read, events and persons I did not know had existed.'[68]

Separating these remarks from personal anecdote, the easier argument for the unconscious porosity of the self is its vulnerability to uncertainty and to the unexpected. It doesn't matter how hard we prepare and plan, there will always be novel events and gaps in understanding making ourselves and the objects we study open to changes and variations. In turn, these diversions from identity call for reconstruction: the inventive work of speculative narrative. The self is therefore open to change in ways it cannot control. It is also dependent on narrative for recreating relative cohesion.

The harder argument is more unusual, yet also more robust. Our knowledge is not only limited by future unexpected and unknown events. It is also vulnerable to false confidence about its past and present: the influence of 'events and persons I did not know had existed'. This latter argument falls under the paradox of knowledge. How can you be guided by what you do not know? Ginzburg's solution depends on the role of hindsight in detecting unknown stimulus. When looking back we can see effects we once did not know. When we see it in this way we can connect the known to the unknown and understand more clearly how they interact. A blind hunch turns out to be the premonition of an important causal connection. A book we never read brings dimly lit ideas into focus, showing more clearly how they were working on other thoughts.

One of the books Ginzburg had not read and yet was being guided by was Siegfried Kracauer's posthumous *History: The Last Things Before the Last*, where he discusses the difference between macro and micro history, earlier than the Italian historians Ginzburg worked with. Kracauer teaches two laws governing the relation of micro to macro: the law of perspective, whereby some part of the micro evidence must be ignored from the beginning; and the law of levels, according to which the micro level conveys possibilities missed in the macro-level account of the identical event. These twin necessities dictate that 'part of the evidence drops out automatically' and the 'available evidence reaches its destination in an incomplete state'. This means history is always a 'nonhomogeneous structure' comprising 'fields of varying density . . . rippled by unaccountable eddies'.[69] The challenge for microhistory, and for the microcritique of the sublime I wish to defend, is how to construct a method suited to these restraints on history and freedoms for philosophy.

Patterns of fragments

Instead of fully adopting the methods of microhistory, my definition of the egalitarian sublime connects to other ideas of the sublime through a variation of the methods I'll call microcritique. The change in name indicates a difference in topic alongside continuities in techniques. Where microhistory is anchored by historical evidence and given impetus through speculative narratives, microcritique employs many of the same procedures, but on conceptual material and problems.

Narrative is too linear for the ideas of the sublime; it is still too close to the model of storytelling about human lives. Conceptual problems do not have the same restriction to life and death, to growth and decay. Their passage through time doesn't have to be linear or limited to organic development. I will therefore turn to diagrams as more abstract and flexible ways of giving structure to relations.

The ground was prepared for this shift from narration in my critical remarks on Ginzburg's humanism. However, it would be wrong to assume that this transfer to diagrams is easy. There's a challenging counter to the turn from the human, in pointing out how concepts require human minds and human environments. When I say concepts have a different way through time, I invite the objection that concepts can only move through time in line with human minds and physical causality. Is there any sense in giving diagrams for concepts shorn of human actors or independent of physical causes?

In Chapter 4, we'll see that since the mid-nineteenth century the sublime has become associated with technology and with the experience of a technological sublime. This electrical sublime is now familiar to us; for instance, in the awe we feel when first arriving in Shanghai or Hong Kong at night:

> Spectacular lighting made possible the awe-inspiring manipulation of both nature and the man-made. As electrical lighting transformed the appearance of streets, bridges, skyscrapers, public monuments, the Natural Bridge, and Niagara Falls, it became not only the double of technology but also a powerful medium of cultural expression that could highlight both natural and technological objects and heighten their sublimity.[70]

The sublime contradictory feelings of distance and closeness – of repulsion and attraction – are conveyed by our identification with each set of lights as a sign of humans just like us, and by uneasiness at the realisation that all of us are but small illuminations among many, not special individuals, but replaceable units, on a scale that mocks our particular loves, desires and self-regard.

We have seen how microhistory follows the example of film in moving from large-scale vistas, like the view from a plane, to close-ups, such as the anguished faces of actors caught in a traffic jam as they flee the city. Films frequently use this juxtaposition, particularly in scene-setting such as at the beginning of Robert Altman's *Short Cuts* (1993), where we cut between views from helicopters, spraying against flies, to lives on the ground. The aim is to preserve detailed fragments from the dehumanising effect of the overview without denying it. The story is individual in the depth and complexity of its micro detail and yet partly unified by the macro level ideas and lines, binding individuals into the mass, its mechanisms and its logic. The humanist lesson is in how each life is an anomalous resistance to the conclusion that the overview is sufficient.

The difference between microcritique and humanist microhistory can be understood through Ginzburg's claim about the self. The anomalous nature of the micro level depends on the multiplicity and intricate extension of the self. Each human self is a paradox for the general view. This is because the self is porous, making humans a point of complexity and resistance to generality and to overviews. You never get the human you expect to find and it is incumbent on you to do justice to the individuality you do find, hence the value and importance of microhistory as a political and ethical method.

The metaphor of porosity implies a prior self, open to later transformations from the outside, like a sponge absorbing different liquids. Social historians such as Ginzburg and Davis are interested in this porosity partly because it retains individuality, yet situates individuals within a social sphere with strong effects upon them. My study of the sublime depends on a different assumption. The self doesn't come prior to outside effects; it is constituted by them. This is important because it replaces the idea of the independent value of the human, as multiple and as open to infinite variations, with the value of multiple and open processes that can subsequently, but not necessarily, be identified as particular human selves. It is not a matter of porosity to the outside, but of ongoing construction by it.

This alternative view is the basis for a response to the claims that we should think of ideas and concepts as dependent on human narratives and time. The opposite is the case. We should think of humans as dependent on other processes, to the point where it becomes a mistake to address problems through a human framework. Instead, each problem becomes a matter of selecting and working through the processes involved in bringing it about. Some of these will be associated with the construction of human beliefs, actions, identity, time and narratives, but others will not.

There is a straightforward way of illustrating the reversal taking place when we move from microhistory to microcritique. It is a similar shift to the change from ascribing human qualities and actions to a physical system, such as the weather, and seeking to explain those systems through many other non-human processes. When we transfer from microhistory to microcritique, we are making a similar change to when we stop talking about a vengeful winter and instead look at patterns of winds, pressures and temperatures.

This analogy breaks down, though, if we assume microcritique is about deterministic physical explanations. On the contrary, because explanations are responses to problems coming out of paradoxes generated by a multiplicity of processes, in tension with one another and with general theories, deterministic approaches are unsatisfactory and microcritique is not limited by their laws.

None of this means we must abandon any of the techniques of microhistory. On the contrary, nearly all retain their most important functions. First, the movement between different dimensions keeps macro-level generalisation and speculation in check, thanks to heterogeneity and multiplicity at the micro levels. This micro is no longer about individual lives and external effects upon them, but about micro-level processes. These are the causes and influences participating in the more general ideas and concepts. They can be images, physical causes and natural environments, forms of writing and difference of vocabulary, shared and individual human experiences and sensations (though these are no longer given priority over other factors).

In microcritique, processes of construction take the place of evidence in Ginzburg's account of the role of proof in narration. Speculative diagrams, defined as charts of the relations between processes and between macro and micro levels, replace human-centred narratives. The political impetus remains, but becomes more broad, going beyond what's determined to be important for humans, to anything considered as problematic in the sense of involving tensions and contradictions causing difficulties for future development. Thus there can be problems for animals, machines, systems and even worlds.

I have swapped 'critique' for 'history' in the name for the method in order to mark how upper-level speculations are criticised thanks to their fragmentation at the micro level. Instead of a homogeneous reference for macro ideas, structures, processes and concepts, they encounter resistance in anomalous and discontinuous phenomena in micro processes. This resistance cannot be ignored or set aside because it takes place through forms of emergence and kinds of influence involved in the creation of the macro level. There is a genetic link between the two. It is not only a speculation failing to apply, but an idea or concept proving to be incoherent or contradictory.

Microcritique guides the idea of the egalitarian sublime between general definitions of sublimity and detailed accounts of the sublime in a particular sign. As a frequently used sign indicating value, the sublime becomes a series of fragments impossible to identify with one another. However, in what follows, these fragments are brought together through definitions, diagrams of their effects, and critical consideration of their implications for an egalitarian sublime. Each definition participates in this coming together, but it also keeps it in suspension, in the sense of keeping it in question, in relation to individual cases and experiences of the sublime. Furthermore, other general definitions of the sublime are included in the diagram, but subjected to similar critical inspection. We are then left with a new definition within a network of historical ones, and this novel pattern remains problematic through its difficult relation to singular instances.

Chapter 3

Nietzsche Against the Egalitarian Sublime

Only for the few

What if the sublime and the highest values are only for the few? What if it is an experience only available to a minority, or to a small number of exceptional individuals? If the sublime is restricted to the few, not just sometimes but in every possible case, then it will make no sense to speak of an egalitarian sublime. The sublime will be a mark and place of division, where the chosen ones separate from the masses. Some will experience or create the highest values and others will be destined for the ordinary and the merely beautiful.

Looking back through the history of the sublime, it is odd to even ask these questions about the few and the many. It also seems perverse to want to suggest that the sublime can be egalitarian. The name has stood for exceptional men: great orators, the kings of divine right, those to whom and through whom gods speak – our greatest artists and leaders.

The domain of the sublime has been described as exclusively masculine, with women given over to the 'beautiful and picturesque'.[1] This depiction was always inaccurate and the exclusion has invited feminist responses, redefining the sublime as feminine. Yet the need for this countermovement against the banishment or elision of women also demonstrates how the sublime has served the few in their claim to higher powers.

At the end of the eighteenth century and beginning of the nineteenth, the English poet Anna Seward made frequent use of the sublime in her letters to Sir Walter Scott and others. Scott was the editor of her letters after her death. Seward traces her affinity with the sublime to early childhood, 'the first scenery which struck upon my infant perceptions, with wonder and transport, is brought back by poetic pictures of wild, uncultivated, lonely nature'.[2] Seward extends the sublime to Haydn's music: 'First, by that wild and complex dissonance which sublimely represents the tumult of chaos',[3] and distinguishes Milton and Dante over sublime horror: 'Why should we impute this simply-grand portrait of a demoniac countenance to a conception in the Italian bard too grotesque and monstrous to be sublime?'[4] There is further evidence in her literary debates, where she sides with Burke against Addison: 'while Burke, on a subject much of the same nature, his discrimination of the sublime and the beautiful, awakens and energizes, interests, and entertains me'.[5]

Even when the sublime has not been a sign of rare creativity but of more inclusive transformative experiences, natural events and phenomena of the sublime have not only been exceptional, they have also required extraordinary circumstances. Mountains and canyons cannot be sublime for goat herders or park rangers, as they tend flocks against wolves or maintain paths in the intense heat, because sublime feelings depend upon detachment from everyday tasks. The sublime is a forceful interruption of contemplation, or of idleness, by events we are not accustomed to.

Landscapes are sublime for tourists and travellers, for artists and philosophers, when their senses are overwhelmed by uncommon and terrifying vistas. This experience is about gazing over a flood or a landslide, not the fight to survive it. Burke defines the sublime as coming after danger has passed: 'In all these cases, if the pain and terror are so modified as not to be actually noxious; if the pain is not carried to violence, and the terror is not conversant about the present destruction of the person.'[6] Delight – itself defined as release from pain – replaces terror as the danger subsides: 'as these emotions clear the parts, whether fine, or gross, of a dangerous or troublesome encumbrance, they are capable of producing delight'.[7] The important point is that terror and delight are co-dependent and hence delight cannot be pure pleasure, 'but a sort of delightful horror, a sort of tranquillity tinged with terror; which as it belongs to self-preservation is one of the strongest of all the passions. Its object is the sublime.'[8]

There's a remnant of the historical sublimity of peaks and chasms, witnessed by wealthy travellers on a grand tour, in our fascination for images of modern-day adventurers, as they fly, jump, ski, skate and cycle from mountain tops, supplying sublime images to distract us from the everyday. The feeling of the sublime is for the spectator, not the acrobats, whose deep concentration on the task at hand keeps them from feelings of awe or terror. In popular usage, for instance in sports, it is reserved for commentators or viewers expressing admiration for exceptional performances and moves: a sublime pass; a sublime shot; a sublime player.

The same requirement for detachment is true for political events and conflict. Revolutions and battles are sublime at a safe distance, but not when you have to duck bullets to seek provisions, or when mud slows you down while fleeing tanks. Sublime nature and sublime political upheaval are not only necessarily out of the ordinary they also tend to be rare experiences. To be experienced safely, they require comfort, wealth and leisure, since not only must feelings of terror be balanced by delight, they must also be accompanied by refined ideas. These depend on distance from immediate threats and pressures. The sublime is for armchairs and galleries, coffee tables and high-definition screens, not workshops, farmyards and factories.

Burke's argument for safety follows from the power of the drive for self-preservation and the pain caused when it is thwarted in the face of danger: 'The passions which belong to self-preservation, turn on pain and danger, they are simply painful when their causes immediately affect us.'[9] Later thinkers, and above all Kant, will introduce ideas into the sublime for moral reasons, but Burke is rigorous in seeing their more formal role in ensuring the safe presence of an earlier threat: 'they are delightful when we have an idea of pain and danger, without being in such circumstances; this delight I have not called pleasure, because it turns on pain, and because it is different enough from any idea of positive pleasure. Whatever excites this delight, I call *sublime*.'[10]

Again prefiguring Kant, Burke argues that in apparently simple experiences of the sublime, imagination and ideas frequently play a part in ways requiring knowledge and leisure; for instance, in the contemplation of infinity or in the imaginative leap from an unbound view or large object to the idea of infinity: 'Infinity has a tendency to fill the mind with that sort of delightful horror, which is the most genuine effect, and truest test of the sublime ... the parts of some large object, are so continued to any indefinite number, that the imagination meets no check which may hinder its extending them at pleasure.'[11]

In his empirical and physiological reflections on the sublime, Burke describes a tension caused by pain and danger followed by a rapid release. We are then caught in a balance of the idea of pain and the feeling of delight: the feeling of the sublime. His studies are prescient when set alongside modern forms of media in cinema, music and digital entertainment, with their rollercoaster effects of waves of tension and release. His language also runs ahead of Gothic and later forms of sublime horror: 'a sort of tranquillity shadowed with horror'.[12]

The most troublesome instances of the sublime, as a product of safe and comfortable viewing, are when the few gaze over the misery of the many. Vast hillsides covered in precarious shacks, or the mass movements of refugees across sea and land, induce a safe terror and awe in onlookers when media convey the scale and horror of tragedies to more secure locations. For an assessment of the divisiveness of the sublime, it does not matter that these images can sometimes be a prelude to sympathetic actions and sometimes invite fearful rejection, since these effects still depend on a distinction between those who experience the sublime and those who undergo misery.

The deepest question in this initial critical overview of the exclusivity of the sublime is not about how sublime political events move us to act. It is whether we should look to sublime feelings as grounds for political action at all. If we begin with the sublime as a feeling for spectators, we end with a politics of spectators and sufferers. This is a politics of external actors led by sentiments and ideas removed from the people whose pain the action is meant to alleviate. It is a politics lacking in equality twice over: first, in the privileged position required for the sublime – the luck of security and relative wealth; second, in the distinction between actors and beneficiaries – where the former at the very least start with ideas and feelings that the latter cannot afford to have.

Viewed this way, the sublime cannot be an egalitarian creation, sign or event. It is not to be experienced or made by the masses. Worse, it is against the interests of the many, in their opposition to the few who control and exploit them, even when the intention is to help. Put most starkly, the sublime has always been a plaything and an instrument of power, where the many are given sermons under high vaults or among colonnades, or enticed to dream along with the follies of the rich, or to tremble at the devastation of repression, or receive charity given on a basis of continued subservience.

Burke is alert to the expression of power in sublime architecture, preferring its classical manifestations. Discussing the sublime in buildings, he praises the sublime effect of succession and uniformity for conveying grandeur, believing this effect is partially lost when religious buildings are based on a cross, because the vision of infinite succession and distance is lost when lines slant: 'there is nothing more prejudicial to the grandeur of buildings, than to abound in angles'.[13]

In his diatribe against the sublime, James Elkins proposes a moratorium on the use of the word. His arguments are sometimes contradictory, since when highlighting the weakness and contradictions of the concept some of his points match those made here about dangerous political power. The sublime can take people away from the gritty worlds of politics and society, of meaning and narrative, of culture and value, but this does not mean it is not a powerful phenomenon that introduces new ideas of value into those worlds, for better or worse.

According to Elkins, the sublime is an elitist concept associated with emotions of distance and nostalgia. Its detachment protects 'postmodernists from having to make difficult judgements', for instance about their own privileged position and ideological commitments.[14] Postmodernists aren't quite the right target here. They may well discuss the concept of the sublime, going back to Burke and Kant. Their critical discussion may also betray a nostalgia for the sublime. But the more pressing danger comes from old and new positive definitions of the sublime, with their far-reaching effects on the way we think about and apply values.

The sublime as effect

To begin to find a thread out of this apparent dead-end for sublime egalitarianism, I'll turn back to the idea of microcritique, or critical remarks alternating between micro-level observations and macro-level speculation, designed to draw differences between positions within a line of ideas and objects. The sublime isn't simply one thing or another. It is a history of many threads and many shades. These minute differences need to be inspected close-up and only assessed for their implications thereafter, and in relation to new concerns. No matter how attached the sublime seems to be to a lack of equality, it is possible to distinguish definitions through degrees of division and unfairness.

With the aim of unpicking different strands of the sublime, I propose diagrams as models for contrasting effects. Each definition of the sublime implies different results on boundaries and inclusions for these models. When translated into dynamic movements on a diagram, aspects of these definitions indicate how different meanings and features imply stronger and weaker opposition to egalitarianism, sometimes with unexpected and counterintuitive consequences. These repercussions only appear in relation to new concerns, such as a desire for equality respecting differences in values, or the command to sacrifice our values for those of others.

Later, I'll suggest critical and constructive diagrams, showing the way to an egalitarian future for the sublime. However, the first diagram is mainly negative, since it highlights ways to inequality. It begins with a fourfold division around space and activity:

Outside	Inside
Passive	Active

I have described the sublime as experience and as creation. The two upper quadrants indicate this distinction according to whether the sublime comes from the outside, as an experience, or from the inside, as creation. Is the sublime something caused by an external event or phenomenon? Or is it something happening inside us, as a creative force?

This initial division is insufficient. When an experience comes from the outside it can either be something we are submissive to, or something we need to work for. It is either a passive reception, or active interaction. For example, we are passive when we are simply struck by a sublime event, such as an avalanche seen at a distance, but we are active if the external event requires effort from us, like the consideration of the idea of revolution on receiving news of an uprising, or an awareness of the scale and properties of a galaxy observed through a telescope.

The same is true for the internal sublime. It can strike us passively; for instance, as inspiration or ecstatic inner experience where we are taken beyond ourselves, not necessarily against our will but certainly outside of our control. This passivity is conveyed by the idea of a sublime muse, arriving from nowhere and conveying divine inspiration. However, the internal sublime can also be the outcome of a painstaking creative procedure: a conscious effort to make something sublime. In this version, the sublime might be the outcome of everyday efforts and communal techniques; slimy clay reappearing with the purest sheen and shape from a hot oven, born from communal learning over millennia.

We need all four quadrants to account for different types of the sublime. Yet the notions of types and quadrants are another trap, this time concerning the nature of the diagram. Every definition of the sublime is an intervention on three things: a series of ideas, a world, and the future potentials of both. The writer reacts to earlier thinkers, tests ideas against the world, and aims to bring new potential into it. As such, no definition of the sublime is simply one thing or another. It begins in a mix, applies to muddled worlds, and seeks to drag all of this into something new. A novel hypothesis is always an interaction with a complex and tangled series of processes.

This implies that independent quadrants and types cannot do justice to any definition of the sublime. These definitions never belong simply to one type and hence to one quadrant, even when they claim to. Statements about unoriginated purity are false, because they are always interventions on impure lines of ideas and events. If there is purity, it is fabricated and does not come from nowhere. Here, the absolute necessity of any exclusive value for the sublime is undone, since the exclusion of the many is always imposed, rather than natural or essential. It is a claim to something, like fencing off land or resorting to property law, rather than a natural divide or value.[15] The sublime is made to be divisive. Microcritique is the tracking of different effects of this manufacture.

Though the diagram consists of four quadrants, we shouldn't situate a definition of the sublime as a point on a particular quadrant. Each definition is an operation across quadrants, but in each one to lesser and greater degrees, and with different styles and character, dependent on its effects on the ideas signified by 'active', 'passive', 'inside' and 'outside'. The definition is like a slash across the quadrants: a process relating them in a singular way. The diagram communicates the degrees and manner in which each quadrant is touched, transformed and set in relation to the others. In this transformation, all the quadrants are expressions of changes in series of ideas, worlds and new potentials.

I choose 'slash' as the image of the effect of a definition on the quadrants, rather than 'point' or 'lines', in order to indicate the dynamic and extended effects of a new definition. In the next chapter I will also use gravitation in a similar manner. The effect is an ongoing material process, like a painted arrow across a map, a rip through a plan, or a swirl of ingredients in a mixing bowl. To offer a definition of the sublime is more like matter painting than the specification of abstract ideas.

Though it pre-dates him, the description 'matter painting' has often been applied to works by the Catalan artist Antoni Tàpies: 'In theory, I use wood pulp because I want to experiment with the *material*, a similar impulse to the one that makes me use marble dust, varnish or wood. The fact that creased and folded paper tears easily or that wet paper is soft and organic are phenomena that attract me as much as the material properties of marble dust or varnish.'[16] His paintings offer a good way of understanding the difference between an ideal location on a grid and an event on a diagram: 'a dynamic presence rather than a symbol', he says.[17] His works often consist of grainy and mixed fields of materials and simple figures (including a fourfold division such as a cross), impacted by slashes and apparently accidental brush strokes, sometimes deep, sometimes bare touches. In a definition of the sublime, as in a matter painting, 'names, colour, gesture, movement in depth, have been condensed together in an emotional explosion, static, timeless, alive'.[18]

It would be easy to think of these marks on matter or across diagrams as a puncture or defacing of the material, but that would be to miss the wider effects complicating the initial injury into positive transformations, where spaces are not divided but rather 'seem to be wanting to pass from one to the other'.[19] Each new definition of the sublime is a transformation of connected historical series, worlds and their futures. The change introduces new values, surpassing earlier ones. Whether something has been defaced, in a negative sense, depends on pragmatic perspectives on the old and the new, between a slash across a much-loved landscape, or the cutting of an escape from a desolate and rotting valley.

In the mid-twentieth century, in his text 'The Sublime is Now', the abstract expressionist artist Barnett Newman advocated a return to the sublime in art. He did so not as a nostalgic recapture of the past, but rather as a revolution through the sublime. The title expresses this overturning as a turn to the present. The sublime is *now*. It also proposes it as something created today. The sublime is *made* in the present. Yet the sublime is also to be now as a present experience. The sublime is *felt now*.

To draw a diagram for Newman's ideas, we can take account of two related moves. The old sublime is denied: 'We do not need the obsolete props of an outmoded and antiquated legend.'[20] The new sublime is to be the highest experience, freed from external conditions: 'We are reasserting man's natural desire for the exalted, for a concern with our relationship to absolute emotions.'[21] This is a rejection of the past and yet a reconnection with something eternal and absolute. How can something natural and eternal not also be in the past? Why did it become lost?

Newman's answer depends on sublime emotions as responses to art. The absolute heights are produced and they can be made well or badly. His text defends a sublime art free of the mistakes of the past: 'We are freeing ourselves of the impediments of memory, association, nostalgia, legend, myth, or what have you, that have been the devices of Western European painting.'[22] The sublime should not come from meaningful symbols recovered from the past. But how can art and the sublime avoid past signs and their meanings?

New sublime works will achieve an immediate connection between the sublime feelings of the artist and of the viewer: 'The image we produce is the self-evident one of revelation, real and concrete, that can be understood by anyone who will look at it without the nostalgic glasses of history.'[23] This direct and physical transmission of absolute emotion cannot depend on signs and meanings, since these will vary according to culture. Past signs and meanings feed nostalgia and division, like an old flag or a memorial.

Taken alone, nostalgia can never be sublime, because it fosters a sense of loss around remnants of feeling and significance, barring the way to the new and to more intense sensations – resisting them. The artwork should therefore be without meaningful forms, consisting instead of pure feelings expressed directly in abstract works: 'Instead of making cathedrals out of Christ, man or "life", we are making them out of ourselves, out of our own feelings.'[24]

I draw attention to Newman's short manifesto for two reasons. First, it is a precursor to a more egalitarian sublime. There is a natural capacity for sublime feelings in everyone, so long as this feeling is liberated from past meanings. This leads to freedom and to liberty, both shared equally: freedom from nostalgia, and liberty to act in a different future accessible to all. For Newman, the egalitarian sublime must break with historical sense and connect to universal emotions, through sublime artworks.

Second, the manifesto is a slash across the four quadrants of the diagram I have proposed for the sublime. It transforms inner experience into something pure and independent of sense-laden historical forms, from outside to inside. This experience is triggered by abstract outer forms made by the expressionist artist.[25] The construction is active, involving a will to break with the past in the act of painting. It is also passive, in its openness to a pure and absolute emotion, a transformation of the relation of active to passive.

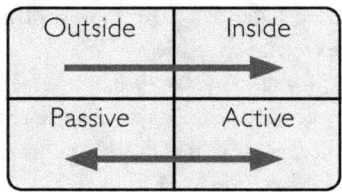

However, on closer inspection of this diagram, Newman's attempt can't shake off division, despite its universal aims. As egalitarian, Newman's ideas are a failure. Across the active and passive quadrants, they rely on a distinction between artist and spectator, where the passive experience of the latter contrasts with the refined activity of the former. The artist (as well as the museum curator and architect, the critic and the patrons) stages the passive experience for the spectators.

Newman wanted to escape from nostalgia, but his challenge depends on a very old distinction between those who make and those who experience. Far from being a resistance to division, this deepens it. Those who experience the sublime do so only on condition that the efforts and considerations of the making, staging, justifying and funding of the work are hidden. This is much closer to the deceptive purity of the religious sublime of Gothic cathedrals than the absolute experience Newman seeks. Over the course of this book, we'll see how the idea of deception is both important and easily missed in any assessment of the sublime.

There is a more hidden failure. The idea of a natural sublime emotion – latent in all – is only egalitarian at the cost of imposing a single hierarchy of value and a single type of emotion on all. What if for some the sublime is drawn from meaningful forms? What of all the older experiences of the sublime that Newman rejects as nostalgic? Do they not have sublime potential in new creations? What of people who do not or cannot experience the sublime in expressionist works, but do so rather in the cathedrals Newman scorns, or in works from cultures and places distant from European and American ideas of the sublime?

Newman's fields of colour are split by shimmering 'zips' to maximise the sublime effect of infinite succession and uniformity, yet avoiding both broken figures and mere simplicity. This leads to a sublime of infinity and interruption, where the disruption to the infinite colour gradient breaks into its attraction tinging it with a distressing uncertainty and lack. However, this imposes a restricted model on the sublime. Burke is much more inclusive and open in his description of its causes, allowing them to range across many physical sensations, from sounds and sights to natural and built environments. Against Newman's claim for a break with earlier traditions, his abstraction can be seen as a more extreme version of the distinction Burke draws between the gradients and variations of beauty and the monolithic nature of the sublime. Where Newman's concrete sensation and abstract works are limited and exalted in form and content, Burke's sublime is free-ranging and democratic.

As such, Burke is much closer to an egalitarian sublime than Newman, despite the former's glaring exclusion and distinctions around gender, the sublime and the beautiful. In her softness and deceitfulness, woman is beautiful and not sublime:

> Observe that part of a beautiful woman where she is perhaps the most beautiful, about the neck and breasts; the smoothness; the softness; the easy and insensible swell; the variety of the surface, which is never for the smallest space the same; the deceitful maze, through which the unsteady eye slides giddily, without knowing where to fix, or whither it is carried. Is this not a demonstration of that change of surface continual and yet hardly perceptible at a point which forms one of the great constituents of beauty.[26]

I will return to these forms of discrimination based on the sublime in later chapters, but it is important to note them early. Above all, the terrible distinctions made around race and the sublime by Burke, where his causal account of the sublime is particularly violent in its claim that darkness and blackness lead to terror, due to what he claimed were the naturally terrifying effects of black skin on the basis of nothing more than reported stories: 'upon accidentally seeing a negro woman, [the blind boy newly given vision] was struck with great horror at the sight'.[27] This racism in the sublime is far from restricted to Burke. Kant's deeply ignorant discussion of sublime feelings for different races is even more damning: 'The Negroes of Africa have by nature no feeling that rises above the ridiculous.'[28]

When I return to these instances of discrimination, I will argue that they aren't contingent and expendable parts of definitions of the sublime. They are effects of those definitions. The importance of diagrams or maps of these effects is therefore to show how a simple definition plays out in wider cultural, social and political fields. For example, Newman's diagram for the sublime is a version of sublime individualism and of the imposition of hierarchical values cloaked under claims for the universal. It transforms inner and outer experience through the imposition of a single model of abstraction for the outer, and single mystical revelation for the inner. Though he rejects religious imagery, there is still the same religious desire to share (or dictate) a single religious experience. He adopts the language of sameness in the universal, but this comes through the individual and exceptional creation of high art. Society remains a pyramid, with its tip hovering unattainably away from the base.

Despite the actual divisions in taste and ability implied by Newman's version of an abstract sublime, it might be argued that everyone has the potential to share the experience of sublime art and the capacity to make it. This would depend on types of education and training working as kinds of cultural imposition on a diverse population. Were it possible, such an achievement would still fail as egalitarian, this time by snuffing out diverse experiences, desires and abilities in favour of a single higher model. The sublime would then arrive at a false equality, on the basis of a pedagogical restriction of potential.

Does this mean that when we seek to take the sublime in an egalitarian direction, we must always end up with distinctions between creators and consumers, leaders and followers, active participants in the sublime and those enabled to experience it, and consequently with forms of deception and indoctrination, even in education?

Untimely, sublime

The sublime's tendency to lead to a distinction between creative individuals and the mass of humanity is a challenge to the project of an egalitarian sublime. Even if sublime individuals bequeath sublimity to the rest, even if their sublime creations lift the whole of humanity, the dependence on a minority of individuals means the sublime cannot be equal in distribution, potential, control or power. Some lead and some are led. Some produce and some consume. Some wield the sublime and others submit to it.

Nietzsche is the deepest thinker of this inequality between sublime individuals and the masses. However, the combination of exceptional individuals and future goals for humanity constitutes a paradox in his thought. The sublime individual is *for* humanity in struggling *against* it. In my search for an egalitarian sublime, I want to learn from Nietzsche's arguments as they relate to the idea of the sublime as necessarily untimely. Nietzsche's combination of untimely effects with earlier individual efforts is the most sophisticated attempt to explain why the sublime is necessarily individual, but also elevating for humanity as a whole.

To track these arguments I will study them in Nietzsche's essay 'On the Uses and Disadvantages of History for Life'. There, commenting on

Hartmann, Goethe and Schopenhauer, Nietzsche denies that the sublime goal of humanity could be the result of a communal effort. Humanity cannot be sublime as the aggregate result of historical development, whether this is as a society, as a particular culture, or in a more spiritual shared end such as judgement according to gods, reason or moral values.

A society is diverse; it has achievements alongside failures, and precious moments among many tawdry ones. In all of these, if we follow Nietzsche, it is in conflict with itself and always therefore prone to decadence, through a struggle between creative and reactive forces where, given time, reaction wins. In the unequal distribution of these forces, only sublime individuals have the strength to separate themselves from the negativity and decay of their epochs. Only they can become untimely, outside time and free of the way the masses yearn for survival, comfort, salvation and pleasure in communities built around shared aims.

Reflecting on the sublime and history, Nietzsche justifies the necessary separation of the masses and creative individuals by arguing that history presents humanity with an overwhelming profusion of conflicting demands. There is not only too much information and too many values, but too many different and competing parties: 'Historical knowledge streams in unceasingly from inexhaustible wells, the strange and incoherent forces its way forward, memory opens all its gates and yet is not open wide enough.'[29] The forward motion of history depends on a surge from the past that exceeds our powers of understanding. This hinders our command over the future, because we cannot comprehend how it comes from the past.

The sublime individual possesses superior forces to harness profusion and chaos. Among these strengths, Nietzsche lists artistic creativity, the power to select and to forget, a willingness to suffer and to face danger, the ability to transform the past into something new and different, powers of consistency and endurance, and perhaps above all, a sense for universal values that don't equate to simple knowledge.

Why, though, is it necessary for the masses to lack these strengths? Individuals can rise together to respond to uncommon challenges and adapt speedily to new circumstances – we see this frequently in times of stress when an external threat challenges a community to unite and resist. Why can't they do so as a mass? Haven't they done so in war, revolution and peacetime communal efforts? Isn't progress the work of masses, rather than individuals whose inventions and ideas depend on communal labour and organisation?

According to Nietzsche, the problem is about persistence over time in relation to history. The mass or community either fractures or fails to elevate itself when struck by the 'incoherent forces' of history: 'nature travails in an effort to receive, arrange and honour these strange guests'.[30] The difficulty is in responding to a struggle between different claims, where 'they themselves are in conflict with one another' and therefore demand a superior force 'if one is not oneself to perish in their conflict'.[31] There can be great common achievements in history, but they lack the superior coherence and consistency needed to stand as sublime values over time, against a backdrop of conflict and chaos.

The dilemma is between a risky individual response, set against others, or an answer as a mass, but at the price of failing to live up to new forces. This failure comes from settling for controlling but self-defeating reactions to new challenges: 'Habituation to such a disorderly, stormly and conflict-ridden household gradually becomes a second nature, though this second nature is beyond question much weaker, much more restless, and thoroughly less sound than the first.'[32] If the first nature is to be set in motion by conflicting forces, the second is to become used to them, to lose sight of them. Why is this weak, restless and unsound, if it is part of a successful strategy to cope with the challenge of conflicting demands?

The flaw in the coping strategies of the mass follows from a turn away from new challenges that subsumes them into knowledge. Conflict is filed away as known through its components, even if knowledge has to maintain the contradictions of that conflict. This type of knowledge dissipates the energy and creativity of earlier efforts, in favour of strategies of organisation and control, like a tired revolutionary movement giving way to the management of threats it once sought to transform and overcome, or like a tired industry holding on to old forms of manufacture as new entrants slowly destroy its markets, or a scientific body resisting new hypotheses that run counter to a successful theory.

When this happens, knowledge 'no longer acts as an agent for transforming the outside world but remains concealed within a chaotic inner world'.[33] Threats are brought inside and create internal turmoil, as knowledge seeks to manage them rather than transform itself in an external response, leading to a self-destructive process of internal purges and debates about redundant dogma. This inner chaos explains the restlessness, since the internal conflict has no route to resolution or transformation because the external threat remains and grows, operating unconsciously within knowledge.

The mismatch between external challenge and restless interior, incapable of transforming itself along with its environment, explains why the mass and its strategy are unsound. Surviving through an accommodation with contradictory demands, rather than seeking to overcome them, the mass is undermined from within. It has internalised conflict, like the different factions of a revolution arguing fruitlessly over the future, as enemies gain strength, or like the accountants and engineers of a firm arguing over the cost of refurbishing old machinery while their competitors shift to new production lines.

Given this understanding of conflict and response, it is a mistake to confuse Nietzsche's sublime with two more familiar versions, both from

Burke, but running through Kant and on to later writers, including Lyotard's poststructuralist sublime. First, Nietzsche is original in extending the sublime beyond terrifying events, the stormy thunder and lightning Lyotard retains in his discussion of Heidegger's version of the event in *The Differend*.[34] When Nietzsche uses the phrase 'rolling thunder', as opposed to a single thunderclap, he is defining the sublime as an enduring and robust creation.[35] There's something of permanent revolution and transformation in Nietzsche's sublime. Later, we'll see that this is very important for understanding what he means by eternal values for the sublime.

All this is quite different from the traditional view of the sublime as causing momentary awe; for instance in violent explosions or the terrifying cracking sounds announcing an avalanche. Nietzsche's sublime isn't a passing external sign we learn from; it is a superior power we become. We don't live the sublime in the passive experience of the lightning strike. The sublime individual must become rolling thunder, a continuing energetic outflow, more robust and powerful than those who might seek to know the storm and hold it at bay.

Second, against the association of the sublime with terror and delight, for Nietzsche the sublime isn't in the three-stage unfolding of fear and attraction, respite, and subsequent reflection. The terror and danger accompanying it aren't sublime at the moment when we are released from them by higher ideas, or periods of safety. The release never truly comes, whether in ideas (for a transcendental approach to the sublime) or in moments of blessed peace (for an empiricist reading).

Burke defines the sublime negatively, and in two stages. First, there is a restriction where 'the pain is not carried to violence, and the terror is not conversant about the present destruction of the person'. The physical violation never takes place and, though terrified, we remain untouched. Second, there is a moment of relief and delight in the lifting of this restricted pain: 'as these emotions clear the parts, whether fine, or gross, of a dangerous or troublesome encumbrance, they are capable of producing delight'.[36] This isn't a pure positive pleasure, but rather gladness following a lifting of pain and danger.

Terror and delight determine the sublime in two negations, as a feeling of release (*no longer* in pain) and following relative terror (*not amidst* actual destruction): 'not pleasure, but a sort of delightful horror, a sort of tranquillity tinged with terror; which as it belongs to self-preservation is one of the strongest of all the passions. Its object is the sublime.'[37] Burke's sublime depends on these negations, contradictions and limitations: 'not', 'delightful horror', 'tranquillity tinged with terror' (and terror tinged with tranquillity), 'self-preservation' and 'passion,' understood as a passive response to an external cause. When contrasted with Nietzsche, Burke falls into a fundamental misunderstanding of the sublime as a source of superior values, since those values and the sublime become negations relative to destruction and troubling passions, rather than positive on their own terms. The sublime serves to ward off, rather than create.

For Nietzsche, the sublime is not determined by pain but by joy. It is not to be found in periods of respite but in periods of creative transformation, since to withdraw from the danger of the sublime is to internalise it and make it more dangerous over time. Ideas and passions determined negatively with respect to sublime horror are not confirmed and upheld by it, but are rather illusory protections weakening us. To be truly overcome, a passion must be elevated into an action such that it no longer counts as a negative force. Against Burke's definition, making the sublime a common experience of mitigated threat followed by relief, Nietzsche defines it as an uncommon accomplishment, only achievable by rare individuals.

This turn to an affirmative sublime in Nietzsche is not without costs and threats of its own. In a lecture from 1969, through an appreciation of Yeats as formed by both thinkers (and by Machiavelli and Blake), Conor Cruise O'Brien answers Nietzsche on behalf of Burke: 'There is no doubt that Burke would have loathed Nietzsche, not merely – or I think mainly – as *Antichrist*, but because of Nietzsche's taste for extreme instances, paradoxes, love of the shocking and the original, and above all because of his disrespect for, and reckless inroads on, the socially conserving fund of *prejudice*.'[38] Burke's negativity and passivity, his concern for relief and for the lifting of threats, can be extended to the dangers of Nietzsche's unbridled creativity. The creative sublime is an attack on the conservative value of prejudice, given an affirmative definition as a shared concern for preservation and identity defining a particular society and ensuring its survival.

Ending his lecture, O'Brien voices a prescient warning for future generations of the dangers to come from new 'crypto-Nietzscheans' on the right, with their understanding of new modes of communication and new technologies. His insight reminds us of the need to reflect on the deeper meaning of creativity and on the ethical limits we ought to apply to it, if we are to speak of an egalitarian sublime. Is the political creativity and propaganda implied by the manipulation of new forms of communication a legitimate form of the Nietzschean sublime, or is O'Brien's use of 'crypto' enough to indicate some distance between them?

O'Brien gives a convincing version of how Burke might have loathed and feared Nietzsche, though I would add 'sympathy' to 'prejudice' as ideas Burke might have wished to protect from Nietzsche's critique and alternative approach. Burke's sublime gives rise to social sympathy in two ways. There is the sympathy of common threats experienced in different ways; for instance, the sympathy spectators of a shipwreck feel for those clinging to life as the ship goes down. We'll see that this is still a topic of study today, when we turn to Žižek's critique of the sublime in relation to the sinking of the Titanic.

There is also the more cohesive sympathy of a community warding off danger and the sublime together. This grows into a political consequence of the sublime that Burke applies to the French Revolution. In this politics, the sublime becomes something to avoid and evade. It is the sublime of mobs and of extreme violence, of the disintegration of social norms and practices. Once the sublime is defined negatively, the idea that it should be suppressed is always a possible outcome. As such, the sublime then serves a socially and politically conservative role, far removed from Nietzsche's conception of the creation of a new humanity.

These oppositions lead to two different versions of my diagram of sublime processes, mapped according to their effect on the concepts and practices of inside, outside, active and passive. Importantly, it is not only which direction each thinker draws the effects of the sublime to, but also how each transforms what those directions mean.

Burke draws the diagram strongly to passivity, making the sublime a human passion of terror and delight. In so doing, he restricts the inside to a physiological apparatus of tension and release in humans, while dividing it from the outside – experiences that happen to humans – themselves limited and split into the threatening and sublime, and the beautiful and pleasing. However, activity still features, but as a force for warding off danger and achieving sympathy. As such, activity becomes external and social.

Nietzsche pulls the diagram strongly towards activity, making passivity a bar to the sublime and weakness in the face of danger. He then gives two versions of the inside and outside. For weak passivity, the distinction between inside and outside remains, but it is unstable, because the outside is still at work internally and destructively. For the creativity of the sublime individual, inside and outside are drawn together, to the point where they become indistinguishable, except when the outside is defined as weakness and negativity. On this Nietzschean diagram of the sublime, the masses must remain within passivity and a self-destructive distinction of inside and outside, masquerading as self-preservation. They cannot attain the sublime as creative individuals.

This picture only makes sense if we accept that mass responses to modern challenges fail and lead to decadence. Were a revolution, a social movement, a religion, a science taken as a shared good and achievement, or a new form of political organisation to succeed in answering turmoil with a sublime and communal transformation, both robust and consistent, then the claim for the uniqueness of sublime individuals would collapse. It is for this reason Nietzsche compares some types of democracy, modern science, history and political organisation unfavourably to the works of sublime individuals. It's not that the individuals are superior because wholly different, but rather that they respond better to a common condition and environment, by avoiding knowledge and control in favour of a head-on creative response.

By studying a key remark on science from 'On the Uses and Disadvantages of History for Life', we can follow Nietzsche's original way of articulating the sublime. He begins his point with standard sublime images of earthquakes and volcanic eruptions: 'cities collapse and grow desolate when there is an earthquake and man erects his house on volcanic land only in fear and trembling'.[39] The value of science could follow from a Burkean lesson to be drawn from such sublime experiences. Thanks to scientific knowledge we can make the world a place of delight and safety after the sublime warning from nature.

This isn't Nietzsche's conclusion. Those well-worn images of impending destruction cannot be sublime because they cause fear and not elevation. Furthermore, there is no elevation in the scientific response to possible destruction and the subsequent technological and social progress. Despite its material benefits, the scientific revolution brings weakness: 'life itself grows weak and fearful when the *concept-quake* caused by science robs man of the foundation of all his rest and security, his belief in the enduring and eternal'.[40] Science protects us from sublime threats through a shift in concepts and values (a quake) towards knowledge and technical mastery. This change comes at the expense of more valuable ways of living according to enduring and higher values.

The true values are those created by sublime individuals. When science promises us health and happiness, sublime individuals 'will undermine the concepts this present has of "health" and "culture"'.[41] This isn't a gratuitous act of destruction, but rather a twofold response against an elision of values and towards a new creativity: that of 'an active power that fights, excludes and divides and of an ever more intense feeling of life'.[42] The sublime is neither in sublime events, nor in their avoidance through science and knowledge, but rather in the transformation of our values away from negative passions and towards intense creativity.

Sublime individuals against cohesive communities

Nietzsche's repudiation of science was untimely when it was uttered, appearing absurd or reactionary, but it was designed to grow ever more accurate as a diagnosis of the future, not of science proper, but of a future reliance on knowledge. It fits contemporary life well, as a critique not of our discoveries, but of our dependence on mass media and information as sources of knowledge rather than creative inspiration. We are supplied with difficult news and facts across all fields, but cope with them as something we come to know yet do not respond fully to, in the sense of incorporating them into a new life.

For example, our technologies are for recording, storing, sorting and reproducing information and commodities – they develop an inward eye directed to images and objects. News sources keep us informed, but this knowledge leads to little change through truly new values on the basis of that knowledge. This is weakness for Nietzsche because, though the coping mechanism keeps us secure as knowers, it works against us as doers, locking us into circuits of knowledge exchange, information processing and mean-spirited comparison: 'his head is crammed with a tremendous number of ideas derived from a highly indirect knowledge of past ages and peoples, not from direct observation of life'.[43] The strategy and its systems internalise flaws and weaken us in the face of external threats – including those presented by the very sources of knowledge meant to enlighten us – in preventing us from achieving sublime and critical creations.

Despite their contribution to protection from destruction or pain, each of the values of security, ease, hope and release from pain are negative for Nietzsche. In their operation through cohesive communities – through sympathy, care and sacrifice – they are directed against external and internal threats rather than towards positive self-overcoming, in the sense of using our greatest strengths to attain the highest values we are capable of. Negative values are thereby also directed against creative change, where it doesn't contribute to protection, or puts it at risk.

Positive values, such as culture and creative energy, are affected by this negativity if they are made secondary to the construction of cohesion. When culture becomes an institution it loses its capacity to elevate and transform us, becoming instead an instrument of identity: a means to unite in nationhood, social order, or group identities. If humanity is judged according to an end point, internal drives are subjugated to a single external outcome. Positive values are then bartered for that outcome and controlled by it, through actions aimed at eternal deliverance, or lives bent to fit an abstract criterion of reason, or moral and spiritual norms, taken as inviolable rules for how we should live.

There is a deep opposition between the place Burke assigns to sympathy within the workings of the sublime and Nietzsche's critique of its role in the construction of social cohesion. For Burke, when we witness another's pain, or the pain of a whole society, and project ourselves into it while remaining safe, we experience the combination of terror and delight characteristic of the sublime: 'For sympathy must be considered as a sort of substitution, by which we are put in the place of another man, and affected in a good measure as he is affected, so that this passion may . . . partake of the nature of those which regard self-preservation, and turning on pain may be a source of the sublime.'[44]

This feeling then forms the basis for fellow feeling and communal elevation against suffering, since sympathy and delight combine in a desire for shared self-preservation.

The use of the sublime for communal preservation is controversial in the interpretation of Burke, in particular in connection with colonialism and the sublime. Sara Suleri criticises Burke's sublime because the sympathy and communal values it underpins are those of the historical continuity written by the colonial power: 'The sublime, therefore, functions as a conduit between the delusional aspects of empire-building or breaking and the very solidity of history, which appears to suggest a continually stable hold on what the proper course of events may be.'[45] Luke Gibbons, in contrast, gives a positive gloss where the sublime improves sensitivity and sympathy: 'the politics of the sublime affords the possibility of a more grounded, ethnographic Enlightenment, sensitive to cultural differences, inherited loyalties, and the contingencies of time and place'.[46] It is true that Burke's sublime is distinctive in deducing a type of sympathy from the sublime, but this does not refute Suleri's point, since the sympathy comes out of sublime terror and delight. It is a feeling born of strangeness. Its sympathy radiates from a self-possessed individual or nation confronted by a combination of allure and fearsomeness.

Nonetheless, Gibbons is right to detect a tempering of the confidence and insensitivity of Enlightenment colonialism in Burke's sympathy: 'Though easily construed as a counter-Enlightenment, it offers the possibility of an alternative vision of social change which questions the logic that modernity only extends to the victors, leaving the powerless casualties of history in its wake.'[47] This moderating of the violence of colonialism through sympathy is a possible step to a more equal politics but, if it leaves the sublime untouched and defined once and for all by the colonial power, it is a very modest step and one that fatefully fails to account for the possibility of many other sublimes going beyond the limits of sympathy as a basis for political action.

Though Nietzsche's analysis of the sublime is much closer to Suleri than Gibbons, it offers critical additions to both. The colonial power is weakened by the sympathetic sublime. Action on the basis of sublime sympathy is necessarily a misunderstanding of the higher values attainable in the clash of cultures. A similar argument to these analyses of the sublime and colonialism can be made for Burke's sublime and revolution, as argued by Ronauld Paulson:

> [Burke's imagery of revolution came from] the terrible of his sublime, with precisely the aesthetic distancing implied in his formulation that pain and danger 'are simply painful when their causes immediately affect us; they are delightful when we have an idea of pain and danger, without being actually in

such circumstances'... Burke could come to terms with the Revolution by distancing it as a sublime experience, even while denying its sublimity and realizing that it might not keep its 'distance'.[48]

For Nietzsche, were the sublime to function through sympathy based on self-preservation, leading to delight in the overcoming or forestalling of terrors, or dignity in succumbing to them, then this would be no superior value at all. Each of the moments in this chain is an internalisation of weakness based on misunderstandings. Sympathy comes from a mistaken representation of others and connects us on the basis of negative passions such as pity. Self-preservation seeks an unchanging identity, where the threat demands self-transformation. Delight is merely passing. It is a moment of relief and relaxation making us unaware of a growing menace. There is no dignity in terror, only in active resistance.

Burke's sublime sympathy is marked by a prurient lamentation and a desire to conserve. This is at odds with Nietzsche's concern for renewal and his determined thrust to a new future and to higher values. In describing sympathy, Burke gives two lively and telling examples. First, he remarks how a theatre would empty rapidly at the news that 'a state criminal of high rank is on the point of being executed in the adjoining square'.[49] Sublime delight in art is weaker than real horror. For Nietzsche, it must be the opposite. The sublime is where reality is made, not observed in fear. This is another reason the sublime is not for the masses, because the mass is constituted by a shared gaze and, if we follow Burke, a desire for imitation that 'forms our manners, our opinions, our lives'.[50] As a mass, we are spectators working through comparison and identification; we watch and the sublime individual performs – a tightrope walker or an athlete, and a gawping crowd of passive fans.

Second, Burke conjures up an image of London, 'this noble capital', ruined by an earthquake. Before the quake, none would have been happy to see the city destroyed, but afterwards 'what number from all parts would crowd to behold the ruins'.[51] Here, Burke is in tune with the fascination of the Romantic sublime for classical and imaginary ruins; for instance, in Turner's visions of Italy, following Claude Lorrain. The attraction is explained because in the sublime we 'delight in seeing things, which so far from doing, our heartfelt wishes would be to see redressed'.[52] The desire for redress carries the terror, while the picturesque situation of the ruins conveys the delight.

Nietzsche's objection to this argument is that the sublime cannot be our most supreme elevation if it is a secondary passion, a desire to protect rather than create. Burke's sympathy and the aim of preservation are conservative and backward looking (although supplemented by improvement and ambition), whereas Nietzsche's sublime is a destructive and constructive drive to a different and better future. It is a clearing away of the past to make space for elevating innovations. This does not mean Burke has no place for change.

There is an interesting twist in the argument, here, since Burke's short study of ambition is notable, in a Nietzschean context, for its reference to eternal return of the same as a reason for ambition and change: 'yet if men gave themselves up to imitation entirely, and each followed the other, and so on in an eternal circle, it is easy to see that there never could be any improvement among them'.[53] The study of ambition is also one of the main places where Burke refers to Longinus on the sublime.

From his social, artistic and historical observations, Nietzsche concludes that 'the *goal of humanity* cannot lie in its end but only *in its highest exemplars*'.[54] It is necessarily the case that the sublime can only be achieved by rare individuals, since only they have the strength and daring to stand out from history and make something new. This is what Barnett Newman did in risking an art at once unpopular and revolutionary, even though he claimed universality for it. The universality wasn't in the present. It couldn't be, since it was needed rather than available. It was always to come.

For Nietzsche, the sublime is necessarily conducted through a few untimely individuals, yet they create the highest value for the future of humanity. The paradox of standing for and against humanity is strong here, because the sublime individuals are in combat with present and past humanity. They need to stand out from it in order to create new values for a future humanity they at once deny, depend upon and stand for.

Yet these sublime individuals cannot simply be hermits or exiles, though periods away from others may be necessary to nurture their creativity. They are closer to misunderstood seers or healers, carrying humanity with them against its will.[55] The future those individuals create cannot be solely for themselves. To think this thought would make them poor artists, with an eye to the outcome distracting them from the creative task and with a delusion of independence from a world their art grows from. This kind of bad faith and self-deception would destroy sublime creativity from within. For Nietzsche, the sublime is neither an end, nor a result, nor an absolute.[56] It is always in the creating, as continuing and open overcoming.

The paradox of the sublime also holds in reverse, for humanity itself. It only has a sublime future if all its internal differences and powers can be released from constricting ends and judgements. How can this occur, though, if those differences hold sway in the present and lead humanity to conflict, tempered by compromise and middling values?

Nietzsche's mistrust of democracy comes from the risks of this averaging out of differences and cancelling of rare novelty. He foresees a failure of the sublime in the egalitarian politics of equality and majority, because the highest novel values will be resisted in favour of conciliation and moderation or, more seriously, because in times of stress the highest values will be mistaken for worn out and false ones – the fake leader (such as cynical dictators or thieves), the search for scapegoats (in outsiders or minorities), the illusion of freedom in compromised forms of liberty (in consumerism, for instance), or enslavement to a false ideal (the nostalgia of decadent nations).

Only exceptional individuals are capable of determining a true future for humanity, because they have the capacity to stand out from humanity and lead where it does not want to go – like unpopular artists, reviled in their age, but celebrated many years later; or liberation fighters, seen as agents of social disintegration until a new society is built around their ideas; or scientists at the dawn of a new paradigm, denigrated for denying the patently true. Unlike these innovators, false leaders and ideas take humanity backwards to something it has evolved away from, thereby also amplifying past disasters and mistakes.

Burke remarks how the sublimity of the stars depends upon a perceived absence of order and care: 'The apparent disorder augments [grandeur], for the appearance of care is highly contrary to our ideas of magnificence. Besides, the stars lay in such apparent confusion, as makes it impossible on occasion to reckon them.'[57] It's this perception of disorder and the impossibility of reckoning (of understanding) that forces sublime creators out of humanity for Nietzsche; were they understood and were their works signs of recognisable care by the majority, they would not be sublime. This is not the case for Burke, since he offers an associative account of poetry as sublime in Book V of his philosophical enquiry.[58]

The contradiction of communal elevation through singular individuals locks humanity and sublime individuals into profound oppositions. It is important not to lose sight of them when considering the idea that sublime individuals create for humanity. First, on the level of social interactions, the desire to conserve and avoid conflict encourages us to seek shared values. For Nietzsche, this exchange of individuality for similarity is opposed to life, because the desire for all to be the same makes us weaker, not only as individuals, but also as a whole. Life evolves by risking many different creative changes. Societies thrive through this innovation, since it allows them to renew themselves and be adequate to unexpected threats. We should therefore work against our desire for compromise and encourage divisiveness, not in old divisions or apparent diversity, but in separation from ourselves for the sake of something new and higher.

Second, on the level of social hierarchies, the need for exceptions depends on the division between the masses and sublime individuals. These individuals must stand apart from the masses, in order to be able to create new works the majority cannot understand, appreciate or value at the time of creation. For Christine Battersby, this impossibility of understanding is constitutive of the sublime, even for the sublime individual: 'Like the Kantian sublime, Nietzsche's reconfigured *sublim* disarms conceptual understanding; but, unlike Kant, Nietzsche links the sublime to "difference" and to those aspects of an event, a subject, or an object that are registered at the level of the pre-conscious, but that our framework of assumptions stop us from seeing.'[59] Where the Kantian sublime will compensate this lack in understanding through a single moral vision, Nietzsche replaces it with a more mobile and open sense of difference.

The focus on difference – and disagreement about what constitutes difference – is important here for understanding the complex nature of the sublime event and its ongoing nature, rather than finished perfection. New works are challenges to current ways of life. The majority must fear and reject them, because living as a collective depends on order and common agreement to ensure cohesion. These are put at risk when a novel idea takes shape, such as an innovative industrial process threatening redundancies, or a new kind of love upsetting social order, or countercultural ways of life cutting away from economic, bureaucratic and political dependencies. Battersby is sceptical about this challenge. Having recognised the commitment to a kind of difference in it, she doubts how far it takes us and whether it really shakes the old order: 'Nietzsche's reconfigured bodily sublime involves an encounter that does not take us outside the realm of representation. Nor is there simply a disruption to a single linguistic or symbolic reality that is the "truth" that is always, everywhere the same.'[60]

To the objection that sublime artists and leaders have been followed widely at the time of their highest creative activity, Nietzsche explains how this adoption still involves misunderstanding and a distortion of the sublime creation; for instance, in the uncritical fanaticism of the followers, or in their desire to draw the sublime creator back into humanity through base forms such as an obsession with biographical details, rather than an effort to take the new work even further. Here too Nietzsche is original in diagnosing how the sublime defined as a passion will have a tendency to destructive and regressive types of enthusiasm, as was manifest in twentieth-century uses of the sublime in propaganda such as Riefenstahl's *Triumph of the Will* and, differently, *Olympia*.

Third, on the level of values over time, the untimely quality of the sublime and its opposition to present values and to future ends implies inequality between settled values and emergent ones. This might seem an unimportant disparity but it is more consequent than the others. It means that what we think we know in the present and what we think we should aim for in future are of lesser value than the creation of the new as something ongoing, unfinished and uncertain. By extension, it also implies a difference in value between living according to settled values, whether current or future, and living in the midst of the creation of new ones. For Nietzsche, the sublime cannot be an end point.

If the sublime is necessarily untimely, it seems that it must be opposed to egalitarianism and committed to the emergence of individuals or subgroups away from the mass. The argument depends on defining time as a kind of historical continuity and order. Time cannot be a simple succession of independent instants, because then the idea of succession would make no sense either, so something must bring it together. From the point of view of humanity this cohesion depends on shared memory and practices. Continuity with a remembered past gives us time and history, but it also means we depend on the identification and preservation of joint memory and tradition.

Paul Ricoeur's reading of Aristotle in *Time and Narrative, Volume 1* leads to a succinct version of the argument for narrative and plots as collective forms of wisdom, leading to shared universals that overcome discontinuity in time and ensure the coherence of myth: 'They are universals related to practical wisdom, hence to ethics and politics. A plot engenders such universals when the structure of its action rests on the connections internal to the action and not to external accidents.'[61] This view depends on a belief in the sharing of practical wisdom and agreement about plots that Nietzsche's sublime rejects. Not only is history about the decay and failure of so many instances of practical wisdom, but there is never agreement about plots or narratives, except where the assent is imposed.

The untimely is a break with time defined as continuity with the past in the present through memory, itself defined as collective narration, justification and activity. Alexander Rehding argues that, counter to the commemorative role of monuments in the nineteenth century, Nietzsche sees a void at the core of monuments, not a continuity with the past but rather its undoing in favour of nothingness.[62] In his distinction between monumental, antiquarian and critical species of history, Nietzsche sees the critical as the most elevating in relation to the future, but not in the guise of reforming critique, since this would aim to fill the void. He means critique as an expression of the void and of creative attempts to deepen it, thereby increasing its untimeliness.[63]

The untimely individual is therefore outside time from two perspectives: for the individual and for the society dependent on shared memory. The individual falls out with the mass, since the sublime life needs to break with historical values and judgements in order to be able to create anew. The mass is threatened by the individual's untimeliness, because it perceives danger from ways of life and creations threatening the shared stories, values, practices, norms, truths and types of order that prevent time and society from fragmenting.

When Nietzsche describes his thought as dynamite, he is doing more than admitting to the risks it presents to him and to others. He is also recognising how it must appear to others in its threat to the common stories and truths needed for continuity and cohesion over time: 'It is always a dangerous process, especially so for life itself: and men and ages which serve life by judging and destroying a past are always dangerous and endangered men and ages.'[64] This might seem distant from a direct threat to common ideas of equality, but it strikes at their foundation, since the sublime individual 'must possess and from time to time employ the strength to break up and dissolve a part of the past'.[65] This strength is unreachable for the mass, as a challenge to the norms and laws they must hold dear as conditions for community.

Even if the sublime is to point to a new equality to come at some future time, it must be at the expense of current ideas of equality. The problem is yet more severe because, were sublime individuals to advocate a new equality, this would rest upon a denial of the possibility of making that plea according to current values. The new equality would be inconceivable according to older truths. The sublime individual is therefore necessarily born of inequality, and the mass is incapable of living according to the new sublime idea of equality at the time of the birth of the idea. This is why 'untimely' also means 'too early' for Nietzsche. Sublime individuals always appear before their sublime creations can be accepted and valued.

The untimely nature of the sublime reinforces the paradox of the continuity of time for the sublime individual: time must cohere through independent instants. For continuous historical time, memory and connection with the past ensure the present isn't a clean break in time. Though each new present is different, from the point of view of memory it is only different within the limits of the past. Every change is a variation within a recognised order and a connection to the logic and reason of historical development.

However, for the untimely sublime, with its rebellion against past patterns and values, time is once again at risk of shattering. The solution to this paradox is to make the sublime a reconnection of time but not through the continuation of past values and reasons. One of Nietzsche's most difficult and powerful ideas is that the sublime isn't simply untimely as outside time or as a break in time. It is rather that the untimely sublime is also a recasting of the whole of time: not new and different from here onwards, but new and different for all times.

The sublime is eternal in this transformation of all times – not eternal in the ideal sense of an unchanging idea, but eternal as a change across the whole of time. When Nietzsche alludes to a common eternal realm for all sublime creators and creations, it is not through a common receptacle, a paradise for all things sublime, but through a shared property. All sublime creators and creations recast the whole of time. There is therefore a connection between Nietzsche's definition of the sublime and his thought of eternal return.

The sublime must pass the test of eternal return, or it will have failed. Nietzsche makes this argument in *Thus Spoke Zarathustra*. In 'Of the Vision and the Riddle', he first presents the certainty of failure in the most superior men and values: '"O Zarathustra," he said mockingly, syllable by syllable, "you stone of wisdom! You have thrown yourself high, but every stone that is thrown must – fall!"'[66] Eternal return is the reason for this necessary fall: 'and must we not return and run down that other lane out before us, down that long, terrible lane – must we not return eternally?'[67] Sublime individuals can rise, but their rise will be followed by a fall taking them back from whence they came. The riddle is then the challenge of how superior individuals can live through the test of eternal return: 'No longer a shepherd, no longer a man – a transformed being, surrounded with light, laughing!'[68]

The most original reading of eternal return, as allied to sublime values, is by Pierre Klossowski in his analysis of eternal return as a selective doctrine. Of greatest interest here is Klossowski's remark that eternal return has to be selective against equality and against the preservation of humanity as a whole, in order to counter the repetition of the same that takes place through modern industrialisation: 'To the degree that humanity seeks consistency in and through its conservation alone, it falls even further into inconsistency. The increase in the number of *agents* of existence is proportional to the decrease in power of each of them.'[69]

There are Malthusian overtones to this translation of Nietzsche's argument into population numbers. I will not consider them beyond Klossowski, other than to note how the arguments about inequality and the sublime become far more violent and opposed to equality if we suppose that the sublime is in some way rationed or, even worse, in diminishing supply. This isn't Klossowski's or Nietzsche's argument, since for them the sublime is created and the question is more about the balance of power between creative individuals and the masses; but it is one way of thinking about the sublime as a store of value, a way certain to be in play at a time when resources are diminishing, the world is unstable, and traditional measures for the sublime are in shorter supply.

In 'On the Uses and Disadvantages of History for Life', a work earlier than those containing his ideas of eternal return, Nietzsche renders this step into eternal values, and out of the despair of eternal return, through the selection of a 'familiar, perhaps commonplace theme, an everyday melody'.[70] The everyday is sublimated into eternity by 'elevating it into a comprehensive symbol' fusing all times together and 'thus disclosing in the original theme a whole world of profundity, power and beauty'.[71] Again, this requires a rare and refined skill, 'great artistic facility, creative vision, loving absorption of the empirical data, the capacity to imagine the further development of a given type'.

The sublime individual is unlike common humanity, in changing objectivity from a cool assessment of the present into an artistic 'inward flashing eye' for the future of that present. In Nietzsche's original twist, the sublime is brought inside as a flashing creative insight, transforming the whole of time but starting from an internal and individual creativity, rather than passivity before an external source.

This power to see into the future and change the values of the present and the past is a further reason for the exclusivity of sublime individuals: 'Do not believe historiography that does not spring from the head of the rarest minds.'[72] The difficulty of the task calls for exceptional abilities, in its amalgamation of great imagination for the future, powerful critical analysis of the present, and reconnection to universal ideas from the past: the 'genuine historian must possess the power to remint the universally known into something never heard of before'.[73]

Four different but related definitions of the untimely therefore determine the sublime for Nietzsche: the untimely as rupture in time and break with the past; as an idea that arrives too early; as an eternal truth outside any given epoch of historical time; and as a recasting of the whole of time in a new way, as a new perspective on life. Each of these definitions is also a challenge to ideas of egalitarianism, defined classically as equality across all members of a society. As break in time, the sublime is a rupture in society across the dividing moment: individuals creating the future, separated from a mass preserving the past. The idea of arriving too early depends on a distinction between those who cannot recognise the sublime at a particular epoch and those who create it. The eternity of the sublime as truth is not available to all, only to sublime individuals, because the eternal truth is in creation, not in a finished work or idea to be consumed or assented to.

Finally, the recasting of the whole of time in the sublime takes place as a struggle determined by the other divisions brought about by untimeliness. A sublime creation is at once eternal in its truth and fragmented in its historical manifestation since, though it changes everything as truth, the way this truth takes hold over historical time is through difficult and often violent conflicts between the old and the new, between the desire to conserve and the dangerous drive to make things different. For Nietzsche, there can be no social equality in how this conflict unfolds.

Through the few, but for the many?

There's a possible answer to the negative conclusion on Nietzsche's sublime and egalitarianism. It is that humanity is redeemed through the creations of sublime individuals. Keith Ansell Pearson has developed this idea while stressing the importance of the sublime for Nietzsche.[74] He agrees that the sublime corresponds to the highest values but adds that this connects untimely creation to the future of humanity: '[Philosophy] is a sublime exercise and operation in that it entails elevating individuals to greatness and nobility and creating a people, or a humanity, equal to this concept.'[75]

Ansell Pearson focuses on activity ('exercise and operation') in the sublime. He also notes how equality, if it is to come, must emerge from a division between sublime individuals and others. The sublime is not a thing. It is an action to be accomplished by some, not all. The consequent divide is overcome through the idea of equality arriving as a consequence of greatness. However, for a critique of Nietzsche's sublime, everything turns on the meaning of equality in greatness. Is it equality in the same way for all, or some kind of participation in the greatness of others? Or is the equality only for a few?

Philosophically, the sublime is a significant thread through Nietzsche's works, explaining his reactions to other philosophers such as Plato, Hegel and Schopenhauer, his conception of the artist, and his criticisms of past and contemporary epochs. It leads to the philosophical project of a future humanity, where sublime individuals and humanity can be reunited through sublime creation.

This future cannot be given in a single representation, or through utopian images, or in the description of a perfect city, culture or human being. As sublime, the future never arrives at a finished state, but is rather to be lived as an increase in sublime creativity. There can be many different sublime activities and peoples. There can't be a single sublime outcome. Like the life of the sublime individual, this future will not be a smooth path of ever-increasing greatness, but a winding one, with its setbacks and suffering, followed by outbursts of creativity. Again like the sublime individual, these fluctuations follow from internal complexity: not one drive, but many competing positive and negative ones. They also follow from a difficult relation of this complexity to changing environments: not isolated activity, but a struggle with changing situations.

Given this difficulty and struggle, inequality in powers and circumstances are conditions for the sublime. Its heights require 'superior perception of vision', 'extraordinary states of mind and action', 'dangerous conditions', 'rare and impressive resources', and 'daring that is both desperate and hopeful'.[76] This leads to a life 'pushing itself further and further, upwards',[77] and this effort is away from the mundane life of the masses because it has to be exceptional: 'to become what one "is" where this refers to what is "unique, singular, incomparable"'.

It would be wrong to conclude that these exceptional individuals are struggling just for themselves: 'one is not simply a lawgiver for the sake of oneself. Nietzsche is inviting the empirical individual to elevate itself, to become equal to what is best in life and in itself, and for the sake of life.'[78] The sublime individual is part of life and stands for it. To forget this would once again be weakness through lack of understanding. Nietzsche is not defending a thesis built around selfish or self-obsessed individuals, unaware of their debt to and dependence on life.

Nonetheless, elevating oneself for the sake of life is not to strive for all actual living beings, or even for all future ones. The argument can be put in biological terms. Ansell Pearson is an interpreter of the influence of biology on philosophers; he shows this influence for Bergson and Deleuze, as well as Nietzsche. Biology changes over time and the relevant biological theories are historical, corresponding to the epochs of each thinker.

Influenced by early Darwinism, yet also critical of it, evolution for Nietzsche depends on exceptions standing out and attempting something new. This does not mean being absolutely different. Biological and philosophical exceptions are living beings: 'All living things require an atmosphere around them, a mysterious misty vapour; if they are deprived of this envelope, if a religion, an art, a genius is condemned to revolve as a star without atmosphere, we should no longer be surprised if they quickly wither and grow hard and untruthful.'[79] The efforts of sublime individuals contribute to life, belonging to how it evolves and what it evolves to, participating in how life perfects itself: 'philosophers, artists (and saints) as the perfection of nature . . . "a most sublime order"'.[80]

John Richardson argues that 'The key point Nietzsche takes from Darwin is a different model for teleology, which he extends and applies.'[81] In stressing the epistemic aspect of values as kinds of self-knowledge and knowledge of nature, and in arguing that 'genuine philosophers have always also created values *for society*', Richardson offers an interpretation apparently at odds with the one given here.[82] For the sublime creator, values are always untimely and valuation is always strategic rather than epistemic: a creative struggle rather than the search for and sharing of knowledge.[83] Nonetheless, the two interpretations are not as far apart as it might seem. Knowledge does follow from sublime creations, but the key thing is that it is not sublime once it becomes knowledge. The fall into knowledge is one of the ways in which sublime values become entrenched and dangerous. We'll see examples of this decay into damaging distinctions in Chapter 6, in critical discussions of Kant and Descartes.

In considering how sublime individuals redeem the whole of humanity, it might be thought that since all of life evolves through exceptional individuals, every part of life is equal to every other, once evolution has taken place. The mass would have absorbed exceptional qualities and become equivalent to earlier sublime individuals. This argument conflates evolution through exceptional individuals and a state of evolution at a later date. Were sublime individuals to be great artists contributing to the evolution of culture, this would not imply that future humans would all be great artists, but rather that future humans would benefit from this shared culture, even if they did not create it.

Martin Ryle and Kate Soper are therefore right to see Nietzsche as opposed to their defence of general creative elevation through sublime culture: 'Matthew Arnold's conception of culture as offering "sublime" experiences from which all could in principle benefit.'[84] Nietzsche's sublime is counter to the contention that we can all be elevated into makers of culture by learning from sublime works. When defended by Ryle and Soper, 'the best cultural works are "sublime" . . . in the more limited sense of giving us access to a more comprehensive authorial or writerly perspective'.[85] Nietzsche's argument is the exact opposite. As untimely and sublime, cultural works cannot be absorbed into the perspectives of the masses without losing their sublimity.

Nietzsche denies the hope for wide cultural improvement through general access to creativity, in the strong sense of everyone becoming sublime creators. Sublimity must remain closed to the masses, because it is necessarily for a few untimely individuals and must therefore be rejected by the mass as a threat and as beyond sense. This does not mean Nietzsche is always opposed to cultural education, or that he rejects the idea of universal improvement. It means that he does not believe such an education can increase sublimity, since the sublime must always remain rare. It is worth noting how this argument also implies different definitions of sense for sublime individuals and for the masses; and different ideas of sense as untimely and historically located. Some will feel differently. The way they feel will make them alien.

For the mass to evolve through them, exceptional individuals must stand out from the mass. However, even at a later date, when evolution has taken place, the mass cannot be equivalent to the earlier individuals, since it still does not have the quality of being exceptional and since it requires new exceptions for its own evolution. The mass evolves, but it is never a mass of sublime individuals. Inequality remains.

Nietzsche's point goes further than natural evolution, defined as the evolution of a population through exceptions from a norm or majority. Sublime creation must remain exceptional in the strong sense of removed from the laws of nature, if they are understood as applying in the same way to all. A further sense of untimely is important here. The sublime individual is outside physical and biological time, if time is defined as unfolding lawfully, regularly and predictably (according to a statistical mean or a range of probabilities) or progressing rationally (according to logic and reason) or unfolding organically (following patterns of evolution). Sublime individuals are philosophical, saintly or artistic, when these are understood as partly free from the laws of nature.

An interpretation of the redemption of humanity falls at this point. We could assume that Nietzsche is arguing for elevation thanks to reason. Sublime creators would contribute to reason and to enlightenment as shared by later humanity. But this would be to misunderstand the nature of reason and enlightenment for the sublime individual. Neither takes a form shareable at later times. Reason for the sublime individual is not about a replicated content or method, but about a manner or way. It is attached to the individual and prone to perish when copied by others.

Modes of mass learning, such as imitation, are not appropriate for the sublime. The sublime individual cannot be successfully imitated. The sublime is not an eternal ideal, object, style, concept, figure or measure that could be adhered to. For Nietzsche, the sublime is solely eternal as a manner and energy of art that transforms the whole of life in the act of creation. Its secret is unveiled through experimentation, only guided by example but never complete as copy or model. The sublime is the highest value, not as norm or standard, but as a superior evaluation, always in new ways and through new works.

The sublime individual therefore defies law, logic and reason in ways implying strong opposition to Enlightenment ideals around common reason and humanity. If there is to be a redemption of humanity through the sublime it will not come from a shared common sense or rationality, or from actions based on laws following from them, such as Kant's categorical imperative or a rational basis for human rights. The sublime individual is not sublime by proffering or pursuing just laws – true and good for the whole of humanity – because creative powers are negated by such laws and rights, in their general sense of moral restrictions and in the practical sense of requiring political and social apparatuses designed to uphold and impose them.

Paul Guyer tracks this shift from transcendent rationality to the transvaluation of the value of rationality itself, from Kant to Nietzsche:

> In Nietzsche's hands the sublime becomes an experience of the transcendence of rationality rather than that of a transcendent rationality but remains, as it had for Kant, an affirmative experience: in what he would later call the 'transvaluation of values,' Nietzsche sees human redemption in transcending the limits of individual reason and identifying with the absurd and contradictory nature of existence.[86]

The sublime turns from a superior freedom and law, transcending nature, to a creative transformation of all values, a transcendence of rationality itself. In so doing Nietzsche counters decadence in the idea of the sublime after Kant, where it turned into a negative value: 'Nietzsche, in effect, returns the sublime to the position of importance that it had enjoyed under Kant and Schiller but gradually lost in the work of Schelling, Hegel and Schopenhauer.'[87] Guyer's emphasis on the absurd and contradictory aspects of the sublime is important for understanding why sublime individuals are out of step with their contemporaries. The sublime must appear contradictory and absurd, since it is a radical challenge to the values and knowledge of its age.

Nietzsche has disdain for the masses, not out of unthinking disgust, but because the masses are a threat to sublime creations, always leading them into decay or opposition: 'The masses seem to me to deserve notice in three respects only: the first as faded copies of great men produced on poor paper with worn out plates, then as a force of resistance to great men, finally as instruments in the hands of great men; for the rest, let the Devil and statistics take them!'[88] The sublime individual does not redeem humanity or the masses by gifting enlightenment or reason to them. They would only make poor copies of these gifts, or fight against them, or become fodder for them.

It would also be wrong to think the sublime redeems because humanity will inherit from sublime individuals. Nietzsche's version of evolution goes beyond genetic explanations, since sublimity is about creation as evaluation, as a new way of interacting with life by enhancing it and transforming it. The relation between beings and evaluation is not one of cause and effect; it is more loose and tentative. Among Nietzsche's most important insights on the sublime are its resistance to repetition, since each iteration erodes the sublimity of the original, by dragging it into new environments it is not suited to and by taking it away from the individual source of its energy and truth.

It does not matter what sense of inheritance is used, from genetic, to intellectual, to cultural and artistic. The inheritors are guaranteed not to be sublime in the same way as their ancestors were, because they will always require different powers for different challenges and because every power wanes within and across individuals. This is why Nietzsche insists that sublime individuals are outside the process of history. The worst thing we could do is try to be sublime in the same way as our progenitors, to imitate them, thereby rendering ourselves incapable of the untimely. Yet the masses must live by imitating in order to stand as a homogeneous group.

The contrast with Burke's sublime is at its strongest where Nietzsche defines the sublime individual as taking life further but at great risk and against the rules and laws designed to protect the species. For Burke, delight is the sign of the sublime through the operation of sympathy and imitation. This pleasure through sharing encourages community in two ways: imitation of works, and, more importantly, imitation of nature through observation, for instance, of human physiology.

When Burke applies his definition of the sublime to the arts, he arrives at a statement that could stand as a summary of his conflict with Nietzsche: 'The true standard of the arts is in every man's power; and an early observation of the commonest, sometimes of the meanest things in nature, will give the truest lights, where the greatest sagacity and industry that slights such observations, must leave us in the dark, or what is worse, amuse and mislead us by false lights.'[89] For Burke, value in the arts is available to all and found in the most comment experiences. Nietzsche gives us the reply that the sublime cannot be in every man's power, because true observation is only achieved by a few untimely individuals with the energy and powers to escape imitation and the mundane. Sublimity depends on leaving the masses, risking their mistrust and loathing.

Given sympathy and correct observation of nature, Burke's sublime fosters conservation and community: 'the passions belonging to self-preservation are the strongest of all passions'.[90] If we follow Nietzsche, this sublime community of shared safeguards is an error, since the sublime cannot be shared by all and isn't a passion. More importantly, as defined conservatively by Burke, the sublime is a mistake about life. Life and humanity evolve and survive because some individuals discard self-preservation as conservation, replacing it with the risk of sublime creation, eschewing imitation of others and imitation of nature.

If the sublime individual is exceptional for Nietzsche, it is not strictly as an exception or variation within a species. It is rather as an untimely individual, where to be different is not to vary in one way or another across a range of possibilities, but rather to create something new that is wholly exceptional. In so far as the sublime is a matter of truth, it is as a truthful individual evaluation. In this sense, we can only have examples of truthful evaluation, rather than truths themselves. Truth is neither about known truths (facts, laws or methods) nor about the production of future truths (the discovery of as yet unknown truths).

This explains Nietzsche's ambivalence about truth and science when he discusses the sublime. If truth amounts to established scientific truths, or to a scientific method, the sublime individual is beyond truth, because the sublime creation is a challenge to given truths and methods as ways of ordering and limiting life. Nietzsche expresses this in terms of the roles of forgetting and of eternal truths in sublime creation: '[science] hates forgetting, which is the death of knowledge, and seeks to abolish all limitations of human horizon and launch mankind upon an infinite and unbounded sea of light whose knowledge is of all becoming'.[91] It is a mistake to see the sublime redemption of humanity as salvation through progress. The truth of sublime individuals is eternal because it forgets and destroys, in affirming individual creative powers and not our common store of knowledge.

Jeffrey Church therefore restricts Nietzsche's argument when he defends the claim that 'the aesthetic justification Nietzsche offers . . . is not through artwork but rather through the beautiful lives of exemplary individuals, who become immortalized as permanent parts of humanity's memory and identity'.[92] Memory as permanent record misses and obscures the sublime as untimely. Individual lives are sublime exactly because they are not beautiful. This is not only because there is no aesthetic judgement adequate to such an evaluation, but also because evaluating lives in this way, according to common norms, is contrary to sublime creation as eternally unique, and because the sublime is not about lives but about creative processes. The immortality of biography – the lowest form of humanism – is fundamentally opposed to the sublime, because it preserves the life when it should be transforming the creation.

Church claims that 'humanity can transcend its own origins and devote itself to the eternal'.[93] This is to mislead us about Nietzsche's sublime. Devotion to an 'eternal ideal'[94] will fail as sublime creativity, since sublimity depends on destroying ideals, creating new works and abandoning faith in permanence in favour of individual acts of rebellious creativity. Humanity cannot share in the sublime by idolising sublime lives. This act of devotion is a misunderstanding of how those lives stood out from the masses by breaking with them, in order to create eternal evaluations rather than ideals. Devotion is dependent on hagiography, purification and replication. It is the business of religions. The sublime requires betrayal, realism and distortion. Humanity is at its most tawdry, slow and self-deceiving – least capable of living up to new challenges – when it worships and imitates the lives of the great: 'In relation to such dead men, how few of the living have a right to live at all!'[95]

Nonetheless, Nietzsche speaks of the sublime as for humanity, rather than simply for life, because sublime metaphysical creations go beyond life understood as natural evolution. Humanity stands out from other life forms, animals in particular, because humanity can rise with the sublime individual. For Ansell Pearson, 'The "sublime" is the moment of perception or vision when we experience the elevation of the human beyond the merely animal, when life raises itself up through the conquering and overcoming of need and makes "the leap of joy".'[96] This is not an elevation of all humans, but rather a perspective on some humans becoming different by overcoming the forces compelling the mass of humanity to decline and fail.

This is not an elevation of humanity as individuals or as a whole. It is that some human acts can be sublime. The important point of interpretation is where Nietzsche makes this claim: 'Not to bear their race to the grave, but to found a new generation of this race.'[97] The sublime new generation is not the race as a whole. The race as a whole is always heading to its grave because it becomes maladapted and decadent. The new generation must therefore be a subset standing out by sharing sublime powers and eternal creativity, a power to rise to new challenges, rather than the need to pretend they are old ones.

Rising through perception does not mean passively looking or seeing; it is rather in the experience of living differently and better in a given environment – closer to the sense of living in an environment in a novel manner than to the sense of perceiving a set of stimuli. Similarly, rather than the elimination of wants or scarcity, or the satisfaction of material desires, the overcoming of need must be understood as an overcoming of negativity and nihilism.

In Ansell Pearson's interpretation of Nietzsche, 'need' is shorthand for a consequence of negativity: to live life according to opposition and lack. The sublime individual rises above this dependence on negative values, such as judging oneself according to what one isn't or what one does not have. This is another reason to reject the interpretation of humanity rising through its devotion to the beautiful or sublime lives of exemplary individuals.

The sublime is a self-overcoming in its double meaning of overpowering negative drives and self-transformation, as rising above oneself. This cannot be achieved through devotion to masters or through copying their lives or works. Like Nietzsche himself, to avoid the temptation to imitate, sublime educators of the future will have to disappoint and elude their pupils, while transmitting creative values.

There are two further misunderstandings to avoid about the elevation of humanity through the sublime. The first is to think that humanity is not part of life understood more widely. Though humanity is raised through the sublime human individual, this does not mean humans aren't animals or that all of life is not raised with the human. On the contrary, the sublime individual creates in ways that also elevate the animal and nature, but only do so by transforming the human, in the superman possessing higher powers of perception as a transformation of nature.

In avoiding the second misunderstanding, we are also able to respond to a critical point against Nietzsche stemming from the first mistake. Sublime creations must not be confused with scientific and technological inventions, pitting humans against nature, or assisting them in transforming nature. This is a response to the critical point that factory abattoirs and eight-lane motorways through mountain ranges hardly seem to elevate humans, animals or nature. Industrial development based on science and technology, rational justifications for industrial exploitation, and the spread of megacities over nature are not what Nietzsche means by sublime.

The sublime should therefore not be confused with the strict identification of humanity with either its animal or mechanical aspects. Nietzsche is working against the sublime of scale and reproduction, if it is understood as the product of modernity in either its anti-spiritual or technological guises: 'It is a sublime vision of the human being . . . that Nietzsche offers in contrast to other images of the human we find in modernity, such as the image that glorifies its descent into bestiality or the image that seeks to tell us that nothing more is at work or operating in the human than a robotic automatism.'[98] This distinction is significant because it means Nietzsche cannot be allied to the idea of a sublime reached when humanity is transformed by technological enhancements or reduced back to some state of nature.

It is a fundamental mistake to confuse Nietzsche's idea of the superman with an increase in physical or intellectual powers, as measured, understood and valued by a particular society. We might read Nietzsche's argument as superficially connected to modern concerns with physical and intellectual feats in sport, games, intellectual tests and warfare. This would be incorrect since they all miss the thoroughgoing nature of creative transformation in the sublime. Nietzsche's superman has nothing to do with those who excel according to common measures, the successful entrepreneur or sportsperson, for instance.

A project for superior humans based on technological implants, biological improvements and mechanical or virtual extensions would also having nothing to do with the sublime individual, if that project is about increasing powers we already have: better sight, faster limbs, greater strength, more longevity, fewer passions, less weakness, faster minds, better memory. Those values are well understood by all; they are the values of the mass. In no way do they make humanity different as a creator of values. Nietzsche's sublime individuals must seem weak and imperfect when compared to these technological trans-humans. Their missions are different: to elevate by making things different, as opposed to the appearance of elevation in the inflation of known strengths.

Excellence in established sports, games, tests and warfare are the epitome of negation from the perspective of the creation of new values – for participants and spectators. The only way those fields can be sublime is through participants whose moves transform the activities into something different. If this leads to 'winning', it is not about victory within the rules but in the overcoming and creation leading to a win (or to a loss). It isn't that the game or race was won, but that a different way of thinking and acting, and different values, emerged in the winning (or losing).

Ansell Pearson often returns to the importance of art for Nietzsche's sublime, including the idea of philosophy as art. Though sport can be given sublime imagery and vocabulary, it is a false sublime, because the actual achievement is only a marginal gain, or a pushing back of a limit, therefore far from exceptional in manner or measure, according to Nietzsche's more radical sense. Creative overcoming in sport is judged according to goals and limits, where statistical performance within the rules (further, faster, higher) matters more than a style or manner. The opposite is true for art. The artist working faithfully within the laws of a given school, with the goal of producing fitting art, is always further from the sublime than creators of new styles, techniques and experiences.

As an example of the sporting version of the sublime, taking cues from Kant, Tim Gorichanaz argues for a constant search for more sublime forms of running as ways of resisting the take-over of sport by technology and commodification. He therefore advocates a form of sublime wild running: 'The wild turn of ultrarunning seems to represent an effort to heighten the sublime experience of sport: Though ultrarunning in all places can be sublime, ultrarunning in the wilderness can be all the more sublime.'[99] The problem with this argument, from the point of view of Nietzsche's definition of the sublime, is that the sublime should be neither about giving a higher meaning to life by pushing back current physical boundaries, nor about seeking to attain the sublime by returning to nature and wilderness. There is a contradictory combination of escapism, conformism and nostalgia in this sporting sublime. It entraps the sublime in current states of knowledge and in reactionary values, misunderstanding the nature of infinity by defining it as a receding limit to strive for.

Sublime creation and elevation imply rising above merely destructive and negative forces in the human, where 'mere' indicates how destruction and negation aren't secondary aspects of a higher and positive creation. The sublime is not a release from impediments or an increase in the strengths required to overcome them. Though scientific, technological and cultural creations can be sublime, by making humanity different and better, this is not achieved if the goal is simply an improvement of current states and values.

It would be easy to take Nietzsche's expression 'the leap of joy' and think of joys and achievements for all humans. The meaning is exactly the opposite. The sublime is not in the ideas of faster, stronger, happier, cleverer and more populous humans. If equality is defined as an equal share in such general increases, then the sublime does not aim for that equality. This is important because it distances Nietzsche from political systems based on an equal share of growing resources and from utilitarian conceptions of a general increase in happiness.

The sublime is not in general freedom from needs, or shared wealth, or even in the artistic products of a society of leisure. This means Nietzsche is also distant from the science of economics, where it maintains its utilitarian roots and measures success according to growth in productivity, leading to an increase in aggregate happiness or comfort. The sublime cannot be measured in this way, since it is a challenge both to the idea of measurement of quantities, as assessment of value, and to the idea of a common measure between historical progress and the untimely sublime.

This opposition to collective improvement relative to standards such as shared wealth or ease runs deeper than a difference in aims. Collective values work against the sublime. For Ansell Pearson, Nietzsche is 'inviting us to value the rare and the unique, in which humanity works towards the production of great individual human beings as its most essential task'.[100] The effort is towards the individual, not for all humans.

The important relation here is between the ideas of 'rare' and 'unique' and the 'great individual being'. We could imagine rarity and uniqueness to apply to the possessions or experiences of a collective; for instance, where all participate in their own ways in valuable pleasures, practices or products, in a comfortable and cultured life available to all. None of those valuables are sublime.

Sublimity lies rather in the way a sublime individual appears, bringing new and strange values. Again, this is instructive for our late-coming society, with its attraction to sublime antiques and past achievements – to rarity grasped as increasing scarcity. Collected works, museum pieces, past acts and feats are only sublime when they contribute to new creations. If we value something for what it was, rather than for how it participates in new and uncertain sublimity, then we are dealing in nihilistic processes, sure to inhibit our creative powers.

This implies a counter-intuitive definition of humanity. It does not include all humans. It lies in the exceptional values that indicate the way to a superior and different future for humanity. The appropriate images for humanity are therefore not found in collections of many different faces and bodies, but in greatness coming out of waste: the short film produced by discarding countless outtakes, or the inspiring artwork standing out from more numerous mediocre and expendable reproductions, or supermen barely recognisable as human to the humanity they rise from: 'The goal is neither a large number of specimens and their well-being nor those specimens that are the last to evolve... Great human beings "redeem" nature and evolution... "not for the benefit of the majority"'.[101]

Individuals and masses

To study the effects of Nietzsche's original take on the sublime, I propose another simple fourfold diagram. This time the four quadrants of the diagram are occupied by concepts of groups, from a single-member group, to types of multiple associations:

Collective	Multiplicity
Classification	Individual

A collective is a grouping where the things grouped together share an internal property justifying the grouping; for example, the group of free humans. A multiplicity is a grouping of different individuals through an external accident; for example, everyone moving towards a particular attraction. A classification is a group of different other groups, involving at least one collective; for example, a class-based system dividing aristocrats from plebeians. An individual is singular, different from all others, such that the inclusion of the individual into a collective is reductive in some way; for instance, an individual forced into following the belief system of a wider collective.

The point of the diagram is to show effects on different types of equality. For a collective, equality can be determined according the internal property given to its members; freedom, for instance. For a multiplicity, or for an individual made to belong to a collective, this would be a false imposition on the different individuals involved; for example, when an arbitrary binary distinction (either A or B) is imposed on a group of individuals. Classifications impose inequalities between their classes; for instance, where there is a distinction between a master and a servant class.

Nietzsche's definition of the sublime takes the diagram strongly towards the individual, while ascribing negative properties to the collective and setting up new classifications. The sublime individual is essential to Nietzsche's argument as the creator of new works that are themselves sublime evaluations of life. However, since these eternal valuations are shared between sublime individuals, Nietzsche's sublime also constitutes an eternal multiplicity. This subgroup redeems humanity. Understood in terms of positive values the diagram takes this form:

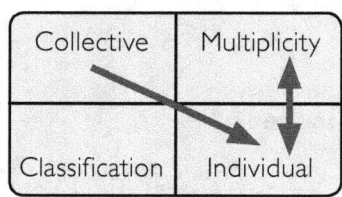

However, in terms of negative judgements the diagram is quite different, because the collective is drawn to a classification dividing sublime individuals from the mass:

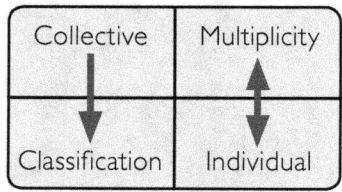

Even if we grant the redemption of humanity through the individual, there is still a deep inequality implied by these effects, where the mass and its values are judged negatively and classified as lower than the sublime individual. Any redemption is not for the mass or even for the majority. So long as we follow Nietzsche in dividing society along creative lines, the sublime will be a force for inequality. If his definition marks the high point of the sublime as the source of exceptional creations and values, characteristic of the post-Kantian sublime, then it is not surprising that the concept gradually fell out of favour in later epochs searching for greater equality.

Chapter 4

The Return to the Sublime

The search for value

Remarkably, for a concept ignored for much of the twentieth century, the sublime went through a resurgence of interest in the 1980s. Earlier mistrust of the idea was understandable, given the wartime and political horrors of that century. Hope for progress and enlightenment through scientific, technological and practical reason, allied to democratic institutions, as antidotes to mysticism and ignorance, partly explain why the sublime became obsolete. When sublime values are implicated in the disasters of conflict and exploitation, it is wise to look elsewhere for ways to a better future.

As an example of this association of the sublime with wartime enthusiasm and propaganda, in her book *Dietrich's Ghosts*, Erica Carter demonstrates how the sublime was used in two ways to further the war effort and aims of the Third Reich. First, the sublime served the cult of Hitler: 'the perception of the *Volk* or *Führer* as sublime objects that seemed to promise some possible reintegration of self and collectivity'.[1] Second, with the films of the Swedish singer Zarah Leander, the sublime bridges between an aesthetic experience of dislocation and an imagination of righteous violence: 'an experience of disintegration and disembodiment that was prolonged spatially and temporally, and that ... found one cognate cultural expression in the potentially limitless violence of the *Blitzkrieg*'.[2] The argument, here, is not that Hitler and war were actually sublime, but rather that films, speeches and images turned them into impossible yet longed for resolutions to unbearable tensions, within the people, their lives, their aesthetic experiences, and their hopes and fears for the future.

Updating these associations between propaganda, the sublime and totalitarian regimes, Julie Ongved Amundsen connects them to the quite different 'ritualistic theatricality' of the Arirang Festival in the Democratic People's Republic of Korea as well as to recreations of the battle of Gettysburg. The massive performances of the Arirang games support the North Korean ideology and system since 'the performance was a reminder of the totalized system of the state, sublime in size and monumentality, and terrifying in its lack of presentation of a necessary surplus'.[3] The idea of unpresentable surplus is drawn from Žižek's work on Hegel and Lacan. Amundsen shows how the pleasure generated by the mass participation in the performances is accompanied by a repressive terror caused by negative ideas of unknown external enemies and by intimations of the void that would be left were the national leader to disappear.

If science and technology, tempered by common humanism, can take us to a better world, then the supposedly higher values afforded by the sublime seem to have no place. In fact, the sublime is suspect when contrasted with the new rationalism, because sublimity harks back to an earlier irrationality, to the violence of divisive fanaticism and misplaced enthusiasms.[4] Why return to the sublime after all that?

Subsequent to its demise in the turn to more grounded types of reason, there are two broad motivations for the reappearance of the sublime. One is internal to the world now supposedly free of the sublime. The other is external and opposed to it. The two are frequently combined, since the internal critical moment prepares the way for a shift to different values. The new sublime supplies the critique with a positive goal. Together, these motives work to show how a world without the sublime is neither what it claims to be, nor superior to sublime alternatives.

The internal reason splits into two further arguments: the world without the sublime still conceals dangerous incarnations of the sublime within rationalism and pragmatism; it therefore needs alternative values and practices. These reasons work in tandem. A rational world has an unconscious or hidden set of mistaken sublime values within it, so it requires correct ones to counteract those mistakes. The step to external values takes place if it can be shown that no such values are available from within.

For example, in the midst of rational and humanist development, practical activity can seem rightly free of sublime or higher values other than the reasonable norms and guidance behind the good conduct of development. Good work is being done, for good practical reasons, towards common sense goals, aided by free markets and technocratic government and according to empirical methods, so nothing more is needed. If anything, the greatest risk comes from the temptations of higher sublime values, with their abstractions and extremism.

The everyday research undertaken in scientific laboratories and research departments of companies and governments can be seen in terms of such practical and down-to-earth endeavours. Their medical, social and technological breakthroughs contribute to a generally agreed-upon improvement, thanks to science and market economies, and with no need for any higher justification – or, put more strongly, in opposition to past justifications based on religion, revolutionary ideals, or divisive values such as nationalism or other ideas of exalted destiny. However, the confidence and upward path of this prosaic and steady progress is fragile. And this fragility invites the return of the sublime.

If developmental activities encounter difficulties and suffer setbacks, if doubt sets in, two defence mechanisms take over. First, there is an effort to sidestep problems by referring to more distant images and goals; freeing the world of inequality, or developing wild and unused lands, or ever-increasing growth, for instance. Second, the activity can continue despite hindrances and reasons to be unsure, because it is driven on by desires, images or instincts it is not conscious of but that nonetheless help it overcome obstacles. Fear of failure, dread of shame and death, hatred of an enemy, horror at the approach of something disgusting or evil, lust, ambition and greed can all function in the background to keep a threatened activity going when it encounters resistance.

A laboratory has a local aim based on its direct research, but fear of redundancy, the need for success, hope for a better world, horror at suffering, the requirements of funding and rewards, and competition with other laboratories can all contribute to the drive to achieve its main practical objectives. The same is true, and to a greater extent, for companies, where successive laws have been necessary to tame greed and mendacity, whether on the part of mining companies, banks, manufacturers, insurance brokers or pharmaceutical companies, even though all of these firms can justifiably claim to have valuable practical roles.

These mechanisms for ensuring continued effort appear to be quite different. The first depends on positive aims or ideals and the second relies on drives frequently seen as negative, such as sinful passions. Nonetheless, theories of the sublime can identify them as the operation of higher values. For the imagery of distant success, such as great future cities and contented peoples free of suffering, the value is directly accessible. The images and goals are the ultimate sublime ends for which we strive despite obstacles and reverses. Each effort we make is in some way a step towards the heights, sacred in its own small way because it brings us all closer to a better world.

However, to think that the negative and unconscious cannot be sublime is to miss the terror and awe in historical definitions of the sublime. It is also to miss the way negative causes can drive us to higher achievements. Though we might assume that base motives and passions, or things that horrify, terrify and disgust us, cannot be sublime, we only do so by forgetting how the sublime depends on certain kinds of excess and contrast. This extreme aspect is shock inducing. It takes us beyond the ordinary and, according to some definitions of the sublime, leads to later reflection on higher ideals.

When considering the sublime potential of negative experiences we should recall that the sublime is frequently opposed to the beautiful. Different from pleasure in the beautiful, the shock of the sublime forces us out of stable states. The sublime is not something we bask in, but something we pass through or undergo. Furthermore, the sublime isn't simple like the beautiful, with its straightforward connection to the pleasurable.

The sublime combines passions such as terror and delight, or pain and relief. As such, though it involves negative effects, these can serve positive outcomes coming as a result of the initial shock. Resembling a horrifying fairy tale with an edifying lesson, the sublime can turn terror into positive growth. Also as in such tales, the operation of the terror and its sublimation into something more positive need not be conscious. The sublime can operate in the background, as a hidden sense of terror and release, perhaps revealed only in dreams and fiction. These contrasts and tensions between positive and negative passions in the sublime explain why it is frequently seen as more truthful than the beautiful. There's a hard realism to the sublime missing in the monotonous pleasure of the beautiful.

For a critique of the return to the sublime, signs of fragility in a world deemed to be free of the sublime explain how it came back into favour when it seemed finished. If the main historical thrust of the sublime is to supply the highest values for a society, and if the sublime can no longer convince in this role, then it ought to be discarded. But if the alternative world is prone to failure and has concealed sublimity within it, then it becomes a matter of assessing which sublime values are the right ones and how they should guide activity.

The sublime can be thought of as having four critical resources beyond the straightforward appeal to a need for value. First, at the point where the highest values are installed, there is a critical tension between old and new. Historically this came to the fore when, for example, French seventeenth-century critics revived the sublime from its classical roots. In so doing, they became involved in a quarrel between ancients and moderns. This dispute between traditional or classical values and innovative or revolutionary ones is locked into the sublime once there is a disagreement over supreme values – not only because the new is a threat to the old, but because each has an implicit critical position on the other, justifying their own assessment of what comes highest.

La Bruyère, one of the main defenders of the ancients against the moderns, allied himself to Boileau, who produced a loose and highly influential translation of Longinus on the sublime, in a counterattack on the modern French style emerging in the seventeenth century; for them 'the sublime only paints truth'.[5]

Picking up on the deep problem of deception in debates around the sublime, Théodore Litman draws attention to the role of a force of truth in the classical sublime, allowing it to counter artifice in modern art forms: 'La Bruyère sums up well the tendencies and aspirations of erudite critics in the second half of the seventeenth century in the dominance of a deep disdain towards the "Moderns" who seek to replace simplicity of expression and force of emotion with the affections of spiritual poetry.'[6] The sublime thereby becomes a vaguely defined rallying point for the values of a threatened old order: '[La Bruyère] allied himself to Boileau and his disciples hoping to save poetry and sacred eloquence; to do this he was obliged to condemn violently the tastes of his contemporaries and in turn to support that vague but imposing ideal of the sublime.'[7]

Second, given the interaction of positive and negative causes and effects in the sublime, new philosophies of the sublime can choose to emphasise the role of the negative or the role of the positive. Is the sublime primarily the product of pain and terror, or does it follow delight and exceptional pleasure? Depending on the answer, does this mean the sublime should be avoided or at least tamed, or should we seek it out and unleash it?

Third, the sublime has always operated on an unconscious level, in the sense that it has depended on powerful emotional and physical effects prior to conscious reflection. Once this level of operation is understood in terms of new theories of the unconscious, and new physiological and philosophical accounts of concealed motivations, then different kinds of definition and critical deployment of the sublime become possible.

This shift is between senses of the unconscious, either defined as what is not yet brought to consciousness, or as always operating beneath consciousness and out of reach in some way. Each of these definitions offers a critical angle on the other, since the former can accuse the latter of falsely exaggerating the scope and invisibility of the unconscious, while the reverse claim is that the boundary between the conscious and the unconscious is much more complicated and porous than is supposed by a simple distinction ascribing superior value and power to consciousness.

The unconscious sublime becomes a way of explaining behaviour and values not through direct and clear effects, but through complex and hidden pathways. This opens up two explanatory methods. There can be an analysis of how the sublime operates unconsciously behind conscious values. There can also be an evaluation of the unconscious sublime as something to be sought out or repressed, or rejected as unnecessary or as invented.

The fourth critical resource stems from the oppositions, alternatives and distinctions following from the contrasts highlighted in the first three. The sublime does not need to stand for the highest values of society as a whole. Instead, the sublime can be an indicator of difference, of minority, or of individual values. Sublime experiences, events, objects and creations thereby become sites and causes for resistance and revolt because they demarcate differences between groups and between individuals. For instance, in his essay on the postmodern sublime, David B. Johnson describes the unconscious aspect of the sublime in Deleuze's work on Francis Bacon and the critically divisive power of the sublime in Lyotard's deduction of incommensurability and 'irresolvability' from the impossibility of giving a presentation of the sublime event.[8]

These oppositions occur in many and often surprising forms; for instance, when the sublime becomes a dividing line or barrier between different creeds, or when it stands for the abject and horrifying, or when it leads to distinctions between the natural and the artificial. None of them are straightforwardly new. It is rather that difference is celebrated in the new sublime rather than taken as something to be overcome. In Chapter 5, we'll see how this turn towards differences in the sublime can lead to egalitarianism independent of a single universally applied standard of equality.

These critical aspects should not be understood as arriving late in the history of sublimity. For instance, all four are analysed in Rodolph Gasché's study of Burke's sublime. The unconscious works through the body in its relation to mind through a form of catharsis: 'In sum, terror not only has a cathartic effect on the body and the mind; it is above all the means to regularly, if not constantly, reanimate, that is, re-create, the bodily and mentally vital principles.'[9] Gasché turns to the positive value of the sublime, against some of Burke's suspicion of sublime events: 'Terror and pain, if they do not press too close, accomplish this animation and thus produce a state of sublime delight which strongest form Burke calls astonishment. Astonishment, the state of "delightful horror," is nothing but the sudden awareness of being alive.'[10] This focus on astonishment leads to a deconstruction of Burke's distinction between the sublime and the beautiful, and of the priority given to the former.

The supreme value lies in an intensification of life against a drift into inertia: 'Quickening the life forces, terror is at the service of self-representation, of which the body and mind are in constant need not only when they are threatened with annihilation by outward objects but also because of the tendency from within to render the mental functions inert.'[11] By replacing terror and delight with a gradient between inertia and intense quickening, Gasché inserts the same gradient between the sublime and the beautiful, thereby replacing their opposition with a form of continuity. Finally, since this intensification is not general, but rather the starting point for differences and divergences, different causes of astonishment and their hold on different bodies and bodily parts or properties lead to variations in types of astonishment and hence in the values ascribed to different occasions for vivification. Hence Burke's categories and distinctions are deconstructed into a more fine series of individual and mobile differences.

The most thorough deconstruction of Kant's sublime is given by Jacques Derrida in *Truth in Painting*, a book that brings together many of his influential mid-period articles on Kant, with a long reflection on painting (notably on Goya's Black Paintings), some of Derrida's favoured artists (Valerio Adami and Gérard Titus-Carmel), and further work on Heidegger's philosophy of art. As deconstruction, Derrida's reading of Kant aims at undermining the absolute in the sublime, returning it instead to measure and to finite scales: 'Kant will have introduced comparison where he says there should be none. He introduces it, lets it introduce itself, in an apparently very subtle manner. Not by re-implicating magnitude in the comparable, but by comparing the comparable with the incomparable.'[12]

This is a familiar argument about the paradoxes of how to represent something that cannot be represented. In Chapter 5, we'll see Žižek develop similar points against Kant via Hegel. Those points are also made by Derrida in his reading of Hegel's *Aesthetics*: 'Hegel criticises Kant for starting from size rather than from that which has no size. To which Kant would, in principle, reply that to be able to think about that which has no size it must present itself to us, even if this presentation is inadequate, even if it is only, and precisely, presented in the *Aufhebung*.'[13] Derrida is playing Hegel and Kant against each other, in order to demonstrate how their own arguments depend on the very points they want to criticise in the other.

In his *Aesthetics: Lectures on Fine Art*, Hegel claims the sublime is an 'outward shaping which is itself annihilated in turn by what it reveals, so that the revelation of the content is at the same time a supersession of the revelation'.[14] The phenomenon reveals an ideal content, but disappears in the revelation, thereby transferring the sublime from a subjective experience to absolute substance as ground for all subjects and objects. The annihilation in the revelation and supersession (*Aufhebung*) is what Derrida is denying. He claims instead that the initial subjective presentation remains a condition for the revelation supposed to supersede it.

Hegel separates his sublime from Kant's on the grounds that the subject is not where the sublime is situated: 'This, therefore, differing from Kant, we need not place in the pure subjectivity of the mind and its Ideas of Reason; on the contrary, we must grasp it as grounded in the one absolute substance qua the content which is to be represented.'[15] Derrida's rejoinder to this statement negating the subject in favour of Hegel's version of absolute substance and spirit (God in some but not all interpretations) is that the sublime isn't first thought and represented through the absolute, but rather experienced as a limit to thought, as in Kant.

In terms of the egalitarian sublime, the deeper merit of Derrida's argument for a critique of the effects of the sublime lies in his insights about economies of comparisons, representations, values and rankings. His deconstruction undermines any move to extract the sublime from a wider circulation of measures and symbols he calls 'economimesis'. The deconstruction through close reading tracks connections back to these economies in metaphors, examples and arguments meant to ensure the exclusive nature of the sublime.

The Kantian sublime is a claim to universal moral law, as independent of material and ideal economies and yet as rightful legislation over them. I will return to these arguments in later chapters, but a good way of understanding them is through Kantian universal institutions such as the United Nations. The universal moral basis for the UN is meant to be independent of specific economic and national interests, yet it serves as a basis for regulating conflicts between nations and between economic entities. How can the UN be independent for the source of its lofty principles, yet engaged in worldly pragmatic interests and powers when it applies those principles?

The required independence is achieved by claiming the moral law is founded on something beyond the limits of understanding, the constraints of nature and the pressures of base purposes and interests; hence the role of the sublime. However, Derrida denies this externality by demonstrating how the idea of measure, and in particular the idea of the column as unit of measure, is always implicated in any presentation of that which should be infinitely beyond measure, the colossal as symbol of the sublime. Against its own aims, the Kantian text thereby provides tracks from the sublime to more mundane economic and linguistic flows, breaking the independence, superiority and universality of the sublime.

Gasché's study is collected in Timothy M. Costelloe's 2012 edited volume of essays on the sublime. The collection is itself testimony to the return to the sublime from the late 1980s to the present. In the search for an egalitarian sublime, Costelloe's introduction to the volume is important in its emphasis on the etymology of the sublime as a token for the highest values, and in drawing together new writers on the topic. Many other collections appeared on the sublime around the same time, but Costelloe's stands out for its breadth and its emphasis on philosophical and historical questions, set in the context of modern concerns.

Other volumes on the subject include Simon Morley's *The Sublime*, David Jarrett's *The Most Sublime Act: Essays on the Sublime*, and Roald Hoffmann and Iain Boyd Whyte's *Beyond the Finite: The Sublime in Art and Science*. Morley offers a comprehensive set of original and secondary texts on the sublime in particular as an influence on contemporary art, and on art and critical theorists. Hoffmann and Whyte show how the sublime extends into science. Jarrett's volume is more eclectic and has rewarding articles from specialist points of view, such as Noel Gray's article on the sublime and geometry. This interest in the sublime is not limited to Anglophone works. On the contrary, it can be seen in new works by French authors and Lyotard in particular, for instance, in the exceptional collection edited by Jean-François Courtine, Michel Deguy and Jean-François Lyotard, *Du sublime*.

Costelloe's introduction also demonstrates how the idea of the sublime as highest value crosses between many different languages. The etymology of the sublime covers the Greek 'height, from high, from above, upwards, and metaphorically summit or crown'; the Latin, 'high up, aloft, elevated, tall or towering, heavenly bodies or meteorological phenomena, denoting the sky or Northern Hemisphere, birds in flight, imposing tall, exalted in rank, illustrious or eminent, with lofty ambition, noble or heroic, elevated style or sentiments'; the English 'sub (up to) limin (lintel or threshold)'; the French 'move up to'; and then 'in the vernacular: to purify (sublimate) fire, violence'.[16] The dynamic quality of the metaphors is one of the underappreciated aspects of this etymology. It is not only that the sublime is about the heights, but also that these heights are reached through a process, or through acts of elevation. The sublime is made or reached, rather than ever-present and unchanging. As such, it is the result of an activity, with political repercussions for how it is shaped and how its effects change society and individuals.

Many of the essays in Costelloe's volume return to Kant for the modern philosophical roots of the sublime; however, in turning to a modern politics of masses, individuals and the search of equality, I want to emphasise the importance of Nietzsche, who refines the critical powers of the sublime and therefore becomes a precursor to changes in political and philosophical attitudes to sublimity. In the paradox of sublime individuals, struggling both for and against humanity, there is the critique of a deceptive sublimity of the masses and an argument for a new individual sublime, redeeming humanity but not all humans. Nietzsche's understanding of the sublime as demanding individual transformations replaces the idea of the sublime as revealing the highest values across a given society and epoch. This shift in definition implies a critical analysis of modern society, through which a genealogy of forgotten yet still effective higher values unmasks many false versions of the sublime, preparing the way for Nietzsche's superior individuals.

Nonetheless, the new sublime emerging in the 1980s and continuing today is different from Nietzsche's individualist definition with its connection to eternal values in creation. After his early essays, Nietzsche alluded to the end of the sublime individual in the sublime itself ('"What do I matter?" stands over the door of the future thinker'),[17] though he always stuck to the idea of sublime overcoming ('Sublimely above oneself?').[18] Nietzsche's solution is to move from the individual to the work, whereas the new sublime does not depend at all on creative individuals, but rather on groups defined by their experiences of the sublime.

Politically, this is an important shift. It escapes the problem of individualism and any dependence on singular genius, associating the sublime instead with either backward-looking resistance or the progressive revolt of groups. For the idea of an egalitarian sublime this is both supportive and problematic, because though inequalities based on individual subjects fall away, differences between sections of society can grow stronger. The sublime then becomes a rallying point, but also a justification for conflict.

To chart these political repercussions and understand the range of positions emerging in the new sublime, I will work through two very different cases, starting from a nostalgic sublime of resistance based on the technological sublime, then moving on to revolt supported by an ecological sublime aiming to hold back the destructiveness of human exploitation of natural resources. Each of these studies follows the method of microcritique, alternating long views and close-up analysis, while suggesting diagrams for the effects of each definition of the new sublime.

Nostalgic social sublime

It is unsurprising to encounter nostalgia for earlier experiences of the sublime in the contemporary return to the sublime. As a longing for how things were done in the past, nostalgia is also a yearning for earlier values. Its tendency to mourn their passing is also their elevation into something pure and of the highest rank, a sadness at never being able to recover earlier greatness – there's a version of this nostalgia in sublime art around classical ruins, real and fictional. David Nye's history of the technological sublime is rare, however, in combining nostalgia with the sublime experience itself, rather than with sublime values. His argument is that the highest achievements and fullest cohesion of a community follow from joint sublime experiences of a special kind.

Due to its recent dependence upon media sent to individual or small group screens, technology has been seen as leading to divisive and individual experiences of virtual worlds, detrimental to the social fabric when compared to interactions in shared physical spaces. Against this impression, Nye's study goes much further back, into the nineteenth century, where he follows a transition from the natural sublime to a technological sublime in railroads, skyscrapers and, above all, the electrical illumination of cities, landscapes and fairs.

To get a feeling for his point, we can refer to common experiences of light shows and fireworks during festivals, where large crowds come together to enjoy and wonder at sublime effects, such as the celebrations of New Year in 2000. These events overcome social divisions in joint celebration. This is only an approximation, since his argument is more progressive than an appeal to simple joint festivity. For Nye, the experience of the sublime in those earlier forms of technology was about the celebration of shared achievement, benefit and hope for a better future, in sublime land and cityscapes populated together. It was not a sublime of simply passive amazement and wonder – both of those effects were to serve social togetherness and progress.

This progressive and communal turn is much more controversial than it might appear at a cursory glance. First, it is an aggressively critical moment in rebelling against elitist philosophical definitions of the sublime:

> Burke, Kant, Schiller and later commentators, too, address an educated elite. While they assert that certain scenes will affect all minds in certain ways, they take no pains to demonstrate that this is the case, being content to let the reader experiment or to reflect on personal experience. And even if all readers of philosophy agreed, historians would still regard them as an interpretative community that might be labelled 'readers of aesthetics,' a group hardly representative of the whole population.[19]

The common people are not to be told what the sublime should be; they are to experience it for themselves: 'non-philosophers developed their own understanding of the sublime, based on nationalism, gender divisions, religious convictions, new technologies, and political values'.[20]

Second, the model land for this sublime is to be the United States. The idea of model is important here. Though Nye is almost exclusively interested in examples from the US, his lesson is universal in how progress was once achieved for humanity through a conjunction of technology and frontier spirit. He identifies making nature safe and reachable with its preservation: 'One appeal of the technological sublime in America was that it conflated the preservation and the transformation of the natural world.'[21] This view would not be consistent with a more strict definition of preservation as keeping free from human destruction. Third, this sublime has passed away in violent and perhaps irreversible ways; the closing of its historical epoch explains the nostalgia for what it stood for and how it came about.

Nye singles out the atomic bomb as the sign of technology going beyond what he understands as sublime, because the shock and amazement at the sublime event of the flash, quake and mushroom cloud are precursors to terminal destructiveness:

> At the deepest level, the existence of atomic weapons has undermined the possibility of the sublime relationship to both natural and technological

objects. The experience of the natural sublime rests on the sense of human weakness and limitation, and on the power of human reason to comprehend the infinitely large and powerful. But when human beings themselves create something infinitely powerful that can annihilate nature, the exaltation of the classical sublime seems impossible.[22]

The reference to power is important here because Nye's concern about nuclear weapons is marked by a shift in power from human reason to the sublime event itself. Gene Ray appeals to similar ideas of overwhelming power in the sublime in his study of nuclear war.[23]

Nye's definition of the sublime is deceptively simple. Even though it can be given in a short formula – as communal wonder in the experience of technology and the realisation of its progressive potential – the full definition is extensive rather than intensive, drawing together historical examples supplemented by critical commentary. This extensive aspect takes a special historiographical form. It is the telling of a transition followed by stepwise progress to a highest moment, in the electrical sublime that 'elided the line between nature and culture and, in the process, dissolved the scale and three-dimensionality of the landscape; yet it could still serve a vision focused on progress'.[24] The technological sublime culminates in the elimination of the nature-culture divide in favour of smooth progress across once difficult spaces.

The narrative of Nye's book is organised around two breaks. An early division frees the sublime from an aesthetic and elite Romanticism. A later cut prompts nostalgia by closing the connection between technology, the sublime and progress. In between, stages of technological development increase the bonds between humanity, place, progress and technology. If we ignore the nostalgia and its causes, this middle period could be a candidate for the egalitarian sublime, where the feeling, objects and effects of the sublime define a new and equal people.

The elision of the line between nature and culture is central to Nye's argument, since it allows nature to be transformed for a community according to shared technology and morality. Although he rejects elitist culture, a popular one emerges as an aesthetic of group experiences of the sublime, in tourism, festivals and fairs. Nature's three-dimensionality and scale are hindrances to this transformation. They make change seem impossible for an ideal based on smooth two-dimensional passage, as represented by road and rail grids, for instance. The scale and shape of North American mountain ranges and chasms seem designed to thwart human will. Where the Romantic sublime saw natural disasters as delivering lessons about our limitations, the technological sublime celebrates our capacity to push back boundaries and make the world ours.

The progress afforded by technology allows us to go around and through landscapes, changing them from a sublimity of gulfs, deserts and barriers depicted in Romantic art, to one of inhabited and edifying social spaces, nonetheless retaining the power to delight us and increase our enthusiasm for progress as a community. Again, the view of city, suburb and distant environment from a plane is a good example of this transition from nature as obstacle to nature as conduit and social space. When the view is of rivers of light running between nodes, space is reduced to two dimensions of potential travel, as opposed to distinct zones in three dimensions without the conduits of lights, roads, bridges and tunnels.

The same exercise, in moving from three to two dimensions, could be accomplished for the cosmos, if distant galaxies taking many human lives to travel between them were brought together by faster-than-light travel. Nye's technological sublime chimes well with the sublime of space travel, represented in popular science-fiction cinema and television as sublime immensity traversed thanks to technology and enterprise. However, the reason for nostalgia is already at work in this shift, because the immediacy of shared experience is exchanged for shared fictions; we move from the enthusiasm of crowds to sharing individual passions. Sometimes it's even worse for egalitarianism, when we are enthused by the ambitions of a single tycoon, a feature missed by Nye, though he could have referred to Howard Hughes or Randolph Hearst for the period of the electrical sublime.

The following passage occurs early in Nye's book and it is the closest he comes to a full definition in relation to historical development:

> The sublime underlies this enthusiasm for technology. One of the most powerful human emotions, when experienced by large groups the sublime can weld society together. In moments of sublimity, human beings temporarily disregard divisions among elements of the community. The sublime taps into fundamental hopes and fears. It is not a social residue, created by economic and political forces, though both can inflect its meaning. Rather, it is an essentially religious feeling, aroused by the confrontation with impressive objects, such as Niagara Falls, the Grand Canyon, the New York skyline, the Golden Gate Bridge, or the earth-shaking launch of a space shuttle. The technological sublime is an integral part of our contemporary consciousness, and its emergence and exfoliation into several distinct forms during the past two centuries is inscribed within public life. In a physical world that is increasingly desacralized, the sublime represents a way to reinvest the landscape and the works of men with transcendent significance.[25]

Firstly, the technological sublime is less internally divided into positive and negative than earlier historical definitions of the sublime. Instead, enthusiasm becomes the dominant emotion as it builds on hopes and fears. Secondly, in public life there is a political horizon of this enthusiasm and a sublime feeling informs public institutions. However, isn't enthusiasm a dangerous emotion for this task, in its frequently unthinking, uncritical and uncompromising devotion to causes?

A response to scepticism about sublime enthusiasm comes from the historical basis for Nye's arguments. Over the course of roughly a century and a half, sublime enthusiasm passed from more dangerous political and religious types of commitment to communal and technologically informed kinds of fervour. That's why Nye's definition begins with an allusion to religious enthusiasm, something he follows up in the parts of his book where he studies sects and religious groups.[26] These are then supplanted by human endeavour supported by technological feats and, crucially, education. So though his sublime is 'an essentially religious feeling', gods fall away to be replaced by the works of men given 'transcendent significance'.[27]

In a similar way, Nye shifts the emphasis away from the natural sublime as described by the Irish, Scottish and English empirical philosophers who influence his approach and as celebrated in the Romantic sublime. This is only a change in emphasis, because nature is not to be eliminated but rather tamed and enhanced. Taken alone, the feeling for sublime nature is too passive and individual for his purposes. He doesn't want humanity to be in awe of nature but rather to be enthused by technology, to deploy its powers of invention and construction in order to communally improve our place in nature, our place in the cosmos.

Democracy and the joint celebration of democratic nationhood reinforce the effect of the technological sublime: 'As technological achievements became central to July Fourth, the American sublime fused with religion, nationalism, and technology, diverging in practice significantly from European theory. It ceased to be a philosophical idea and became submerged in practice. In keeping with democratic tradition, the American sublime was for all – women as well as men.'[28] Amid national celebrations, the skyscrapers and lighting of modern cities in the United States create enthusiasm for a constructive unity, not only of people in the development, application and enjoyment of those technologies, but also of humans and nature, in the way nature is connected to human progress and made reachable for all, while retaining its sublimity. Here, the departure from the earlier divisions of the beautiful and the sublime according to gender, such that women could neither experience sublimity nor be sublime, demonstrates how the new technological sublime achieves social unity.

Diagrams of the technological sublime

With its combination of social progress and democracy is Nye's definition the right model for ideas of the egalitarian sublime? It isn't and the reasons it isn't lead to serious objections to any attempt at an egalitarian sublime. Returning to the diagrams proposed in the previous chapter, the initial impression when mapping the nostalgic sublime is how close it might have come to egalitarianism, progressive politics and collectively shared values.

The diagram for the internal and external situation of the sublime and its relation to passivity and activity indicates a strong emphasis towards the outside and towards activity. Everything gravitates to a diagonal from the top left to the bottom right corner of the diagram: the sublime becomes external and about activity. Gravitational attraction is important for understanding these diagrams. They do not represent a location for the sublime, but rather its dynamic effects. For the technological sublime, the dynamism should be interpreted as community creation, where settings, feelings and ideas are shared rather than closed inside individuals and experienced passively. This sublime calls for activity, a joint transformation of the human condition within a tamed and enjoyed nature.

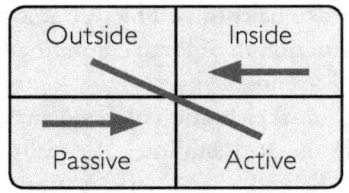

Turning to the diagram on groups, it shows the technological sublime pulling strongly towards collectives and away from individuals, classifications and multiplicities. Though the United States is the paradigm for this democratic collective, with communities, aided by technology, working together to improve their world, in principle Nye's model can be extended to any society. Individuals must take their place within this joint work and it makes no sense for the technological sublime to be claimed as isolated, since technology is dependent on many contributors and users, and designed for collective use. Importantly, classifications are also cancelled by this experience when it takes its unifying national or universal celebratory form, such as on the Fourth of July.

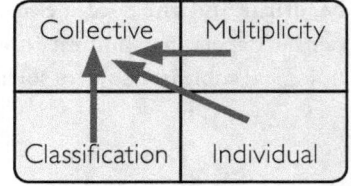

However, both these diagrams are potentially misleading as drawings of the effect of the technological sublime. For the first diagram, though the experience is supposed to be active, a critical reading can point to the stage management of the communal events admired by Nye. Supposedly spontaneous and communal activity is in fact guided and can be defined as a form of passivity induced by political control. The central role of advertising and marketing in celebrations and tourism indicates how demand is created rather than self-driven. Furthermore, the activity is itself subject to constraints, where there are rules and limits to acceptable behaviour and decisions; for instance, when nationalist symbols and ideas are accompanied by an insistence on allegiance at times of celebration and commemoration.

The internal character of this passivity can also be shown when activity is dependent upon prior conditioning and training; for example, where schooling involves immersion in accepted sublimity, from school trips to famous natural sites, to visits to important cultural and intellectual events. The celebrations and tourist events are formative rituals rather than simple manifestations of technical, cultural and political achievement – they have long been mainstays of repressive governments seeking to impose and manufacture unity. As such, the diagram could just as easily be given as a concentration of effects gravitating towards passivity and a type of internalisation. More seriously, this sublime can also have the effect of drawing censure and blame on anyone seen either to threaten or to question the sublime values and unity they are supposed to bring.

According to this counter interpretation, the correct rendering of the diagram would follow the opposing diagonal, drawing effects towards the inside and passivity, and away from activity and external relations, understood as free and open activity:

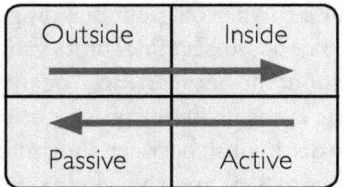

If this version is correct, then enthusiasm in the technological sublime is dangerous, since the togetherness it brings can be controlled and produced. More seriously, this unity could be imposed on a varied population by means of discrimination, expulsion and elimination. If celebration of the technological sublime is used as a means to produce a compliant nation, complacent about the value of technology, then the negative aspects of that technology may be masked or overlooked. For example, the technological sublime and the sense of communal superiority it engenders can contribute to arms races and to an unfettered commitment to technological competition, such as occurred in the space race. More egregiously, evidence of technological achievement can also be used to support racist and apartheid states in their attempts to bolster arguments for superior races and ideologies. If the sublime fosters an uncritical population around a false unity, thereby making exploitation and repression easier, then it will have brought about a less just and less democratic community.

This counterargument also plays out on the diagram of groups. Instead of supporting collectives, the effects of the technological sublime can be interpreted as emphasising classifications. If the collective is illusory and imposed, it distinguishes groups around matters of control, access, belonging and alienation, unconscious training and internalisation. The effect of the technological sublime could then be classifications of controllers and controlled; of those in power and those led; of those accepting or benefiting from the technological sublime and those resisting it, suffering from it, or alienated by it. At worst, this would mean the sublime worked as racist propaganda, shaping a population and defining its outcasts. According to this version, there is no true collective. Multiplicity is replaced by division. Individuals must take their place – or struggle to take their place – on one or other level of the classification.

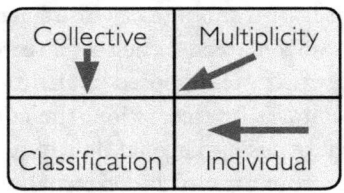

The conflict between these interpretations of the effects of the technological sublime calls for a further diagram mapping how definitions of the sublime can give rise to opposed accounts of its value and effects. The new diagram addresses the spontaneous or artificial quality of the sublime object, and the way the sublime event invites or resists critical reception. I separate object and event here to distinguish between the thing triggering the sublime (the object, such as a raging sea) and the whole sublime process (the event comprised by the sea, the viewers on a promontory, and their feelings, thoughts and later reactions). The components of the diagram are unusual, though they connect to distinctions between natural and artificial sublimes, and to the difference between immediate and intellectual reactions to them.

For example, the sublimity of the cosmos depends on a sophisticated creation of images. Elizabeth A. Kessler shows how the sublimity of images of space depends on simulation, physiological and cultural fit, and political imagination. The colours and perspectives in such images are the result of painstaking manipulation, designed to adapt them to our senses and perception, but also to the cultural history of sublimity and awe: 'It is through trials and errors that the Hubble images have come into being as a labor of both chance and necessity. They need to look as they do, but they must be legible to our senses and imagination.'[29] Politically, these sensual effects and cultural references call up a complicated web of ideas: 'We find in them echoes of the cosmos and reflections of humanity. By evoking the Romantic sublime and the American frontier, they promise a universe of possibilities, a world of exploration, an experience of striving to comprehend.'[30] These are certainly progressive in the sense of promising a new and better world: 'They remind us – as insignificant as we may be – of the potential to go beyond that which may at first seem a limit to us.'[31] However, as I will also show for Nye's technological sublime, and as Kessler acknowledges, the association with manifest destiny and the American frontier is politically tainted by the violent consequences of ideas of a common destiny dictated by the values and dreams of only part of population.

These new categories are important for the egalitarian sublime, and for how the sublime can be misleading and divisive, because they introduce ideas of deliberate control and of openness to critical challenge. The meaning of egalitarian does not need to be restricted to equality of wealth and opportunity, or access to services and education. It can also mean equality as openness to critique. This is a primordial sense of equality. Like a form of welcome or an intention to conceal, it comes before other ideas of equality because it is a condition for them. There can be no equality when one group is deceiving another; whereas a genuine welcome opens the way to interchanges as equals. New questions thus come to the fore in assessing the sublime: Is the sublime object deceptive? Has it been made to be deceptive? Does the sublime event hinder or invite critical responses?

An idea or thing can be manufactured or spontaneous, in the sense of unplanned. In both cases, the way thoughts and objects are presented can either invite or repress critical reception; for instance, something manufactured can be deliberately deceptive, like a con-trick, and something spontaneous can be overwhelming to the point of suspending critical faculties, like a terrifying natural event. In the following diagram, the technological sublime as defended by Nye should be situated towards the right-hand side quadrants. It is made and it contributes to open and democratic communities.

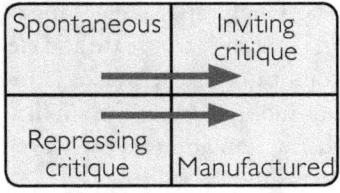

Taken more critically, this diagram is too generous. Nye consistently underestimates the way the sublime event is manipulated by parts of society in order to control others, whether for profit or for political gain, or with unforeseen consequences, or simply as a by-product of another aim, such as perfecting a form of technology at the expense of its simplicity and accessibility. When describing the sublimity of skyscrapers he makes the following claim: '[skyscrapers are] a symbolic structure: from the outside a corporate icon, from the inside the site of a magisterial gaze. To experience either the jagged skyline at a distance, the immense vistas aloft, or the insect life of the street below validates that power. The geometrical sublime and its fantasies of domain thus altered the phenomenology of the city.'[32] The flaw here is that the icon is also a method of control and the idea of validation of power is ambiguous, because it depends on the legitimacy, exercise and effects of that power.

When placed at the centre of a wider and lower periphery, the skyscraper is a centralising symbol, separating upper tiers from lower ones and from the margins, making the heights materially and ideologically opposed to the depths and to distant places. It is closer to medieval dungeons and towers, with their dominance over cities and countryside, than to the egalitarian structures of more communal builds, whether tents or tenements. It might be fine to endorse the idea of new spatial domains allowing better communication, but admiration for the leaders and concentrated power at the top of those buildings can blind a population to the way it is being robbed by them; as, for example, in the lead up to financial crises such as the 1929 stock market crash or the 2008 banking crisis. The most dangerous fantasies are not necessarily about spatial domains. They are also about dominion over a population misled by the sublime iconography of the modern city, modern finance or modern techniques across health, finance, politics, management or education.

At worst these fantasies are about the sublimity of weapon strikes and military parades, designed to convey a sense of power through awe, but without showing blood, burns and broken bodies. Not quite as extreme, but significant nonetheless, the sublime has now become part of the language and symbolism of advertising, where past sublime art, natural settings and technological effects form the backdrop for the selling of mundane objects and activities, from tourism to cars, clothes and alcohol.

Faded sublimity, whether cultural in the form of high art, natural in the form of awe-inspiring landscapes, or digital in imagined worlds, has become an easy way to exploit emotional responses far-removed from the intensity of past sublime enthusiasm. This shift from rare and elevated experiences to an easy and misleading prompt is a further obstacle to the new sublime, or to any idea of an egalitarian sublime. Once the sublime has been reduced to a background image or distraction and to a tool serving deceptive motives is there any place left for it as superior value?

In addition to the risks of social engineering and control, a positive assessment of the value of the technological sublime for building political communion is in danger of overestimating the capacity for unity to invite, tolerate and respond positively to critique. By encouraging a cohesive and sentimental community the sublime can be detrimental to the openness of democracy, because sublime enthusiasm can support ideas of superiority and false reasons for cohesion. This combination encourages the dangerous conclusion that opponents must be deficient in some way, as enemies of sublimely revealed communion and truth.

Compounding this danger, and despite its contributions to forms of communication, the technological sublime is also a menace to deliberation and democratic flexibility. For Nye, the sublime contributes to a sense of national greatness: 'Not limited to nature, the American sublime embraced technology. Where Kant had reasoned that the awe inspired by a sublime object made men aware of their moral worth, the American sublime transformed the individual's experience of immensity and awe into a belief in national greatness.'[33] The problem is that democracy is threatened by a sentimental belief in national greatness, in particular when the nation is defined by a single narrative, such as the technological domination of nature by a particular community.

Democracy must bring together and ensure the coexistence of radically different communities and individuals with conflicting values, origins and claims. It does not follow that because technology enables quicker communication it encourages democracy. The form of the communication is much more important than its speed or reach, since the interchange of ideas must be sufficiently deep and textured to allow views to be communicated comprehensively and sensitively, and challenged radically. We need to sense the presence of other views deserving of space and respect, calling us to change our views fundamentally. A multiplicity of differences is threatened by the monoculture of a shared sublime feeling, even if this feeling is based on a sense of limit or otherness, as it is in the terror of the Romantic sublime.

If a particular section of the community is seen as closer to sublimity, or even as the source of sublimity, then debate on an equal footing followed by inclusive democratic decisions will fail. If some members of the community, or another group of humans, or nature itself, can be defined as contrary to the technological sublime – contrary to the highest values – then an unequal or even violent treatment of them can be justified. This has happened for the sublime, as acknowledged by Nye, in the closeness of the American sublime to a belief in the idea of manifest destiny, where the destiny of some Americans was to extend their ideas, practices, society, technology and political dominion over frontiers and to the detriment of the peoples already present in them. The art and rhetoric of manifest destiny were sublime, but they contributed to land theft and to the removal and genocide of original peoples.

Manifest destiny and the technological sublime are doctrines of the overcoming of nature as an obstacle to human development. By bringing nature under human control and exploitation, they are threats to nature taken as a wilderness to be preserved. Ignoring the terrible conditions for workers building the Erie Canal and the resulting spread of cholera, Nye lauds the unifying sublimity of the project: 'While voters might disagree on the issues of the day, they could agree on the uplifting sublimity of Niagara Falls, the Natural Bridge, or the Erie Canal at Lockport.'[34] Once the viewer knows the suffering of workers behind technological feats such as the construction of railroads and canals, it takes a special kind of wilful suspension to see them as unifying people as different as itinerant navvies, the land speculators profiting from their labour, and the indigenous peoples whose ancestors lived on the land for thousands of years.

Sublimity also comes at the cost of the permanent transformation of natural features and plant and animal habitats. It would be wrong, therefore, to limit consideration of the effects of the sublime to humans. To take account of this, in the age of the Anthropocene, a new diagram is required. Its necessity was not apparent in earlier ages, where wild nature appeared inexhaustible and where the idea of benign technology could be entertained, even though the destructiveness of technology has always been criticised. The categories of this new diagram concern space, nature, control and disaster. They are designed to track the effects of the sublime across different types of space (wild and urban) and in relation to ideas of control (security) and irreversible destruction (catastrophe). The speculative nature of diagrams of effects comes out strongly in this diagram, since catastrophe and control are time-relative ideas. Security can be fleeting and illusory; for instance, when we think we have brought a fire under control but overlook our dependence on a lull in the wind. Catastrophe, defined as irreversible destruction, can appear slowly and through apparently minimal changes, as for example when we approach a tipping point in the spread or control of a virus.

In this diagram, the positive interpretation of the technological sublime positions lines of attraction around urban spaces, defined as technologically advanced spaces for human occupation, and around security, following a shift from natural danger to quasi-urban safety, where beneficial aspects of the city project into nature:

Wild nature →	Urban spaces
Security	← Catastrophe

This positive view invites two different but connected counters. The first is ethical. It argues that there is an intrinsic good to wild nature and that there is something ethically catastrophic about destroying it; for example, that we become inhuman and betray the best in ourselves when we ruin wild spaces rather than preserve them. The second view is practical and can be based on recent science. This is the argument that the Anthropocene, with its species extinctions and climate change, leads to catastrophe for humans as well as for nature, for instance in floods, famine, war and disease. These views can be connected through arguments as diverse as punishment, in the sense of catastrophe as payback for our treatment of nature, or causal connection, where our disregard for nature has brought about the Anthropocene and where a new found regard might give us a chance to mitigate its worst outcomes. On both these counters the diagram takes a form where the technological sublime draws all things towards a catastrophic outcome:

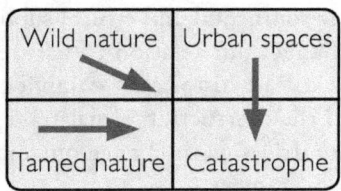

Nye doesn't see the technological sublime as catastrophic, but this is only because he distinguishes between events like nuclear explosions or the lights of Las Vegas, and truly sublime technological achievements. Significantly, for him, the destruction of nature is only a problem for the Romantic sublime: 'The Kantian relationship to the object required a sense of personal security... This necessary precondition evaporates in the superheated wind of an atomic blast.'[35] Destruction is only the end of the technological sublime when it breaks social bonds irreparably in warfare or economic division: 'the billions of dollars spent in Las Vegas represent a financial and psychic investment in play for its own sake. The epiphany had been reduced to a rush of stimulations, in an escape from the very work, rationality, and domination that once were embodied in the American technological sublime.'[36] This distinction explains Nye's nostalgia for an earlier and true sublime in an age that is at once fake and needlessly destructive. On this view, if catastrophe can be avoided, it will only be on the basis of a return to an earlier relationship with technology and democratic unity.

The lesson for the egalitarian sublime is different. The problem with the technological sublime is that it shows how the sublime is always prone to failure as a source of political unity because the sublime is essentially deceptive. It can be manipulated; it gives a false sense of confidence; and it works against critical reception. The obvious reply to this would be that these points only count if the sublime is misleading, but not if it is the communication of truth. The problem is that, historically, the sublime has not withstood scrutiny as truth, whether in ancient rhetoric, in the sublimity of nature or technology, in superior rulers or gods, or in the works of artists or philosophers. If the sublime is to be defined as egalitarian, it will therefore either have to have some new kind of guarantee of truthfulness or incorporate its own critical reception: a sublime doubt rather than certainty.

The environmental sublime

To illustrate the difficulties surrounding the sublime and truth, I'll turn to a version of the new sublime opposed to Nye's definition and appearing a few years later. In redefining the natural sublime for a different age, Emily Brady argues for an environmental and ethical sublime, where the experience of the sublime changes our relation to nature. If the technological sublime can be seen as at least historically complicit with climate change, species extinctions and the destruction of natural spaces and habitats, its environmental opposite drives us to change our moral relation to nature towards a form of sublime respect.

Brady's study is based on interpretations of earlier definitions of the sublime, and recognises a variety of accounts; but, unlike Nye's work, this history is not about empirical experiences but about theories of the sublime. Brady combines a critical reading of Kant's natural sublime with 'the more empirically grounded subject of British aesthetic theories of the sublime'.[37] The label 'British sublime' is common currency and provides an alternative line to the Kantian sublime. However, given the importance of Burke and the variations in the empirical sublime according to Scottish, Welsh, Irish and English locations and thinkers, as well as the fraught relation between the empirical sublime and British colonialism, there is some risk of missing significant differences.

For instance, though James MacPherson was British, having been born in Scotland after 1707, something is lost if we fail to note how the sublime in the *Poems of Ossian* comes from a Scottish writer in the Scottish Enlightenment claiming to have translated the poems from Gaelic.[38] Brady is well aware of these differences, but her argument depends on making a distinction between Kant's transcendental deductions and British empiricism. My concern is that it is exactly at these points that the sublime can eliminate important differences in order to establish more general categories.

The problem here is not simply one of nomenclature, but rather that the sublime is created and varies according to location and history. Which aesthetic experiences count as sublime is therefore not a reflection of simple nature, but rather an effect of multiple changes, both decided upon and natural. Brady has a particular focus on middle-sized mountain landscapes, such as the Scottish highlands, in contrast to more extreme and inhospitable Alpine scenes, whereas Burke has a much broader sense of what can count as sublime, including faces, bodies, political events and art.

James Kirwan is particularly sensitive to this breadth of sublime objects in eighteenth-century studies of the sublime and to the many different figures writing on the sublime at that time: 'Despite the relative fame of Burke and Gerard, it is the latter's approach that is more representative of the discourse on the sublime in the eighteenth century, and we find Priestley, in the last quarter of the century, ignoring Burke's more idiosyncratic inclusions.'[39] The use of 'idiosyncratic' is unfair to Burke and risks underestimating why his fame and legacy went further. For instance, when including smells in the sublime, Burke is being rigorous about the way smells and flavours at the limit between utter repulsion and strange attraction can produce sublime experiences. This is very important when we seek a more egalitarian and multiple sublime, against the prejudices of place, tradition and grandeur.

Though Scottish scenes like the Falls of Clyde and English views of the Lake District have frequently been described as sublime, it is important to note how their naturalness is as deceptive as MacPherson's creation of Ossian. The wilderness has been created by human decisions, like deforestation and nature reserves, changes in animal population such as the introduction or control of sheep, deer and wolves, alterations in climate, like the effect of climate breakdown on precipitation, and changes in plants, for instance through invasive species. Can Brady avoid the critical point that nature is a construct in a similar way to the technological sublime? Is nature prone to deceive and vary in its sublime effect as much as any other created sublime?

The following passage gives a succinct outline of Brady's main argument:

> If the sublime is to have a place in contemporary environmental thought, its value, particularly, will lie in the natural aesthetic qualities it (still) identifies; the way it characterises a distinctive type of intense aesthetic engagement with nature; and the particular aesthetic-moral relationship that emerges through that. It embodies a form of aesthetic response which balances elements of humility and humanity in relation to more threatening or overwhelming qualities and articulates a more challenging kind of environmental experience. The sublime delivers aesthetic responses that potentially ground moral attitudes, where we grasp nature as something that is to be admired, deserving of respect.[40]

I will highlight three ways in which this natural sublime is distinctive within the tradition. First, I want to draw attention to the association of the sublime with superior, though not necessarily universal, moral value. This is different from value as truth, or in the intensity of a lived moment, or in the creation of a superior form of life. In this case, value follows from an ethical consequence of sublime experience. The sublime brings us to respect nature and this leads to moral attitudes; for instance, regarding preservation and conservation based on respect. There are therefore loose connections between Brady's arguments and Kant's transition from the sublime to ethics, though the exact ethical consequences are quite different.

Second, this natural sublime carries many of the marks of historical versions of the sublime, but these are strongly tempered around the opposition of feelings usually found in the sublime. Instead of terror and delight, we are given humility and respect as responses to threats and overwhelming features. This elision of opposites in favour of moral lessons is problematic because it diminishes the intensity of sublime feelings as caused by tension and contradiction.

If the sublime is the result of contradictory feelings of attraction and repulsion, then neither respect nor humility would seem to be satisfactory responses to the tension, because the negative sides of the sublime are not worthy of admiration or humility, but rather lead to wariness and revolve around new ideas, as we saw in the commitment to technology as a way of avoiding threats presented by nature. The sublime is a sign of danger, and though respect and humility can be part of a response to it, they are insufficient and often counterproductive when the danger needs to be overcome, or when it becomes a fateful attraction.

The third point returns to the narrowing of the definition of the sublime in Brady's association of sublime feelings, ethical consequences and moral attitudes with a restricted view of nature. Her approach is close to the early natural sublime of the eighteenth century in its combination of views of landscapes allied to a sense of human figures within it. It is a walk-and-spectate experience of nature.

Yet nature also includes microscopic beings, climate, weather, humans and other larger mammals and all kinds of flora and fauna. Why should our engagement with nature only be sublime when it is overwhelming on visual and pedestrian scales, such as on a long walk between Highland peaks? Isn't there just as much potential for awe in the resilience of moss or mould in a city, or in the number and scale of insect populations, or the number of microbes in a single insect digestive system, or in the capacity of rats to live in our sewers, or in the shearing off of polar ice cliffs, or in the catastrophic effects of the eruption of Krakatoa in 1883, or in the ways humans have devised to dominate and take pleasure in nature and themselves?

Applying the combination of close-up and wide-angle critical views of microcritique, the weakness of an environmental sublime lies in its connection of a contingent selection of the sublime with a general moral position. There is no good reason why an 'an intense aesthetic engagement with nature' should combine awe and admiration only on the specific scales and at the specific locations required to encourage the kinds of 'respect' and 'humility' characterising an environmental ethics. This close-up is as dependent on chance and opportunity as were the sublime experiences of wealthy Europeans on grand tours through the Alps, or the proponents of manifest destiny in the United States during the expansion West in the early years of the nineteenth century.

There can be awe about virus propagation and admiration for cities combining technology and nature to support humans in numbers considered impossible for earlier ages. Why should such awe be less morally significant than aesthetic experiences of nature, since the lessons for humans are as important for survival and based on better knowledge? This means that the deduction from the natural sublime experience – in fact, a subset of experiences of nature – to the general environmental morality is invalid, because the experience described by Brady is particular and cannot be extended generally without imposing the necessity of a certain kind of aesthetic experience where there is none. So when Brady appeals to a 'meta-response theory' to explain the transition from an aesthetic experience (the emotional trigger) to a moral position (the meta-response), she is not making a valid transfer from general experience to general morality, but arguing from a local and contingent reaction to an equally local and contingent morality. This is not to say that there cannot be a general or even universal environmental ethics, but rather that it cannot be based on a particular type of experience of a particular portion of nature.

Brady compares meta-response theory with conversion theory (or catharsis) taken from Hume. The latter involves a transformation away from emotion, whereas the former brings about a new consciousness: 'The meta-response is therefore not catharsis, where emotions are purged and pleasure is felt in that release. Rather, it rests in the awareness of our capacity for moral feeling. We feel fulfilled in connection to our feeling of dread about a brutal character, say, and the fear and pity we have for his victims.'[41] Conversion theory argues for the elimination of a threat to moral behaviour through a dampening of negative passions. Meta-response theory argues for the emergence of morality from a morally elevating experience. The problem is 'Which experience?', and this question becomes crucial to the general validity of the moral position.

The restrictive and contingent aspect of the environmental sublime is most apparent where Brady argues that art cannot be sublime. She gives five reasons that reveal the preconceptions and limits of her definition of the sublime: first, art lacks in 'size and power'; second, the 'frames, forms, settings and conventions' of art mean that it cannot achieve the 'formlessness and unbounded character of the sublime'; third, art does not have 'the visceral "wild" and "disordered" character associated with dynamically sublime things'; fourth, art cannot 'evoke feelings of physical vulnerability, heightened emotions, and the expanded imagination characteristic of the sublime response'; and fifth, 'if we take into account the more metaphysical aspects of the Kantian and Romantic sublimes, art also struggles to present sublimity as such'.[42]

All these points depend on the conflation of the sublime object and sublime feeling as restricted to a particular human experience and definition of the human. For the first, power is in the quality of the emotion whereas size is in the relative proportions of nature and the human body, taken as place of sight and locomotion. It's a definition of the human where the setting for emotion and experience is a landscape of a particular type, with strong effects mainly on vision, sensations of climate and physical location (temperature, wind speed, weather changes) and imagination of spaces (depth and height). If we take auditory qualities instead, power does not equate to size defined as expanse. The error is in supposing that there is something necessary in the relation between a particular set of senses, the scales attributed to them, and a particular setting, when each of these can vary or even be substituted by quite different ones and still lead to the highest values associated with the sublime.

This argument does not even depend on there being many senses. Even for a single sense there are several candidates for excess over normal experiences. Sight, understood as something that can be disturbed powerfully, is not limited to scale for intense experiences; for instance, these can be associated with differences in light and darkness, or variations in colour, or types of perspective, or relations between form and content, or effects of surprise and contrast. Size is not the exclusive cause of intensity or excess in nature or art; even contrast is not enough for that, since deep shock and enthusiasm can be generated by minute variations, rather than stark differences.

Once senses and sublime disturbances are considered in greater range – well beyond the now outdated view of six senses (to which can be added balance, pain, and sense of time, for instance) – the distinction between the size and power of nature and art collapses. Music, architecture, painting, dance and sculpture and are all capable of working through the senses to instigate the most disturbing and powerful emotions without depending on anything like natural scales and forms. Furthermore, these art forms do not need to depend on conscious sensation but can work in the background through senses and artificial settings better suited to unconscious effects and processes of delay, return or repetition.

In his comprehensive study of recent art and theory of the sublime, Stephen Zepke offers a counter to Brady's dismissal of a sublime art, in particular, by showing how art works with the limits and boundaries of representation, sensation and understanding that also determine the natural sublime. Zepke's argument is important here because he insists on the political potential of sublime art. Commenting on Lyotard's definition of the sublime, he picks up on the latter's commitments to technology and the avant-garde as sources for events that give rise to new political awareness and formations: 'A sublime poetics/politics does not mean destroying or abandoning new technologies, but releasing the undetermined freedom of a pure material event immanent in these processes.'[43] This lack of determination and purity sets up an opposition between the politics of sublime art – which cannot make promises about specific ends, yet can give impetus to political and ethical movements by revealing hitherto unseen wrongs – and positions aiming to deploy the sublime with tangible goals such as Brady's respect for nature.

This is not simply to claim that Brady's argument fails because it does not take account of the techniques and works of modern art, in its long and ongoing investigation of intensity and sensual experience, for instance in Abstract Expressionism. The failure is historical as well as contemporary. Even a cursory acquaintance with medieval stained glass (at York Minster, say) makes the statement that art lacks in size and power highly dubious, even before we try to imagine the effects of the Minster's Great East Window on worshipers in the fifteenth century. The size of the window is itself not necessary for such thoughts. In the early days of printing, the first experience of a Dürer woodcut might have not been based on physical size but it is hard to imagine it lacking immense power through its combination of technical brilliance, sensory effects, novelty and symbolic richness.

The argument about formlessness and unboundedness also rests on an error about relations. The clue is in the negations of 'less' and 'un'. Nature is formless and unbounded in given situations in relation to forms and boundaries: in Brady's analysis these are conditional upon the human form and the limits of its vision and motor capacities. If you stand in a desert it appears formless and unbounded in relation to the horizon created by your eyes and sense of distance. When you fly over the same desert, other forms and boundaries are revealed. If you live in the desert, new forms and boundaries appear connected to water, wind, animals and other humans. So the very thing that is supposed to limit the sublime power of art is a condition for the sublimity of nature. The arguments should therefore be reversed. It is because art can work on forms, boundaries and conventions in order to destroy and overturn them while creating new ones that art can arrive at the shock of the sublime.

Similarly limited views of art inform the third and fourth points. It is difficult to maintain the affirmation that art is not wild and visceral when thinking about the straight-to-the-body effects of music or dance, or theatre or film, when a victim screams or a lover laments, or when experiencing the painting of a mouth in mid kiss, or caught in the arc of a dancer's leap, or drawn into syncopated music and movements. We might well feel physical vulnerability in relation to nature, and have our imagination expanded, but existentially that's a thin vulnerability and expansion when compared to the history of the painting of ageing and works such as Rembrandt's self-portraits or Giorgione's *La vecchia*, where flesh is made to speak to flesh.

Nature is blunt compared to art because art reads into us, transmitting and amplifying our deepest emotions and thoughts. It's this circuit that Kant and Brady miss in the idea of nature as closer to metaphysical ideas (understandably for Kant given his post-Reformation religious influences). Metaphysics is born of art in dialogues and meditations. It is through art that it can both grow and founder. Were it not for art, including the art of philosophers writing on the sublime, there would be few metaphysical ideas with a strong hold on us, for nature to then make manifest or destroy.

However, the role of art and of philosophical writing in preparing us for the sublime raises another problem for the egalitarian sublime. If the sublime is a deceptive experience, then proponents of one or other theory of the sublime are liable to amplify and legitimise this deception. This does not mean that writers on the sublime deliberately mislead us. There are few philosophers of the sublime more open and clear than Brady, in the way she carefully presents her position and the arguments for it. It is rather that, in providing support for an experience that already has a tendency to convince us of its truth and rightfulness, theories of the sublime further entrench the deception. The sublime becomes a cultural construct as well as an event, object and experience.

In this context, I define deception as the concealing of contingency and the resulting closing of our critical faculties to different possibilities and potential values. This hiddenness does not have to be intentional. It can be deliberate, as we saw in the risk of sublime propaganda in the discussion of method in Chapter 2, or it can simply follow from a cause with no conscious aim, for instance in the build-up of a cultural image of the sublime. The most serious aspect of this deception is the harm it does to other positions and values. For the environmental sublime and the move from sublime experience to moral positions, an entrenchment of a contingent position as necessary and valuable can be shown on each of the diagrams of the effects of the sublime.

First, outside and inside are conflated in the experience of the environmental sublime, such that inner experience is taken to be a true reflection of something admirable and valuable outside, even though external nature is itself made and the choice of a particular nature is contingent. This then gives force to a movement from passivity to moral activity with a general claim. The three deceptive moments are the conflation, its contingent selection of nature and experience, and the move from experiential particularity to moral activity with a general claim.

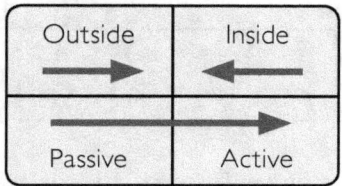

Second, in a similar manner to the technological sublime, the environmental sublime makes a claim for a legitimate collective but in fact introduces many layers of classification on the basis of the initial distinction between sublime and non-sublime nature. As we saw in the rejection of art as sublime, these layers can be highly damaging, forcing individuals and activities into lesser moral positions. So although the environmental sublime presents itself as an ethical philosophy, politically and socially it imposes a closed and potentially violent value system. This violence might end up being physical, since the combination of sublimity and a sense of right carry much force, but it starts with a different definition of violence as an ungrounded rejection of plurality and difference on the basis of a deceptive claim to higher value.

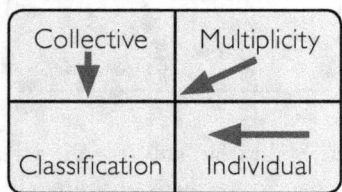

The third diagram is the most simple, in so far as it shows a value shift from tamed nature and urban spaces to wild nature, with the correlate that catastrophe is averted in the moral shift to respect for wild nature. However, if wild nature doesn't exist as such (or indeed if uninhabited space doesn't exist), and if the selection of certain types of nature is not justified by the sublime feeling, then not only is the value shift invalid, but also different kinds of catastrophe can follow; for instance, if the new values and new morality come to justify violent policies such as expropriation, or a limit on economic growth with no redistribution to those who will suffer from it. It is easier to advocate the environmental sublime from a position of wealth and security than from one of poverty and uncertainty, because the sacrifices required by the moral position are mitigated.

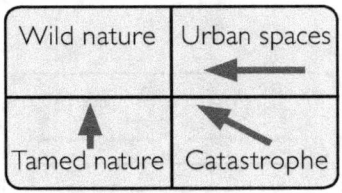

Finally, the diagram on spontaneity, critique and manufacture shows how theory can amplify the effects of the sublime. The powerful hold of the natural sublime – the way it takes us over – silences our critical faculties. It hinders us from becoming aware of the manufactured and evolving aspects of any natural vista or experience. In arguing for a natural sublime, unreachable by art, Brady gives credence to this effect and fixes it as general and truthful. This is then reinforced when the sublime is given moral weight. However, the arrows and gravity in the diagram should be read as capturing, not truthful effects directed towards the spontaneity of nature, but rather a deceitful move away from critique and an awareness of the power of manufactured scenes.

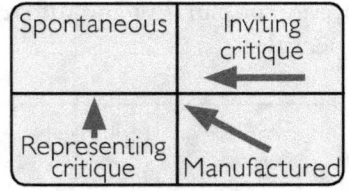

For the project of an egalitarian sublime the relation between sublime effects, experiences, theory and value is both liberating and a challenge. It is liberating because it highlights how the sublime is not only made but also encouraged. The sublime is an effect of art, culture, theory and politics. It is a challenge because, as we have seen in Nye and Brady, the sublime can easily lead to a restriction on equality through the elevation of particular values given the stamp of universal truth through an appeal to the sublime. As such the sublime is politically dangerous in serving the elimination of empirical and practical variations and differences in favour of more limited, yet contingent, values. This raises two questions. First, what is the right relation of theory to the sublime, given their twinned powers of deception? Second, can there be an egalitarian sublime escaping the impositions of particular aims, tastes and experiences over differences in value and circumstance?

Chapter 5

Sublime Miseries

From high to low

The long historical view of the idea of the sublime presents it as carrier of the highest values. The effect of the sublime is to transmit the very best. However, once we move into close-ups of different accounts of the sublime this consistency disappears; first, because there is great variation in what the values are taken to be; second, because, when we move even closer, these values turn out to be deceptive and self-contradictory. The sublime varies from thinker to thinker. Its effects are never consistently positive, even when taken on their own terms.

These findings still overlook a further unexpected aspect of some theories of the sublime, mostly those of the modern sublime, with its attention to the role of the unconscious. Instead of carrying the highest values and transmitting them thanks to positive emotions such as pleasure, joy and delight, although counterbalanced by terror or pain, these theories view the sublime as primarily negative and miserable across some, if not all aspects: the object, experience, emotions, effects and values.

We shouldn't be too surprised to encounter this negative turn in the sublime. As we have seen, the sublime has always had negative components in the form of shock, awe, terror and pain. It has also had destructive effects, for those barred from sublime values, or found to be in the way, or taken as representing the opposite of the sublime. The sublime has given reasons to harm others and other things, when they are judged to be against it or counter to its values.

These negative aspects can be seen as outside the sublime, as avoidable consequences of it, and hence open to remedy; for example, by accepting sublime values but applying them according to practices or moralities that avoid the worst results of an indiscriminate pursuit of sublime experiences. This occurred differently in each of the philosophies examined in earlier chapters. Nietzsche sets his sublime values as untimely, thereby delaying their shocking effects to a time more ready for them. Nye combines the technological sublime with democracy. This democratic input, if open and responsive enough, could mitigate the exclusion and violence of sublime doctrines like manifest destiny. Brady's environmental sublime relies upon a moral metaresponse, capable of guiding the admiration and respect attributed to some views of nature.

Nonetheless, these mitigating features cannot counteract the negativity at the very heart of the sublime. The sublime does not begin with reason and critical discussion, where argument and agreement depend on equality between different participants, such that no one is forced to acquiesce. Instead, it transmits its value not only through powerful effects, but also thanks to great disparities in value and position. The sublime operates by force, from higher to lower.

It could be objected that this force is never direct and is always counterbalanced. The experience is never one of pure fear or pure terror. Rather, the sublime always involves some distance and protection, as well as some positive emotions or ideas. This is true, but it does not cancel out the fact that those who undergo the experience of the sublime are, at least at first, belittled and threatened. The effects are certainly indirect; for instance, where overpowering natural phenomena such as mountains, gulfs and storms at sea are viewed from a safe vantage point, or when explosions or riots are learned about from reports or images. Even so, there remains a communication of great power, beyond our control and out of scale with our capacities.

This disparity in power does not have to have a natural cause, or even involve physical force. From the earliest philosophies of the sublime, art and rhetoric have been ascribed a power to move and convince us in the communication of high values and intense emotions. There is still inequality in this sublime, since the great artist or speaker moves us through means beyond our comprehension and abilities. It would be a mistake to assume that this lack of direct threat and the presence of high values do not lead to inequality and debasement. It would also be an error to think that because these effects are delayed or unconscious their hold upon us is lesser.

The inequality internal to the sublime follows from two linked processes of negation. First, we are passive in face of the negative effects of the sublime: it takes hold of us and involves overwhelming emotions such as pain, awe and terror. Something external to us brings harm to us. Second, the highest values transmitted by the sublime are unattainable, in the sense that we do not produce them and cannot fully grasp them. Something higher than us requires our fidelity or submission.

Even if these negative effects work unconsciously, they still retain a deep hold and lead to debilitating inferiority and submission. Operating unconsciously, the power of negativity can be even stronger, since damaging effects can grow and work unseen, and in ways harder to counter through conscious acts. Terrifying and overpowering things do not have to be present in order to subjugate us. On the contrary, the threat of something terrible – merely hinted at over time and gnawing away – can bring us to heel, or induce us to fall apart, far more effectively than a direct challenge.

The sublimity of the imagined power of gods, rulers and mobs can take this unconscious form of negativity. Absolute power conveyed by palaces, dungeons, secret police, torture and the vanishing of victims has both the terror and relief required for the sublime; there is terror at the possibility of betrayal, but also shameful release at having escaped when neighbours are taken away. Though these forms of rule might seem antiquated, they have far from disappeared and have in fact mutated thanks to new technologies of surveillance and exclusion.

In the sublime, terror must be defined as a combination of fear and dread, in order to signal how it operates at a distance and over time. To define it simply as extreme fear is wrong, because the sublime always combines terror with other affects and feelings, and always introduces some kind of protection from the thing to be feared. So there is no sublime terror when fleeing a threat, but rather when considering the possibility of its return, even stronger, at some future date.

This raises the problem of whether we should think of terrorism as sublime. For instance, Gene Ray's study of terror and the sublime includes terrorist acts as sublime, not in any way to endorse them, but arguing instead for the power of art in supporting acts of mourning, after the trauma of terrorism and other violent sublime events:

> These essays propose that the sublime and its reception are disruptions through which art can link up with and modestly effect practices of daily life, at least within the limits of specific cultural situations. It is argued that in certain postwar artistic practices, sublime evocations and avowals of traumatic history are used to reactivate the disruptive hit or force of such history.[1]

The care and modest aims of Ray's practices of counter-trauma are significant because they indicate the palliative role of art after terror, thereby dividing two moments of the sublime in the horror of the injury and its cautious reactivation: 'Through the artistic mimesis of the structure of trauma, disturbance is reinstalled in the scene and put back into play, spurring mourning back into movement.'[2] The connection between the sublime and mourning is very unusual in the history of the sublime, but the acuity of Ray's analysis lies in its understanding of the extreme nature of terror in the twentieth and twenty-first centuries and the way this excess has changed what the sublime can call up and call for.

Given the history of the use of terror in those centuries, the question of terrorism and the sublime should therefore be considered with rigour and caution. First, terrorism is a term often used with little discrimination and applied to a great range of different acts, actors and events. Second, it is a negative moral and political term often applied according to double standards, designed to carry heavy moral condemnation and sometimes to justify indiscriminate and rapid political action, beyond the standards of legal scrutiny, public reflection and democratic validation applied to other acts. Third, the label terrorist is usually ascribed by states to non-state actors and entities.

Taken together, these points make terrorism a dubious term, in so far as it comes laden with unstable combinations of calculating and hyper-emotional political motivations, meaning that its use can be unreliable and imprecise. For example, the same violent acts, such as the bombing of civilians, are labelled terrorism dependent on whether they are perpetrated by a state or not, or whether they fall on rich communities or poor ones, or whether they occur in close or distant countries. The label terrorist may then be used to justify or forbid arms sales, and legal or extra-legal actions, when the end result is the same for murdered civilians.

Furthermore, the label 'terrorist' is frequently justified on vague and poorly understood accounts of actors' motivations (to terrify) and character (evil). Other explanations for violent acts are well known but not considered, such as strategic and tactical motivations, or extreme principles and beliefs, or desperation. Against the label 'evil', little attention is given to the fact that perpetrators of terrorism are like non-perpetrators, coming from the same communities, but not necessarily from the same conditions. Similarly, little attention is paid to the shifts in the application of the label over time; for instance, where those once called terrorists become agents of a state.

Given the unreliability of the term terrorism, I'll rephrase the question to ask whether the use of extreme and violence-inducing terror can be described as sublime. It can, and theories of the sublime should be tested in relation to this violence. However, it is important to distinguish between calling an event sublime and taking this as the basis for an appropriate response to that event. The point here is to criticise definitions of the sublime, so while I do not advocate Richard Kearney's ethical alternative to the sublime through artistic narratives, my critical approach is in line with his repudiation of the sublime as a sufficient ethical response to terror: 'The sublime, as Kant, Baudrillard and Arendt all concede, does not connect us to any kind of universal narrative empathy. Rather it draws us away from what Kant called "aesthetic reflective judgment" and shatters our *sensus communis*.'³ The key lesson for the study of an egalitarian sublime is in Kearney's conclusion about narrative empathy. If equality is to be based on a shared narration of a common history, then the sublime must break with it because its effect is to make universal empathy impossible.

Against Burke's argument from the sublime to sympathy, Kearney's focus on extreme terror shows how it leads to incomprehension and loathing of others, making us incapable of shared judgements and community. Though the sublime can have a positive role in curbing the hubris of rationalism and over-confidence in individual values and judgements, it leaves no ground for the ethical reconstitution of community: 'if in the process the experience of sublime horror does serve to humiliate the rationalist and narcissistic pretensions of the ego – no bad thing – it still leaves us helpless before the basic question of how to respond ethically to the enigma of terror'.⁴ The twin aspects of terror and fascination, triggered by extreme power, can be attributed to acts and events as varied as nuclear explosions, bombings, mass killings and expropriation, torture and repressive threats. As such, they are sublime in the traditional sense of generating a powerful attraction and repulsion in response to an overwhelming event, but with no escape from the breakdown of our faculties of judgement.

In this way, the sublime can become an instrument of power, contributing to order and to disorder, through a combination of terror and relief operating in part at an unconscious level on our actions; for instance, where the possibility of annihilation, disappearance, deep pain or extreme privation influences behaviour without being a well-defined component of conscious calculation. By breaking communities of empathy, shared judgement and common narratives, the sublime contributes to a reliance on force. This is one of the reasons why, in work by thinkers as different as Lyotard, Kristeva, Adorno and Žižek, the question of the sublime becomes a matter of misery and of the unconscious effects of terror.

From *The Inhuman* onwards, Lyotard's later philosophy investigates different registers of the sublime, combining often small-scale events in art with moments of individual renewal and awareness. This is quite different from the concern for the sublime in extreme large-scale violence. Much of Lyotard's work on a minimal sublime and 'micrologies' follows from his reading of Adorno's *Aesthetic Theory* and the idea that the end of metaphysics occurs on a minimal scale: this is 'the principle sketched out by Adorno at the end of *Negative Dialectics*, and that controls the writing of his *Aesthetic Theory*: the thought that 'accompanies metaphysics in its fall', he said, can only proceed in terms of "micrologies"'.⁵ For Lyotard, these minimal events are sublime and the mark of an artistic avant-garde because they are moments of privation and uncertainty that bring down an old order but do not replace it with a new one, thereby inducing effects of attraction and repulsion characteristic of the sublime: 'Like micrology, the avant-garde is not concerned with what happens to the "subject", but with "Does it happen?", with privation. This is the sense in which it still belongs to the aesthetic of the sublime.'[6] Lyotard's definition of the sublime in terms of an unanswered and unanswerable question accompanying feelings of attraction and repulsion is an attempt to give a limited and highly tentative reconstitution of community around testimonies to otherness and difference, rather than shared narratives in art, as defended by Kearney.[7]

Unconscious threats are not only about the exercise of power. They can also be about its overthrow or absence. The ferocity of crowds in revolt and revolution, or desperation and fury, has the same capacity to terrify without being present. We imagine and unconsciously fear a breakdown of order, with its sublime qualities of the loss of all bearings and familiar anchors, accompanied by life-threatening violence. Once again, none of this has to come through direct experience. Mere reports of revolution (true or not) can play on the unconscious and be used to keep us haunted and compliant.

In his study of critical language about revolution, Burke and the sublime, Steven Blakemore argues that Burke shifts between two ideas of the sublime in relation to the French Revolution. For Burke the violent sublime of revolution destroys the sublime and the beautiful as connected and higher social values:

> Burke moves from an aggressive argument of a punishing sublime in his prerevolutionary writings to an essentially defensive argument in his counter-revolutionary writings. And as sublime authority continues to be attacked, Burke envisions the revolutionaries 'stripping' the social fabric and rending the 'veil' that results in the fall into knowledge and correspondent fall of the European world.[8]

The French Revolution traps Burke between sublimity as sign of great value and the destructive violence of revolution that nonetheless satisfies his conditions for qualifying as sublime. The solution is to attach traditional and enduring values to the definition of the sublime, thereby discounting any sublime that attacks those values.

In a more critical reading of Burke's ambivalence around the sublime and revolution, Tom Furniss points to the contradictions involved in maintaining different degrees of the sublime and takes this to explain Burke's bourgeois sublime and his deep opposition to the French Revolution: 'in attempting to exploit a distinction between the dangers of the sublime in its highest degree and the benefits which might be derived from its inferior effects, Burke becomes embroiled in a series of ineradicable contradictions which may, perhaps, account for his "rage" against the revolution'.⁹ For the egalitarian sublime, the contradictions and the introduction of class are more relevant than accounting for Burke's rage. Once the sublime is attached to the values of a particular class and its interests it fails as egalitarian; if the contradictions stemming from different types of sublime are to be overcome, revolution and a classless society might then be one way of arriving at a shared sublime.

It would be wrong, though, to associate Burke's sublime too strictly with his epoch and the French Revolution. Richard Devetak updates Burke's sublime, and the idea of the monstrous sublime more generally, to reflect on terror and the sublime after the attacks in New York on 11 September 2001. Discussing Burke's responses to the French Revolution, he points to the distinction between true and false sublimes used as a justification for repression of revolution: 'Burke's gothic scene portrays a monstrous republic unconstrained by moral, political and legal limits. To combat this monster, European powers must use force to restore order.'[10] The Gothic scene of horror and monstrosity plays on the imagination and on the unconscious. Devetak's point about its support for force and order extends beyond the Gothic period, applying just as well to the increase in repression and the demand for order after terrorist attacks. This runs counter to the progressive and morally unifying function ascribed to the sublime.

I have distinguished unconscious effects from the unconscious as an aspect of mind in order to separate arguments about effects we may not be conscious of at a given time, or in a given state, from arguments dependent on one or other theory of the unconscious (psychoanalytic or psychological, for example). It is not necessary to hold to any such theory in order to make the point that, since consciousness has different degrees and levels (sleepy, attentive, peripheral . . .), if powerful influences such as the sublime work in the background, then their negative effects can be hidden yet all the more powerful by remaining unconsidered or hard to grasp, like deep fear, dread or other passions.

The role of such unconscious effects is central to debates about the positive or negative roles of the sublime, because it leads to an explanation of how moral versions of the sublime provide an insufficient account of the connection between the sublime and moral order. The paradigm of these versions comes from Kant, but we have seen others in the technological and environmental sublime. The key to their deductions is an implication from the sublime event to a positive moral conclusion. Instead of remaining in a state of terror and fear, balanced by attraction and joy, the person experiencing the sublime is necessarily led to a moral position, so long as that person satisfies certain conditions of rationality and feeling.

Paul Guyer tracks the fortunes of this positive moral role for the sublime in the nineteenth century. It begins with Kant, then fades, until it is revived by Nietzsche. The phrase 'positive moral role' would be misunderstood here, if read as applying to an equal role across all of society. As we have seen, Nietzsche's sublime must work through the few and not the many. When Guyer speaks of human redemption it cannot mean that all individual humans are redeemed. For Nietzsche, only a few are touched by the absurd, and then come to transform it in an untimely sublime creativity, terrifying and incomprehensible to most humans.

Kant: equality in universality

Writing at a time of revolution, and after a careful reading of Burke with his mistrust of sublime enthusiasm, Kant is aware of the threat of the sublime through fanaticism and terror. His task is to show how the experience of the sublime does not return us to nature as a force of unreason, for example in ferocious revenge or a collapse into pure terror. For Kant, though we certainly undergo the sublime, it cannot remove our status as rational moral beings. This means that sublime events and feelings are secondary to the sublimity of freedom and reason.

Sublime revolutionary fervour runs counter to this true sublimity, because the disorder of revolution is the enemy of enlightened reason. Only steady and lawful change can bring about the 'supreme good': 'If we try to give [the best, metaphysically sublime, constitution] reality by means of gradual reforms carried out in accordance with definite principles, we shall see that it is the only means of continually approaching the supreme political good – perpetual peace.'[11] Gradual change is the only means to perpetual peace because radical and violent change breaks the rule of law and thereby sets the cause of reason back, depriving it of the legal setting and relative peace it requires to spread universally.

In 'An Answer to the Question "What is Enlightenment?"', Kant contrasts true enlightenment through freedom and reason with the lack of reform achieved by revolutions: 'A revolution may well put an end to autocratic despotism and to rapacious or power-seeking oppression, but it will never produce a true reform in ways of thinking.'[12] Throughout his writings on law and politics, Kant is not prepared to exchange the rule of law for revolution driven by sublime ideals: 'But no attempt should be made to put [the best constitution] into practice overnight by revolution, i.e. by forcibly overthrowing a defective constitution which has existed in the past; for there would be an interval of time during which the condition of right would be nullified.'[13] Revolution fails because it is a violent cut in time where law is suspended. Legality is essential for progress towards an enlightened constitution since it requires steady steps that appeal to freely exercised reason. This freedom and rationality are disrupted by violent interruptions which then become large reversals.

The necessary role for some kind of steadily improving legal order shows how Kant could not have taken the feeling of the sublime, as experienced in a dynamic and threatening situation, as a positive political force. We need distance from disorder to exercise freedom and reason together. This is a key insight for any egalitarian definition of the sublime. If the definition is to involve the confusion and chaotic states induced by sublime experiences, then politically it will depend on some kind of higher order to make sure the positive aspects of the sublime are not lost to negative forces.

Kant's definition of the sublime changes and becomes more rigorous between the pre-critical *Observations on the Feeling of the Sublime and the Beautiful* and the *Critique of Judgment*. Furthermore, in his writings on law and politics, different uses of the sublime follow a range of critical, empirical and metaphysical examples and definitions of the term. In order to arrive at a precise though limited definition of the sublime in a critical but also moral context, I'll therefore follow a single passage from the *Critique of Judgment*, where Kant discusses our capacity to overcome the effects of sublime emotions, through the apparent contradiction of a free subjection to moral law.

In the *Critique of Judgment*, Kant transfers the sublime from objects to human minds: 'Hence sublimity is contained not in any thing of nature, but only in our mind, insofar as we can become conscious of our superiority to nature within us, and thereby also to nature outside us (as far as it influences us).'[14] Sublimity is not an objective quality. Furthermore, it does not have a causal hold upon the human mind. Humanity retains its freedom to overcome and dominate the internal passions of the sublime. This resists the power of nature as external cause of the sublime. It also controls it as internal nature, in our emotions, instincts and drives.

For Kant, the dynamic sublime can be understood as a clash of forces: of the causal power of nature and the force of our will. This is a contrast between two different ideas of power, where the magnitude and force of nature, exceeding our understanding, meets with an even stronger strength of will and reason, though this strength is moral rather than physical. These different powers should not be confused; true sublimity is only internal, and a property of will, reason and moral law. To call objects sublime is a misnomer: 'Whatever arouses this feeling in us, and this includes the might of nature that challenges our forces, is then (although improperly) called sublime.'[15] When Kant transfers the sublime from objects to human subjects, he also transfers the value of the sublime from physical power and emotional influence to moral determination: the power to choose the good even under the greatest duress.

Modern readings of Kant often downplay the religious aspects of his argument. In the passage from the *Critique of Judgment*, he is also invoking the sublimity of God, as creator of nature and, more importantly, as creator of our will and reason under moral law: 'it is only by presupposing this idea within us, and by referring to it, that we can arrive at the sublimity of that being who arouses deep respect in us, not just by his might as demonstrated in nature, but even more by the ability, with which we have been endowed, to judge nature without fear and to think of our vocation as sublimely above nature.'[16] Having started with the dynamic power of nature, as encountered in mountains and earthquakes, then passing through the mathematical sublime of number and scale, Kant ends with sublimity coming from the combination of will, law and respect for the supreme being. We can rise up to dominate our terror and limitations. We do so by choosing to submit to universal moral laws. Nature, will and law are given by a sublime god.

It is a peculiarity of this argument that God is not necessary for the transfer of the sublime from object to subject, since this depends purely on the human mind and will. A further peculiarity is the combination of freedom and submission in choosing to subject ourselves to reason as the source of moral laws. Neither of these are contradictory, since the idea of God as creator has no direct bearing on will and reason and since freedom can be retained within the framework of moral laws as the free selection of which laws to submit to.

These factors explain how Kant's version of the sublime could be seen as the high point of the egalitarian sublime. The idea that all humans reach sublimity on an equal basis in choosing to follow universal moral laws leads to an egalitarian view of the human (we share the same will), of mind (we share the same reason) and of moral law (the laws we subject ourselves to must be universal or, more properly, universalisable). This last condition, concerning a test of universalisability, adds a further subtle egalitarian twist, since we do not have to be equal under the same laws, but rather when we choose to submit to specific laws they must be universally applicable without contradiction.

The positive reading of Kant's theory of the sublime can be rendered in the following version of the diagram on the internal and external effects of definitions of the sublime:

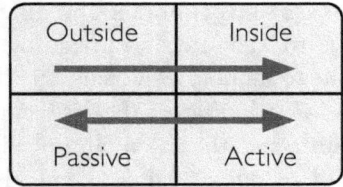

Kant transfers the sublime to the inside and at the same time balances its effects between activity and passivity by cancelling passivity in relation to natural influences, while also tempering the sublimity of human freedom with moral law. The sublime can then be seen as a support for modern cosmopolitan humanism. Safely enthused by the sublimity of our shared will and reason we can construct international and universal moral realms:

> Violence will gradually become less on the part of those in power, and obedience towards the laws will increase. There will no doubt be more charity, less quarrels in legal actions, more reliability in keeping one's word, and so on in the commonwealth, partly from a love of honour, and partly from a lively awareness of where one's own advantage lies; and this will ultimately extend to the external relations between the various peoples, until a cosmopolitan society is created.[17]

Passages such as this one, and others from 'Perpetual Peace' and *The Metaphysics of Morals*, justify claims for Kantian philosophy as the basis for cosmopolitan institutions such as the United Nations.[18]

In his work on the sublime, Lyotard was particularly interested in the role of signs attesting to this progress as described by Kant in 'The Contest of Faculties': The reaction of observers at some distance from the French Revolution, '(because of its universality) proves that mankind as a whole shares a certain character in common, and it also proves (because of its disinterestedness) that man has a moral character, or at least the makings of one.'[19] Lyotard seeks to question and then reverse Kant's analysis of enthusiasm at a distance from the French Revolution. However, despite his interest in Burke's sublime, Lyotard's point isn't to deny the value of enthusiasm at a remove from danger. Writing about enthusiasm for the revolution, Burke claims it is 'better to be despised for too anxious apprehensions, than ruined by too confident a security',[20] whereas Lyotard combines anxiety and enthusiasm in a negative role for 'signs of history'.[21] The signs convey differences rather than commonality.

Lyotard's earlier works on Kant and the sublime explain why he returned to Kant in great depth in his *Lessons on the Analytic of the Sublime*, with its close reading of sections 26–29 of the *Critique of Judgment*. This interest in the Kantian sublime remained consistent throughout his interpretations, where the sublime serves as a sign of unbridgeable differences (differends). As such, Lyotard is opposed to Kant, not in his reading of the sublime, but in Kant's use of the sublime to support universals: 'Neither moral universality nor aesthetic universalisation, but rather the destruction of one by the other in the violence of their differend, that is a sublime feeling. Even when considered subjectively, the differend itself cannot demand to be shared by every thinker.'[22] For Lyotard, thinkers aren't defined by common faculties but rather by uncommon sublime encounters revealing absolute otherness.

In a more historical mode than Lyotard's philosophical study, the ebb and flow of the capacity of the United Nations to facilitate peace between and within nations over the twentieth and twenty-first centuries could be seen as a disproof of Kant's cosmopolitan aspirations. This, however, would be a misreading, since Kant's argument depends on the right conditions being in place for a successful trend towards peace under law. Our recent history demonstrates how those conditions are not yet right and indicates what measures we should take to remedy this at the level of law and rational debate. The deeper problem for Kant's position comes from the idea that this rule of cosmopolitan law either can never be realised or is so flawed that it shouldn't be the basis for cosmopolitan institutions unless thoroughly amended.

The latter point is made by Amitav Acharya, writing for *The Oxford Handbook on the United Nations*. Having raised critical points about the UN's agency and legitimacy in a diverse global order, he argues for a shift away from the universalism inherited from the Kantian Enlightenment and towards a transformation of universalism in the direction of multilateralism. Rather than the suppression of diversity implied by a strict definition of the universal based on Western norms, culture and history, universalism needs to change to reflect a diversity of cultures, norms and practices: 'The future of the UN system lies in this reformulated vision of universalism.'[23]

In this regard, the most interesting arguments come from thinkers of the sublime, such as Lyotard and Adorno, when they turn Kant's sublime against universalism of any form by arguing that sublime experiences demonstrate the impossibility of cosmopolitan order. Taken on its own terms, Kant's argument seems to offer a way out of the dangerous aspects of the sublime in fanaticism and enthusiasm beyond reason. The problem is that this requires assent to his definition of the 'inside': the mind, will and reason. If we lack the will necessary to overcome nature within us, if we do not share the same reason, and if that reason is prone to error, then external nature once again overcomes us and the balance of passivity and activity advocated by Kant is itself an illusion. The critical point can be put very simply. Kant's account of the human being is unrealistic and flawed. It fails to acknowledge the weakness of will and reason. This explains why unconscious effects are dangerous for his argument, because they undermine the power to choose moral laws and overcome natural forces.

This opposition between a Kantian model of the human and ones that situate us more firmly within dynamic nature is the basis for a further critical reaction to egalitarian and cosmopolitan claims. We might have assumed that the Kantian sublime gives rise to a new egalitarian collective, drawing away from individualism and multiplicity, defined as unrestricted freedom to choose and as many natural variations that cannot be reduced to a single human nature. However, if Kant's account of the human is unrealistic, then no true collective emerges. There is instead an imposition of new classification-based distinctions between free and rational humans and those who fail these criteria, and between Kantian universalism and a wider diversity of norms. This is a dangerous split since it can ground negative judgements about weakness, madness and lack of reason while falsely elevating the value of moral laws that aren't in fact universal:

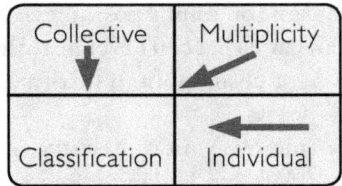

From an environmental point of view, Kant's theory involves a shift from wild nature to nature tamed by reason and moral law. This is justified, from the point of view of the theory, because catastrophe, whether coming from nature or from human nature, can be controlled and eliminated through the construction of legal and cosmopolitan spaces.

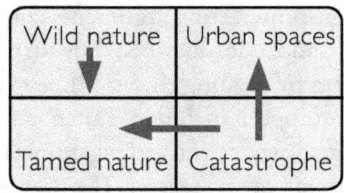

Finally, the most complicated question concerning the effects of the Kantian theory of the sublime is about critical openness and deception. This is because his philosophy is above all critical, in the sense of undertaking a critique of earlier dogmatism but also in the sense of being self-critical. His philosophy draws its strength and lasting value from its relentless search for a justified and robust position. Yet, if we disagree with Kant's account of the human subject, this critical approach can be seen to lead to ideas of the mind and of the sublime that are dependent on a deceptive move from an admission of terror and horror, tinged by pleasure, to their suppression in favour of an illusory human free will and reason. This complication can be shown in two very different diagrams with the same elements. On the one hand, Kant's critical method draws all things towards critique:

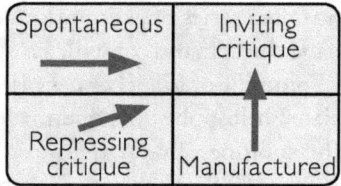

On the other hand, his definition of the sublime and deductions of the faculties of the mind can be viewed as manufactured and as repressing critique in a manner compounded by the very methods designed to ensure a critical philosophy. If a philosophy making claim to the most rigorous standards of critique arrives at false conclusions, then the deception is all the more powerful:

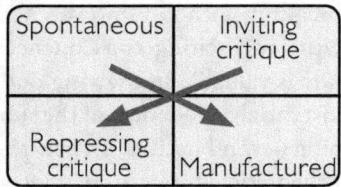

This dilemma is central to debates about the sublime: first, because it raises the question of whether the sublime can be redeemed as event or experience, for instance through an appeal to human powers and moral laws; second, because it calls for an appraisal of the relation between argument, or rhetoric, and the potentially deceptive nature of definitions of the sublime; third, because it is at the heart of debates about scales and types of sublimity. Is the sublime miserable and terrible, or is it an occasion of great redemption or hope?

Schopenhauer's sublime consolations

Schopenhauer gives us an ambiguous answer to the dilemma of critique and deception. On the one hand, his definition of the sublime can be interpreted as avoiding the account of an illusory sublime human will in Kantian philosophy. On the other hand, when viewed from the perspective of progressive philosophies of the sublime such as Kant's, or the more recent technological and environmental sublimes, the highest values advocated by Schopenhauer can be seen as materially futile. Against this ineffectiveness, it can be argued that Schopenhauer turns the sublime into a form of spiritual elevation and consolation through higher knowledge. However, the ultimate value of the spiritual sublime depends on a series of assumptions about pure knowledge and whether we can escape the demands of will.

In the Appendix to Volume I of *The World as Will and Representation*, 'Criticism of the Kantian Philosophy', Schopenhauer gives high praise to Kant's philosophy of the sublime: 'By far the most excellent thing in the *Critique of Aesthetic Judgement* is the theory of the sublime.'[24] Reflecting this admiration, his stated approach is to follow Kant's analysis, 'the general method of investigation', but finally to disagree because '[Kant] does not provide the real solution to the problem'.[25] This self-assessment is not accurate, in so far as Schopenhauer only follows the broadest outlines of Kant's work on the sublime, such as the preliminary distinction between the sublime and beautiful. Even in that case he will eventually move beyond it.

Sandra Shapshay gives a detailed account of the relation between Schopenhauer's sublime and Kant's. She argues that the former transforms the latter, rather than breaking with it. However, if it is a transformation, it is a very strong one with far-reaching consequences for the effect of the sublime. Shapshay's study is valuable in drawing out the contrasts between the cognitive and the existential experiences of the sublime, and the resulting difference in ways of going beyond nature: 'In contrast with Kant's account, which makes use of our theoretical-rational vocation as a source of our prideful elevation, on Schopenhauer's account the subject's limitations are construed more existentially than cognitively: encounters with vast nature instil in us a sense of our smallness and existential insignificance.'[26] For Kant, the sublime is a conduit for higher moral values through reason, whereas Schopenhauer's sublime has an emotional effect on our existence, making us aware of our fragility, weakness and mortality.

This means that the sublime functions differently for the two philosophers. Its excessive scale does not involve a limitation on the faculties of understanding and imagination for Schopenhauer, but rather a form of annihilation of individual will and body, like our sense of irrelevance and futility at the size and inhospitable nature of the cosmos:

> Our frustration does not arise, as it does on Kant's account, from our inability to grasp the totality of the representations. Instead, for Schopenhauer, we are reduced to Nichts by the sheer vastness (in space and time) of the universe. But, similar to the Kantian account, confronted with this painful recognition, there arises nonetheless a pleasurable recognition of the subject's own status as 'beyond' nature.[27]

In my view, Shapshay's claim to this similarity in terms of pleasure is overplayed since the status of what is 'beyond nature' is completely different – freedom and reason versus knowledge and spiritual elevation – thereby contradicting any wider claim for similarities between the two definitions of the sublime.

On a close reading of *The World as Will and Representation* deep contrasts with Kant become apparent: where Schopenhauer detects degrees of the sublime; where he associates the sublime with pure consciousness independent of will; where this intellection is for Platonic Ideas; and where the world of representation does not involve moral acts and decisions bearing on the objective world. Schopenhauer's study of the sublime is a one-way path removing us from the world of bodies and individuals. This is a spiritual path, detaching us from effective action but uniting us in shared knowledge. As such, it is a move towards a strong egalitarianism, in an ideal realm beyond individuals, but it is also a failure for concrete equality due to its remove from material improvement.

Like Kant, Schopenhauer draws the sublime inwards, making it dependent on a modification of subjectivity, of the 'subjective part of aesthetic pleasure'.[28] Unlike Kant, this subjective part is a form of pure knowledge independent of will. This absence of will in a philosophy of the sublime is surprising. Even if the sublime raises us above base motivations, as carrier of the highest values shouldn't it also motivate our will to higher aims, to decisive moral acts, as seen in Kant's moral vocation for the sublime, or move us to flee and be cautious about sublime events, as shown in Burke's wariness of the sublime as a source of terror and enthusiasm?

For Kant, in rising above nature, the sublime will releases our moral potential. Similarly, though on an empirical basis, for the technological sublime there is a socially progressive outcome in collective endeavours that transform nature, spurred on by the joint experience of the sublime. For the environmental sublime, the sublimity of nature introduces responsibility and respect into our attitude to nature. Even Nietzsche's untimely sublime, though divisive, still has the potential to point to a different and better future for the human as a natural animal that can also surpass its nature. These practical collective outcomes in relation to nature are closed off by Schopenhauer.

In his work on the Kantian sublime, Paul Crowther adds to the moral significance of the sublime as an inner experience of our power to go beyond our natural capacities by extending them to comprehension: 'We may know that all human beings have the potential to comprehend things which far exceed their sensible capacities, but to countenance this fact through an experience of the sublime is to experience it, as it were, from the inside.'[29] This leads to a moral humanity, with a moral and political vocation to improve the lot of all humans, together with a sense of the power of understanding: 'Kant saw (however opaquely) that aesthetic experience – and the sublime in particular – has the capacity to humanize.'[30] However, this progressive aim depends on the right moral guidance for the understanding, given that its powers can be used for good or bad outcomes for humanity as a whole.

Schopenhauer is sceptical about this confidence in free will and reason. He turns away from higher acts following from the sublime because he does not believe in purity of will. In holding to a strong distinction between will and representation, Schopenhauer attributes will to bodily and objective motivations, to desire, fear, greed, jealousy, boredom, despair and ambition. We only escape these motivations in the pure contemplation of Ideas – in Representation. For the beautiful, a purely formal aesthetic appreciation of nature 'moves us from knowledge of mere relations serving the will into aesthetic contemplation, and thus raises us to the will-free subject of knowledge'.[31] Movement and relations are central to this argument. There is transfer from dependency on will as utility-led appetite or drive, where objective relations serve the interests of will, to contemplation in pure knowledge.

For Schopenhauer, this purification is necessary because he is cynical about willing, seeing it as always individually motivated and driven by desire. The difference with Kant, and with other thinkers who define the sublime as improving for willed action, is in Schopenhauer's refusal of the idea of an individual disinterested will; for him, there is no such thing as a pure will devoid of its specific causes and aims. The will cannot shake off its roots in self-interest. For egalitarian aims this is important, since the consequence of this suspicion of will is a shattering of group cohesion, due to differences in interest and motivation. Schopenhauer's strongest claim against Kant is that so long as there is will, social, general and universal unity founder in clashes of desires and drives.

However, the absence of will in the experience of the beautiful and in ideal knowledge brings about a deep problem for Schopenhauer's definition of the sublime. It also shows how thoroughly he needs to abandon the Kantian model. If contemplation needs to be will-less, how can this be so in the sublime, with its threats and rewards for the individual? If the sublime involves fear, awe, pain or terror, allied to pleasure, enjoyment or relief, how can it be independent of the interests of will, whether in fleeing threats or seeking thrills?

In solving this problem, Schopenhauer can appeal neither to Kant's combination of will and reason, nor to ideas of collective action motivated in part by objective outcomes such as building a better world or preserving nature, because, for Schopenhauer, not only is the will individual and never disinterested, it is also in the grip of forces that will annihilate it, but that it nonetheless continues to struggle against. The will is therefore divisive and all the more so in the grip of the negative aspects of the sublime inducing fear, terror and a sense of limits in relation to scale and number.

Schopenhauer solves the problem by appealing to a state of exaltation and contemplation alongside an effort of will, where the state and willing are internally independent of one another, while externally dependent. In one of the apparent contradictions of his philosophy of the sublime, there is no will in the exaltation, but there is will in arriving at that state. Christopher Janaway argues that it is not an act of individual will but rather of a general will to life, thereby avoiding the contradiction by describing it as will to life turning against itself: 'The "agent" here is the will to life, which turns against itself. So denial of the will is *not* an act of will of the person in whom it happens.'[32] The effort is required because we have to 'forcibly tear' ourselves (or be torn by will to life) away from the will as negative force; for instance, against the urge to flee a threat at any cost or to seek out ever more pleasure.[33]

Nevertheless the effort leads us to an independent state of exaltation and elevation because it leads to contemplation in 'will-less knowing': 'that state of pure knowing is obtained first of all by a conscious and violent tearing away from the relations of the same object which are recognized as unfavourable, by a free exaltation, accompanied by consciousness, beyond the will and the knowledge related to it'.[34] The sublime object is unfavourable, since it thwarts the will, yet through an effort of attending to it, in knowledge alone, we arrive at an elevated state.

Alex Neill gives a different account of how Schopenhauer overcomes the apparent contradiction of contemplation in a state as dynamic and threatening as the sublime by describing it as a two-stage process: 'involving (first) an active disregarding of the threat posed by the object in question, which makes possible, though it does not itself induce, (second) a passive transition into will-lessness'.[35] My worry about this explanation is that it does not work well for the variety of astute and sensitive phenomenological descriptions of the sublime where Schopenhauer stands out from nearly all other thinkers. As I will show, these descriptions do not fit a structure of stages very well and seem better adapted to an account of parallel processes and matters of degree in an ongoing struggle.

Schopenhauer's study of the sublime is exceptional and original through his insistence on a continued effort towards sublime exaltation, while in the grip of the battle of will with a sublime event and its effect on will. Like Kant, there can be two uses of the term sublime, for the event and for the exaltation, but only the latter is truly sublime. It is attained through a spiritual exercise that's also a spiritual struggle. Kant depends on logical oppositions and analytic distinctions to define the sublime as an independent state: either in it, or not; either beautiful, or sublime. In contrast, Schopenhauer's difficult exercise is much closer to Burke's tension between terror and delight, yet with a deeper appreciation of the many different kinds of effort involved in the many different degrees of the sublime, even in its least intense manifestations.

In *The World as Will and Representation*, vivid descriptions convey this dynamic conflict. A 'violent tearing away' is pursued by 'a constant recollection of the will'. The 'peace of contemplation' is threatened by an anxiety where 'the effort of the individual to save himself supplant[s] every other thought'.[36] The closeness and debt to Hindu Vedanta in this overcoming of the grip and idea of strength of will, through its will-less spiritual overcoming, is acknowledged by Schopenhauer in reference to the 'Upanishads of the Vedas', such that his philosophy comes out of a triangle of very different influences in Plato, Kant and Hindu philosophy.[37] This leads to a theory of degrees of the sublime, due to the different degrees of dynamic struggle involved in the determination to arrive at elevation. It also leads to a philosophy of connected stages, given qualitative differences in the levels of independence from will and in the types of strife on the approach to ideal knowledge.

Mindful of Acharya's defence of diversity against reductive universalism and of Lyotard's insistence on difference in the sublime, it is important not to identify the Indian sublime with Schopenhauer's philosophy. Vijay Mishra draws a distinction between Schopenhauer's reading of the sublime, alongside the Indian sublime, and Hegel's distortion of it through absolute distinctions. The stages to self-extinction in Schopenhauer draw him close to Krishna: 'Self-extinction rather than momentary suspension of the law of reason becomes the cornerstone of the sublime in both Schopenhauer and Krishna.'[38] Whereas, for Mishra, Hegel imposes the absolute on an impossible ideal beyond all representation yet essential for devotional practice and poetry: 'In a clear departure from Hegel, I would want to claim that bhakti or devotional poetry is superimposed upon a sublime narrative where the subject searches for an impossible ideal that is symbolized through a plethora of Gods and Goddesses.'[39] The plethora of narratives and the reference to gods and goddesses are quite different from Schopenhauer's Platonist account of the ideal knowledge.

However, the parallel is still strong in pulling the ideal away from a material world, though it breaks down again with the impossibility of representation in the Indian sublime: 'Although this impossible ideal is represented through the image or the icon, the Absolute Brahman [as opposed to the Brahma] as the ideal ... remains the sublime object that, ultimately, defies all representation in time and space.'[40] In discussing the variety of cognate but still different sublimes, it is also important to note that Hindu thought is not the sole Eastern influence on Schopenhauer. We should also include Buddhism and recognise that both were significant for the development of his thought away from Kant, even if he denies their necessity: 'In short, it is plausible that the influence of Eastern thought accounts for

Schopenhauer's shift from an initial post-Kantian position concerning the thing-in-itself to one more philosophically aligned with what he takes to be the essential tenets of Buddhism and Hinduism.'[41]

The degrees of the sublime in Schopenhauer are also factors in the relation between the beautiful and the sublime. This is never a simple opposition of absolute difference: 'The feeling of the sublime is distinguished from that of the beautiful only by the addition, namely by the exaltation beyond the known hostile relation of the contemplated object to the will in general.'[42] The degrees correspond to the degrees of tension between elevation and the intensity of individual will. They influence the closeness of the sublime to the beautiful according to the strength of the struggle with the threatened will as 'strong, clamorous, urgent and near, or only feeble, remote, and merely suggested'.[43]

Some of the most fascinating passages in Schopenhauer's study describe the degrees of the sublime through a series of sensitive images of sublime experiences. They are crafted with an art and imagination quite unusual for philosophy. They teach us that the sublime can vary and occur with softer and more subtle events than usually thought, in particular in the Kantian tradition. At the lowest end of the scale, Schopenhauer describes the beauty of a city lit by a bright but setting sun. This vista acquires its sublimity when the temperature is low, so we feel beauty, but also a sense of fading life force due to the cold, an intimation of death we must overcome.

In this overcoming, through exaltation in the pure idea of the form, we arrive at the sublime: 'through the faint recollection of the lack of warmth from those rays, in other words, of absence of the principle of life, a certain transcending of the interests of the will is required'.[44] Here, again, Schopenhauer is closer to Burke; they are great stylists and much more receptive to emotional responses, spiritual states and aesthetic conflict than Kant. According to Schopenhauer, this awareness of degrees of the sublime requires a 'vivid' imagination to sense how weak degrees of feeling can still be sublime.[45]

To the objection that the sublime must be intense both in feeling and contrasts, Schopenhauer's study of minimal cases of the sublime responds with a movement from one state to another requiring but a 'slight challenge to abide in pure knowledge and to turn away from willing'.[46] The slightness is enough because the condition for the sublime is the transition towards pure knowledge and the struggle with the will, rather than any particular intensity of feeling or excess over any particular faculty (for instance, of the understanding).

There is a modern parallel to Schopenhauer's sensitivity to degrees of the sublime and the gradient between the sublime and the beautiful in Lars Spuybroek's reimagining of the sublime following Ruskin. In Spuybroek's account, the different gradations of aesthetic construction and experience apply not only to the beautiful and the sublime, but also to a more refined and natural version of the beautiful found in the picturesque. Ruskin seeks to distinguish the sublime from the picturesque while nonetheless seeing their connections and dependencies. The picturesque is parasitical on the sublime: 'This aesthetics is what Ruskin called the "parasitical sublime," and it constitutes his formula for the picturesque.'[47]

Despite these connections, the picturesque lacks the violence of the sublime: 'There is no disgust here, no horror, no rotting, none of the things that have so obsessed us for the last hundred years; no deconstruction.'[48] There are strong affinities between my critical take on the sublime as constructed and Spuybroek's work on Ruskin's sense of an evolution of the sublime. However, in his defence of a new digital sublime in combination with Ruskin's neo-Gothic, Spuybroek is much more positive about the political and aesthetic potential of the sublime than I am. Part of his optimism stems from an aesthetic and ecological, rather than ethical, basis for sympathy among all things. This brings him very close to some traits in Burke around sympathy and the sublime, though the link is not made by Spuybroek. Right at the end of his book, he dreams of a 'pure flourishing'[49] beyond critics, designers, opinions and desires. For me, that's exactly the kind of sublime dream that harbours future disaster. There is no sublime purity, only a construction in history, with varying degrees of negative and positive effects that should be subservient to a politics of equality. The sublime should be a multiplicity, rather than the single glue holding together an ecological aesthetics. Each path through each strand of the sublime should always include self-critique and self-destruction. The sublime is too deceptive, confused and dangerous to be taken as the foundation for a politics or aesthetics with general, let alone universal, claims.

The different degrees of the sublime are emphasised in Schopenhauer's next example, where the sublime occurs in an open and barren landscape: 'Let us transport ourselves to a very lonely region of boundless horizons, under a perfect cloudless sky, trees and plants in the perfectly motionless air, no animals, no human beings, no moving masses of water, the profoundest silence.'[50] In this environment the will is deprived of material; there is nothing to come into conflict with or exploit. We turn to contemplation and inner thoughts instead: 'there is left only the state of pure contemplation'. Those who can bear this, rather than fall into the 'torture and misery of boredom', arrive at 'the state of pure knowing in its peace and all sufficiency'. However, the most important aspect of this argument is that even in this state there is a memory of the misery of boredom and of the existential threat it presents through deathly inactivity: 'a recollection of the dependence and wretchedness of the will in need of constant activity'.[51] The sublime remains an ongoing effort to escape the demands and weaknesses of a will on a path to elevation and contemplation.

This struggle between the needs of the will and elevation into pure knowledge continues through a range of ever stronger cases of the sublime. It ascends through the sublimity of deserts, with the fear of starvation they instil into the will, to the immensity of cliffs and storms and their capacity to break us, to a highest point of a storm at sea and our total dependence on a vessel, where we become 'a vanishing nothing in the face of stupendous forces'. In the next chapter, we'll see a forerunner of this description of the sublime and storms given by Joseph Addison. In each of these situations doom comes to individuals – the etched face staring into a perfect storm. It is felt as a lonely struggle to survive and thrive, experienced by an individual body with its own needs and satisfactions, 'caused by the sight of power beyond all comparison superior to the individual, and threatening him with annihilation'.[52]

This individual willing cannot find salvation in its own efforts or those of others, since they are forced into nothingness by powers far exceeding them. To escape the threat they must therefore abandon the will and elevate themselves through detached knowledge, where they are no longer individuals but rather become united in a pure knowledge of no-will. Again, the detail and degrees of Schopenhauer's study are essential here, because they show how this elevation is itself of one of degrees and experienced in stages, through moves to become 'one with the world, and . . . therefore not oppressed but exalted by its immensity'.[53]

In his consideration of Schopenhauer and the sublime, Dale Jacquette underlines the force of the dynamic sublime on will, but there is a risk that this downplays the degrees of the sublime reaching down to moments as apparently peaceful as the sun setting on a cityscape: 'It is in encounters with the untamed forces of nature that the will to life confronts its limitations, sensing something like the raw energy of the world as Will, while glorying in the superiority of its perception and knowledge over the world as representation.'[54] This is certainly true of untamed forces, but it is also true of minute changes so long as they correspond to elevation and some form of negative effect on will, even if it is as apparently insignificant as boredom or the descending of chill air at sunset.

This sensibility, consolation in knowledge, and release from suffering comes at a high price for conceptions of general, let alone universal, willed moral action. Since the feeling of the sublime is one of 'exaltation beyond our own individuality', understood in the extreme sense of total absence of will at its highest degree and in pure knowledge, the will becomes the faculty to escape from. Schopenhauer therefore arrives at a definition of the sublime exceptionally sensitive to individual differences and degrees, with a universal vocation, yet with no active moral outlet other than knowledge of the nothingness of the world: 'this very real world of ours with all its suns and galaxies, is – nothing'.[55]

Schopenhauer's definition of the sublime is highly unusual for the post-Kantian tradition, but in addition to its influences from the Vedanta and Buddhism it has some similarities with earlier religious definitions of the sublime. There, the experience of the sublime becomes internal and involves a struggle with and then a negation of the will. It then turns upwards and outwards to a higher truth. Éva Madeleine Martin has described this religious sublime in early modern France, and for Pascal in particular, as an elevation towards the divine: 'Pascal, the scientist who writes that thoughts are the consolation and grandeur of man, glorifies here the absence of all thought during an encounter with the sublime.'[56] Martin draws on Teresa of Avila and Agnès Arnauld to emphasise the religious nature of this annihilation through an internal experience of divine inspiration. The parallel with Schopenhauer breaks down at that point, since his elevation is towards knowledge rather than God and since the individual disappears in the sublime rather than remaining in the thrall of divine inspiration.

Unlike the subjective and physical experience of sublime rapture recorded in Pascal's 'Le mémorial' fragment,[57] Schopenhauer's sublime does not depend on subjective interiority, but rather raises the sublime to a form of universal pure knowledge with no individual characteristics: no will, no self, no body, no particular subjectivity. The inwards movement here is radical because it leads to contemplation rather than action. This gives us the following diagram:

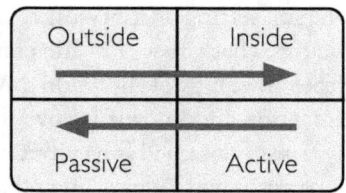

It might be objected that the passivity advocated by Schopenhauer is active in overcoming despair and sadness of the will while it is reduced to nothingness. I have recognised this implication by calling the elevation in his sublime a consolation. It comforts us for the loss of will with a gain in pure knowledge and balances the loss of bodily individuality with universal knowledge. Could this spiritual value be claimed as a kind of positive action? Not if action should have some material benefits. Even if intellectual and spiritual values are involved, I am claiming that there should be some progress in the material conditions necessary for equality: to withdraw from the material world is never enough, even if it is on the basis of some transcendent universal knowledge or faith.

Against my description of the sublime as consolation, Bart Vandenabeele argues for an affirmative role for the sublime, while recognising Schopenhauer's pessimism: 'Even though Schopenhauer's relentless pessimism prevents him from fully recognising this affirmative potential of the sublime and misses the opportunity of adequately developing its relation with the sacred, his analysis hints at it by justly insisting on the metaphysical significance of this type of experience. Life without such experience gets tired of itself.'[58] I accept this definition of affirmation in the sacred, but deny that it stands as truly affirmative, if we have other more pressing tasks for action and affirmation, in particular given my concern for the egalitarian in the sublime and for a material equality rather than one found in an aesthetic sacred state materially denied to many.

The assumptions and conditions I am imposing on egalitarianism in contrast to Schopenhauer's spiritual sublime movement can be shown in the diagram of the effects of his definition for groups.

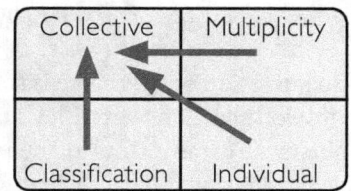

There are two ways of reading this diagram. When interpreted to the letter of Schopenhauer's text, individuality, classifications between humans and the multiple differences between groups and conditions are erased in sublime elevation. In the struggle against will, we all arrive at the same pure knowledge. Sophia Vasalou gives a version of this positive reading of Schopenhauer's sublime as a practice guided by wonder. The strength of her interpretation, beyond its close reading, lies in its accurate rendering of the transformation away from will, caught in suffering, into wonder as transcendence of the misery of individual existence, yet also still attached to the will it must struggle with:

> The wonder and horror tied to the post of individual identity are swept away by the sense of the sublime that directs itself to one's status as a conscious being, one capable of overcoming the domain of suffering through the very act of cognising it. It is a form of wonder whose tinge is darker for containing the terrible as its strain, yet all the more resplendent for transcending it.[59]

My objection to this interpretation is not about its reading of Schopenhauer, but rather about the genuine nature of this transcendence. If it fails to transform the material conditions of suffering, in what way has it transcended them?

When interpreted from a starting point of the many classifications and injustices of all our societies, of the differences between individuals, and of the different multiple aims and transformations drawing us into different and often competing groups, Schopenhauer's sublime can – by definition – do nothing to change them; on the contrary, it serves them, since the will necessary to achieve material change is exactly what must disappear in the sublime movement to exaltation and pure knowledge.

Bela Egyed argues that the contrast between Spinoza's ethics and politics and Schopenhauer's, and Schopenhauer's flawed criticisms of Spinoza, support the view that Schopenhauer cannot contribute to an affirmative and active ethics in the social realm, due to his denial of will:

> What Schopenhauer calls properly ethical follows from his view that the ultimate nature of reality is will. His extreme pessimism about existence – combined with his conception of the double relation the will has with its pure acts (intelligible characters), and with the world of representation – leads him to say that the only truly ethical stance is the denial of the will-to-live.[60]

Aside from the intriguing question of why there is so little on Spinoza and the sublime (until recent work by Genevieve Lloyd to be discussed in the conclusion), Egyed's portrayal of an ethics of denial is devastating for Schopenhauer's sublime. At the very moment where a philosophy shows its greatest sensitivity to life, it turns against it.

Does this mean that Schopenhauer's definition of the sublime is deceptive? This is where his philosophy has the most important lessons for work on the egalitarian sublime, because the answer is that it depends on your perspective. His understanding of the degrees of the sublime and of its many manifestations leads to a large number of different experiences of the sublime and ways of elevating those experiences into higher values. As such it has a great egalitarian potential in avoiding the imposition of a particular standard for the sublime.

However, the sublime nature of those values, the elevating quality of the sublime, depends on accepting his Platonism with respect to pure knowledge and the spiritual direction of his philosophy as 'no-will'. If these highly demanding conditions are not granted, Schopenhauer's philosophy cannot be taken as egalitarian at all because it will depend on belief in and access to a non-existent pure knowledge, and misplaced faith in the possibility of elevation towards a will-less state. Without that faith, the renunciation of desire becomes a false move.

Finally, the value of the scepticism towards willed action on the material world depends on how pressing the situation is in that world and whether we believe in another purely intellectual world. This means Schopenhauer is open to accusations of dependence on a position of privilege (having the luxury of withdrawing into contemplation) or – paradoxically – an act of selfish sacrifice (to withdraw at the expense of others).

Nietzsche summed up these critical points against a decadent world view and morality in a late notebook from Spring 1888: 'the will to nothingness has the upper hand over the will to life – and the overall goal is . . . now, put in Christian, Buddhist, Schopenhauerian terms: better not to be than to be'.[61] If we understand the will to life as the desire to create new values in the world of living sensual bodies, then Nietzsche's ironic answer to the opening question of Hamlet's soliloquy is designed to show the futility and despair at the heart of Schopenhauer's sublime, where *'Desire becomes a state of distress . . .'*[62] In *Dawn*, this critique of Schopenhauer is combined with a dismissal of Plato, on the grounds that both turn away from the world by promising a fictional sublime: 'For the thing they want to show us the way to does not *exist* at all.'[63] In more detail, Matthew Rampley points to the illusory nature of the world as experienced in art and the threat to existence in the sublime, for Schopenhauer, as antecedents that Nietzsche has to work against.[64] Yet it is also important to register the debt Nietzsche's sublime owes to Schopenhauer for the idea of the sublime as untimely.[65] Far from following Nietzsche into new kinds of creative sublime, many contemporary thinkers – most prominently Slavoj Žižek and Julia Kristeva – have been closer to Schopenhauer in taking the sublime into the negative and abject, but without trailing him, at least not directly, into pessimism and denial.

Žižek: a depressing lesson about horror and suffering

Slavoj Žižek has studied the Kantian sublime and its aftermath for most of his career. As a student of Hegel, he is well-placed to chart the shift in German idealism from Kant through Hegel and beyond. As a follower of Lacan, he adds an influential psychoanalytic theory to idealism, thereby submitting philosophies of the sublime to analysis through the unconscious. As a critic of cinema, art and literature, Žižek follows the cultural effects and influences of the sublime, these forming an important part of his work on the aesthetics of the sublime after Kant and Hegel. Finally, his work has a recurring political horizon, where the point of the critical analysis is always political, in its wide definition favoured here as an exercise in social change across all aspects of society and life.

While Žižek's work is explicitly political in its topics and commentary, it is harder to detect an exact position to ascribe to it. Though his concerns can be seen as on the left, in the sense of being critical of established powers of all types from a point of view of social reform (albeit with an obvious, if wary, affection for thinkers on the left), there is a great resistance to adopting a single party or even ideological line. This fits the essentially critical tenor of his analyses, since they are more about a coming to awareness than dictating a clear line and set of political goals for the future. Nonetheless, in relation to the sublime Žižek has a well-determined position: he seeks to sever the relation between the sublime and value across all definitions of the sublime.

In order to break down every ascription of value to the sublime, Žižek's critical readings follow a strict strategy, despite appearances of a more haphazard approach due to his frequent changes in topic and style within arguments and across books. Žižek's study of Kant is a thoroughgoing exercise in negation. First, there is a critique of Kant's sublime involving a negation of the high values assigned to moral law by showing its underside, or the negative consequences of treating moral law as the highest value. This part of the strategy also depends upon a reversal of each step of Kant's argument and their associated values, from the sublime events of nature, to the mathematical sublime and the sublimity of will and reason. Second, the negative or dark side of the sublime is analysed in order to show its pervasiveness and destructive power in relation to the subject. The sublime is a direct and tenacious threat to the subject. Third, each of these steps is given a social and cultural context through interpretations of film, art and literature, thereby supporting the practical reality of the analysis.

From early on in his career, Žižek has offered ground-breaking analyses of notorious events and their cultural representation, such as the sublimity of the sinking of the Titanic, with our fascination for it as the realisation of a horrifying 'impossible' event engulfing the settled order of reassuring values like love, family, culture, class and material possessions: 'The wreck of the Titanic therefore functions as a sublime object: a positive, material object elevated to the status of the impossible Thing.'[66] In these analyses, Žižek expands the classical understanding of sublime terror as connected to absolutes, whether in the eruption of the impossible, in glimpses into absolute otherness, or in a sensation of the real as something horrifying that must always elude yet also unpredictably annihilate what we hold dear.

Fourth, these earlier steps are dotted with remarks about their political consequences, with special attention given to lessons that can be drawn from them. Again early on, in *The Sublime Object of Ideology*, Žižek made the important connection between a critique of the operation of the sublime and an undermining of the symbolic authority transmitted with the sublime object.[67] The value of the object is guaranteed by that authority and they fall together; for example, in Schopenhauer, and in the technological sublime, the value ascribed to lighting effects depends on the sublime symbolic authority of light as life-giving as opposed to the deathliness of darkness, but if the superiority of lighting can be shown to be fake, the authority of light begins to crumble with it. Žižek's perceptive critical reading of the signifying power of religions, and of Christianity in particular, comes from this work on the sublime.[68]

The overall consequence of this fourfold strategy is a shift from sublimity as highest value to sublimity as misery, in the double sense of pain and wretchedness. However, it is crucial not to confuse the aim of severing the sublime from value with an outright denial of any historical relation between value and the sublime. Žižek acknowledges and interprets many past and present routes from the sublime to value, but the point of these critical interpretations is to deny that those connections are well-founded or necessary.

This disconnect with necessity explains some of the difficulty and complexity of Žižek's work, as well as the four steps his analyses go through, since the philosophical question of whether a claim is well-founded calls for consideration of the validity of arguments, of their correspondence to actual things, and of the circular relation between philosophical argument and the constitution of actuality, in the sense that philosophical definitions of the sublime change our perceptions and ideas of the sublime in objects and subjects. The critical examination therefore becomes a special kind of analysis of theory and its connection to reality, combining the study of how things are with the argument that this state is not necessary, and with the aim of making them different.

Since the sublime is a constant figure in Žižek's books, it could make sense to call him a thinker of the sublime. But this would be a mistake. In fact, he is always critical of the sublime, and though definitions of it frequently feature, culminating in a description of the sublime as negative misery, these definitions are themselves rejected, not as real manifestations of sublime effects, but as effects to be sought out and valued politically. Thus, his 2016 book *Disparities* comes to this conclusion: 'We have to abandon the idea that there is something emancipatory in extreme experiences, that they enable us to open our eyes to the ultimate truth of the situation. This, perhaps, is the most depressing lesson of horror and suffering.'[69] There is no redemption in sublime misery whereby its negativity could be turned into a positive value.

In this conclusion, a distinction is drawn between the experience of sublime misery and the highest value of learning to be free through it. The redemptive aspect of the experience is thereby denied. The sublime is rejected as truth-revealing, but only after a study of sublime misery as the culmination of the philosophical and social search for value. The sublime is certainly a truth, but it is not 'the ultimate truth of the situation'. Instead, there is a nihilist tenor to the conclusion, in arriving at a negative state as 'depressing' and in the refusal of any redemptive consequence to the misery encountered in 'horror and suffering'.

There's little doubt that giving up on the sublime can be nihilist, since it involves giving up on the idea of highest values. However, this is not the full story when reading Žižek, because although he arrives at a downbeat conclusion, the point of the analysis is in the unfolding argument and not where it ends. Rex Buttler, in his analysis of negation in Žižek, gives an account of how his philosophy can still be politically active while rejecting the universal of Enlightenment legacy and refusing to posit a fully determined alternative. Buttler's argument turns on distinguishing between the content of a political and philosophical theory and its form. He claims that even though Žižek's work refuses to affirm any specific content it remains progressive in its formal implications: 'In other words, it is because they offer not a specific content but only a certain "form", speak not of something, but of "nothing" for which everything stands in, that they can only (and never properly) be followed.'[70] This position is sustainable over time because, even without content, or in denial of content, the form generates critical positions and undermines the claims of ill-conceived, dishonest or inconsistent political positions that uphold unjust political orders. If there is to be any emancipation, it is in the critical study itself. We should judge Žižek's study of the sublime as a critical working through of the sublime, not as offering a new definition or a simple conclusion.

To understand Žižek's philosophy through negation, among the many discussions of the sublime in his books I will focus on the more extended study from *Tarrying with the Negative*, making references to other works where they make additional points. In this book, his interpretation begins classically with Kant's distinction between the sublime and the beautiful, where the latter is purposive (purposiveness without purpose) and harmonious, and the former is 'chaotic, formless'.[71] Douglas Burnham gives a detailed discussion of the sublime and purposiveness which stresses this 'counter-natural' quality of the sublime: 'In the sublime, the initial experience we have been analysing is one of the counter-natural in the more radical sense of anti-purposive, which nevertheless is not "outside" nature.'[72] Focusing on this anti-purposiveness, in the sense of against the order of nature as having final or efficient causes, Žižek rapidly departs from the standard reading of the sublime, as a go-between between nature and moral law, by shifting to a definition of the sublime in terms of the subject. The sublime then becomes 'the site of the inscription of pure subjectivity'.[73]

This seems a big jump in the argument but is in fact a shortening of Kant's steps to go straight to their implication: from lack of purpose and form to pure subjectivity. The sublimity of free will depends upon independence from external and internal purposes or harmony; if will is subjected to external purposes, or to conditions regarding harmony, it is limited. For example, if we are determined by a natural purpose such as sexual instinct, then our subjectivity will be limited by it; if our existence is governed by natural principles of harmony, as in some readings of Leibniz, then it ought to accord with them. Delight is a perception of harmony for Leibniz but, more importantly, reason is attuned to harmony and the best of all possible worlds is the most harmonious: 'The existence of this world rather than any other possible world is explained in terms of its selection by divine wisdom as the world of greatest harmony.'[74]

Free even of the constrictions of harmony, pure subjectivity should be able to will anything. In the sublime it comes to realise that it can, when confronted by an overpowering lack of form and purpose that it nonetheless rises above – escaping impulses of fear and pleasure, and thinking beyond purposes and harmonisation. Žižek insists on this point in *The Universal Exception*: 'The Kantian sublime is grounded in this gap: it is the very experience of the impotence and nullity of man (as a part of nature) when he is exposed to a powerful display of natural forces that evokes in a negative way his greatness as a noumenal ethical subject.'[75] From annihilation springs a different kind of strength in the realisation of freedom of will as subject of ethical decisions. This confrontation and freedom become the inscription of pure subjectivity, in the sense of its writing or recording as law. This occurs through a realisation of pure freedom as sublime, in the sense of the highest value rising above all other measures, even if we then come to renounce this freedom, rationally and strictly for ourselves.

Yet Žižek does not remain in the Kantian line of argument. He follows his first point about Kant and the sublime subject, moral law and God with arguments from Lacan and Hegel that once again negate Kantian sublimity. Sometimes he puts Lacan first, sometimes Hegel; the order isn't important. Following Lacan, he argues that sublime inscription is not in the freedom to subject ourselves to the moral law. Lacan shows how, if this law is taken to be the imperative to choose maxims to act by that are universalisable, then it entails a violent subjection to law: an imposition rather than a choice. The law is then experienced as evil, in the sense of something we have to suffer as an enforced burden.

Following Hegel, Žižek demonstrates how subjectivity can neither be pure nor have direct access to the sublime. God and the sublime must be experienced through misery rather than grandeur, because the sublime cannot simply appear to subjectivity but must do so through an intercessor. The sublime must be negated to be experienced and the subject must be reduced to nothing in this experience: 'in Hegel we are dealing with a miserable "little piece of the Real" – the Spirit is the inert, dead skull; the subject's Self is this small piece of metal that I am holding in my hand; the State as the rational organization of life is the idiotic body of the Monarch; God who created the world is Jesus, this miserable individual crucified together with two robbers...'[76] The important intervention here is in the necessity of these miseries. They cannot appear in their absolute sublime splendour to limited subjects, so a mediating term must intercede between them; but as severed from the sublime, and required to communicate its absolute nature to the subject, this medium must itself be miserable: cut off from the heights and charged with a message about the terribly reduced state of finite existence.

Drawn from an original interpretation of Hegel, this negative dialectic is a constant thread through Žižek's philosophy. It is a distinctive and powerful take on dialectics because it renounces both major directions of dialectics – up to the Idea and God, or down to the rational subject – and because it opens up a new and rich area for critique of the cultural medium between the heights and the depths. It is worth noting a similarity to Nietzsche's assessment of Plato and Schopenhauer, in this renunciation of two dialectical options and interest in a created middle term. However, where Nietzsche emphasises joyful affirmation in untimely creation, Žižek insists on miserable negation across all dimensions of time.

For an expert in German nineteenth-century philosophy and commentator on art, the sublime and culture, it is remarkable how little Žižek writes about Nietzsche. This is all the more surprising since Žižek is at pains to distinguish his philosophy from contemporaries indebted to Nietzsche, such as Deleuze. The explanation for this absence is perhaps in Žižek's determination to show the closeness of Deleuze to Hegel and thereby to reveal the limitations of Deleuze's superficial repudiation of Hegel (and hence, by association, of Žižek). This comes out strongly in *Organs without Bodies: Deleuze and Consequences* in a discussion of philosophical debts and inheritances in transformative interpretations.[77]

Beyond this text-based explanation, I would speculate that the deeper reason for the gap between Žižek and Deleuze and Nietzsche can be found in the absence of a philosophy of time in the former (with parallels to another Hegelian, McTaggart, and his denial of time), where differences between dimensions of time are replaced, at the highest levels of existence, by a complex understanding of logic and dialectics, in contrast to distinctions between different syntheses and operations of time for the latter. This has implications for the philosophy of the sublime, since Nietzsche's definition of the sublime has an essential relation to a philosophy of time through the complex play of continuity, breaks and cycles of time in the idea of the untimely.

Instead of rising or falling, Žižek's dialectical movement 'tarries' with a necessary and necessarily miserable middle term, caught in a double negation, neither God nor pure subject, but an imperfect body caught between them:

> Herein lies the 'last secret' of dialectical speculation: not in the dialectical mediation-sublimation of all contingent, empirical reality, not in the deduction of all reality from the mediating movement of absolute negativity, but in the fact that this very negativity, to attain its 'being-for-itself', must embody itself again in some miserable, radically contingent corporeal leftover.[78]

Sublimation should lead to elevation, purity, perhaps some kind of spiritual immortality, but there is no redemption, everything remains in misery as failure to sublimate.

The essence of the mediating term as self-constituting, being-for-itself, is in its resistance to sublimation, or transformation into absolute sublimity, and in its resistance to full absorption into the subject, into a fully identified meaning for the subject. The most succinct account of this reversal of the process of sublimation into 'desublimation' is given in *On Belief,* where Žižek analyses it in terms of Christianity and Judaism: 'In this precise sense, Christianity inverses the Jewish sublimation into a radical desublimation: not desublimation in the simple reduction of God to man, but desublimation in the sense of the descendence of the sublime Beyond to the everyday level.'[79] The contingency, and the reason why the intercessor is always 'nothing' for Žižek, is that the two sources necessary for it to have content, rather than function, are themselves closed to it. It cannot take its full identity from sublimity since its role is to drag it down to everyday existence, or from the subject, since its being is to resist its pretensions to absolute freedom. The sublime object must therefore be radically contingent, neither given nor made.

Three candidates for the position of highest value fall in these critical moves on Kant's sublime. With Kant, we lose the sublime object, but should gain the sublimity of will and reason. With Hegel, we lose the absolute sublimity of will and God as they are drawn into sublime misery. With Lacan, we lose the sublimity of law, since it becomes an imposition rather than emancipation. Žižek's contribution is to draw all of these together to enact the fall of all sublime values, including redemption in sublime misery, because they cannot lead to salvation from the negative process they force us through. The sublime is not in the sublime object, but in the subject. It is not in the sublime subject, but in the imposition of law. It is not in the highest laws, but in their most miserable manifestations. Those manifestations cannot be redeemed back to highest values.

In *Tarrying with the Negative*, Žižek reads Lacan as shifting from the Kantian moral law to radical evil through the paradox of the 'free and autonomous subject'.[80] For Kant, the paradox is that though I am free I choose to submit to the moral law. When interpreted with Lacan, the paradox slips from moral law to superego and radical evil: 'yet all this fury of nature pales in comparison with the absolute pressure exerted on me by the superego, which humiliates me and compels me to act against my fundamental interests!'[81] My free acts are the result of a force I am not fully conscious of at the time of acting, since I think I act freely. Yet this force is at work in me. I can become aware of it in symptoms of my subjection, such as my humiliation before the law (though I choose it, I retroactively experience it as an imposition) or my desire to impose it upon others (as a kind of compensation for my own weakness). The subversion of the Kantian argument comes with the characterisation of law as compelling assent by force rather than reason. We experience it in the sublime as the highest and most cruel imposition, rather than submitting to it after reasoned examination.

For Žižek, the selection of universal laws or maxims is not done as a rational conclusion arrived at by a free will. It is done because a terrible power makes us act against our desires and interests. In a sense, here, we all become children again. We are forced to do the right thing, before we can learn to do so of our own free will; except we can never learn. We are always made to do the right thing, even when we convince ourselves of having freely chosen to submit, since, beneath any impression of having acted rationally and freely, there is a deeper unconscious impression of submission and loss.

In another negation of a Kantian motif, this means that the sublime inscription, the transfer from 'sublime' object to the engraving of sublime law on pure will, is a symbol for radical Evil: '[the sublime evokes] the suprasensible, the ethical stance, insofar as it eludes the domain of the Good – in short: radical Evil, Evil as an ethical attitude'.[82] The logic here is that if the sublime is not the Good, as symbolised by the particular purposefulness and harmony of the beautiful, and if the sublime is a terrible imposition that forces me to act against myself for no reason, other than the self-enjoyment belonging to the external force, then the sublime is the symbol of radical Evil: a chaotic and purposeless power taking pleasure in my destruction. Evil is written upon us and not the Good.

A gory and horrifying aesthetic, reminiscent of the monstrous Gothic sublime, accompanies Žižek's negation of Kant. Instead of following the pattern from the overwhelming threat of the dynamic sublime, through the sublimity of will and onwards to the sublimity of universal law (and a rediscovery of God in law and human society on the way to a cosmopolitan ideas), Žižek descends ever lower, forcing us into a spiral we cannot pull out of. In *Disparities*, he reads Kant against the positive Kantian sublime through a reading of his *Anthropology* and of the passages on the monstrous in the *Critique of Judgement*. The point isn't to advocate this descent into horror, but rather to drag the highest values down into it.

Not only are the highest and lowest 'two sides of the same coin' for Žižek, the coin itself is weighted to fall ever more often on the side of horror and negation, as shown in his telling of 'two properly sublime moments' in Jeunet's space-horror science-fiction film *Alien: Resurrection*. In Žižek's interpretation of the film, the reversal takes place through the conjunction of a redemptive sublime image and destruction. The torching of failed clones by a perfect one, in a 'destruction of horror', should lead to redemption by the purification of fire, achieving perfection by shedding lower selves. However, this perfection is doomed to final destruction through absorption into the alien:

> Then, there is the unique scene, perhaps *the* shot of the entire series, in which Ripley's clone 'is drawn down into the embrace of the alien species, luxuriating in her absorption into the writhing mass of its limbs and tails – as if engulfed by the very lability of organic being that she had earlier attempted to consume in fire.' The link between the two scenes in thus clear: we are dealing with two sides of the same coin.[83]

The sublime should be revealed in our attainment of purity, but this high state is drawn down to the very otherness and materiality the ideal ought to have escaped. This upending of the path to improvement is a shocking reversal of the Kantian sublime which starts with overwhelming force but ends with moral law: 'The sublime, also, is understood by Kant as essentially a moral experience.'[84] Instead, we go from overwhelming force to the realisation that there is an even greater power seeking our annihilation for no reason other than enjoyment.

Why should we believe Žižek's analysis? First, there is a rigorous logic to it: if we have to submit to a higher law, and if that higher law is consistent with overwhelming events, and if that law knows us better in our weaknesses than ourselves, and if the only purpose it seeks is enjoyment in our painful obliteration, then the sublime is the symbol of Evil. The first two conditions in this argument are consistent with Kant's position, but only if we grant to Žižek that freedom in Kant and in his version are the same, and if we accept the equivalence drawn between law and overwhelming force. Neither of these are straightforward concessions, because freely choosing to submit is obviously not the same as bending to a higher power, and because the sublimity of the moral law can be seen as different in kind from a power that can annihilate us.

In effect, Žižek's point depends on not accepting the full version of Kant's definitions and claiming that ideas involving greater compulsion and threat are more plausible. I'll return to this claim to believability later, through the aesthetic and empirical sides of Žižek's critical work, but at this stage it can be understood as a sceptical approach to Kantian moral law and subjectivity, depending on relations of force they do not admit to. Where Kant sees the enlightened potential of will and reason, following from an internalisation of the sublime, Žižek detects the work of humiliating compulsion.

However, the second two conditions coming from Lacan are also unconvincing when taken from a Kantian point of view, since Kant's position does not allow for unconscious forces that can overwhelm reason (given certain conditions, such as distance from direct threat and being sane), and since it retains an ideal of a future society consistent with universal moral law (as discussed earlier in the important role played by Kant in Enlightenment cosmopolitanism). In short, reason can convince us on its own to act according to the moral law, and there is an ideal purpose to law in its universality, even if this is not supported by evidence at any given point in history.

For the latter two points, Žižek could depend on Lacan's authority as a psychoanalyst and theorist, but that's not what he does in *Tarrying with the Negative*. Instead, having adopted the Lacanian conceptual approach through the superego and law, he moves to an explanatory approach designed to shift attention to social and cultural reality through interpretations of art and culture. For this particular argument, he turns to Thomas Harris and John Ford, offering explanations for our fascination with their repulsive characters, Hannibal Lecter (from Harris's *The Silence of the Lambs*) and the French governor De Laage (from Ford's film *The Hurricane*).

It could be objected that at least in the earlier *The Sublime Object of Ideology* Žižek depends on Lacan more strongly for a logical argument from psychoanalysis about the sublime object:

> This is also the fundamental feature of the logic of the Lacanian object: the place logically precedes objects which occupy it: what the objects, in their given positivity, are masking is not some other, more substantial order of objects but simply the emptiness, the void they are filling out. We must remember that there is nothing intrinsically sublime in a sublime object – according to Lacan, a sublime object is an ordinary, everyday object which, quite by chance, finds itself occupying the place of what he calls das Ding, the impossible-real object of desire.[85]

My view is that this argument is still dependent on empirical examples from culture and aesthetics to be convincing and to escape the narrow assumptions of Lacan's psychoanalysis; for instance, Žižek's critical study of the Titanic story extends and transforms Lacan's psychoanalysis into wider social critique.

The key explanatory move is to trace the attraction of the cultural works to their revelation of the real power of evil superegos. The parallel to be drawn is between this power and the power of law. We are drawn to the cruelty of Lecter and to his hold over Clarice Sterling because of the way he entices her to give up the core of her being:

> Lecter is truly cannibalistic not in relation to his victims but in relation to Clarice Sterling: their relation is a mocking imitation of the analytic situation, since in exchange for his helping her to capture 'Buffalo Bill,' he wants her to confide in him – what? Precisely what the analysand confides to the analyst, the kernel of her being, her fundamental fantasy (the crying of the lambs).[86]

There are forces powerful enough for us to submit to them, exactly where we have most to give and to lose. According to Žižek's argument, this is how moral law, how any law, works in reality: they play on our weaknesses in order to get us to submit to them.

Nonetheless, it could be argued that Clarice gets something in exchange for submitting to Lecter. In response, Žižek is rigorous and self-critical in his analysis, pointing out that the flaw in Harris's book is that Clarice gets something positive in exchange for handing over her innermost secrets, since this deal allows purposiveness to return into sublime evil. The return to purpose does not confirm the Kantian argument, but rather challenges Žižek's point about evil. We can't have arrived at radical Evil if we submit to it in a purposive calculation (as we do in relation to monetary exchanges, for example).

Žižek therefore moves on to Ford's film, where the force of the hurricane can be seen as a sublime symbol of punishment for evil acts and a lesson in following the moral law. This is because De Laage has relentlessly pursued the convict Terangi throughout the film, yet once the hurricane hits the governor releases him. In a Kantian interpretation, the sublime force of the hurricane turns into the sublime force of an overcoming of unjust laws and a turn to universal ones. Consistently with this view, having been driven by cruelty and error, the governor realises he has lived badly when confronted by the natural sublime, thereby discovering his own higher power to choose a different and just law.

For Žižek, this Kantian reading is fundamentally mistaken. In reality, Terangi's home is destroyed by the hurricane while the governor's is spared, so there is a further reversal missed by the positive interpretation: 'He is able to grant amnesty to Terangi not because he has gained an insight into the nullity of human laws in comparison to the forces of nature as they manifest themselves in a hurricane, but because he realized that the hidden reverse of what he perceived as his moral rectitude is radical Evil whose destructive power overshadows even the ferocity of the hurricane.'[87] Moral rectitude is but a cloak for evil.

It is strange to use the phrase 'in reality' when interpreting a film, but Žižek's argument is an appeal to cynical experience, closer to Machiavelli's *The Prince* than the *Critique of Judgment*. We know that great disasters do not spare the good or bring the bad to do good deeds. On the contrary, tragedy strikes the weak and the poor hardest and releases the most violent and base drives of the rich and powerful – the sublimity of law and legal process is often a cloak for the exercise of wealth. This sceptical view of the sublime leaves no space for positive value and no space for redemption. At each reversal, negative forces grow and any hope for a return to positive values diminishes. Though pessimistic and cynical, note how Žižek's analysis is entirely accurate as an account of disasters following from climate breakdown: they are not occasions for a moral reckoning with the rich and powerful, at the level of nations or individuals, but rather strike hardest at the poor and dispossessed.

However, there are still two weaknesses to his line of argument. First, the appeal to specific cases as banners for reality makes this an empirical argument. For every example and explanation about evil we could choose other films and artworks exhibiting hope and salvation. Second, as we have seen with his positioning of God in relation to the sublime and the parallels between the moral law and Christian morality, Kant's definition of the sublime dovetails with a more general religious and moral account of sublime values and moral action. If our arguments are going to have an empirical element, why shouldn't we turn to this narrative about moral action in relation to the sublime rather than one about evil?

In responding to this accusation of empirical contingency, Žižek deploys a logical analysis of the role of representation in the sublime. In a departure from a strict reading of Kant's sublime, at least in *Tarrying with the Negative*, he turns to Hegel to address the question of the sublime in Christianity. The argument should not be seen as pertaining solely to religion, since there is a more general context of moral orders drawing their power from sublime sources beyond human understanding and powers of representation. This excess over understanding can follow from law, as in forbidding images of God, but it can also follow from natural or aesthetic experiences of the sublime, where the sublime event points to something beyond it that cannot be represented.

The sublime can be defined as the medium of transition between that which cannot be represented and representation itself. For Kant, it is manifest in the struggle of our faculties – imagination and understanding – to take in immense appearances, or powers, or scales, or numbers, thereby pointing to a different kind of sublimity in will and reason (though as we have seen Kant never strays far from Christian morality and a Christian God).

As interpreted by Žižek, Hegel's argument is that the sublime does not indicate something beyond appearance, but rather that it generates this beyond: 'Hegel insists again and again that there is no special "suprasensible realm" beyond or apart from our universe of sensible experience; the reduction to the nauseating "little piece of the real" is thus *stricto sensu* performative, productive of the spiritual dimension.'[88] Here, sublimity changes from a sign of transcendence to a process of immanence – sublimation – where the process is one of generation, in the sense of bringing about higher values. This is central to Žižek's argument against value in the sublime, because in one stroke transcendent value (value out of this world) falls away to be replaced by process within it.

In *The Sublime Object of Ideology*, Žižek makes the same point slightly differently by insisting on the negativity of the noumenal, though this still depends on performativity in an experience: 'Hegel's position is . . . that there is nothing beyond phenomenality, beyond the field of representation. The experience of radical negativity, of the fissure between the two – this experience is already Idea itself as pure, radical negativity . . . the negative experience of the Thing must change into the experience of the Thing-in-itself as radical negativity.'[89] The difference is the idea of production in the later philosophy, as opposed to experience in the earliest book. This matters because there is a greater sense of the sublime as destroyed by a malevolent agency in *Tarrying with the Negative*.

Either way, there is a negation of the higher sublime since, instead of pointing towards otherworldly greatness, it is drawn into and depends on the misery of this world by way of contrast and desublimation: 'the point is not only that God's embodiment in a ragged creature renders visible to us, human mortals, His true nature by way of the contrast, of the ridiculous extreme discord, between Him and the lowest form of human existence'.[90] More importantly, the sublime as higher power is only in this apparent contrast between highest and lowest, rather than any purely positive ideal value. Sublime power is negation: 'the divine power of absolute negativity'.[91]

The process and its performative aspect are significant because the sublime is no longer a sign, or an object, or a subjective property, or something made present at the limits of representation. Instead, sublimity is brought about through an extreme contrast and a process of negation. It is rendered by misery. This adds to Žižek's destruction of the link to value because the highest values become dependent on a misery they cannot be separated from. He calls this a 'downward synthesis' as opposed to a 'triumphant synthesis'.[92] In this negating synthesis, reason as the way to moral sublimity becomes trapped in a miserable and failing spiritual substance.

Why can't this miserable substance be redeemed in the sublime, as Christian (and Hegel's) accounts claim? Why isn't misery a way to superior values? To answer these questions Žižek once again turns to examples from film and literature, while also exploiting the nature of absolute immanence as forbidding any appeal to something external to the unfolding of the world. He selects two works in which cruelty and death are final, allowing no afterlife or redemption: Paul Newman's *The Effect of Gamma Rays on Man-in-the-Moon Marigolds* and Philip Kaufman's film of Milan Kundera's novel *The Unbearable Lightness of Being*.

In studying these films, the aim is also explanatory, but this time in order to convince us that sublimity has to stick within misery with no positive step up to a higher value. In the first film, a humiliated child carries her murdered pet while the soundtrack creates a sublime effect. Sublimity is only a background to murder. In the second, a couple are shown as already dead even in a moment of loving happiness. Love ends in death. The sublime lesson and the transition to higher values are not allowed to happen in this misery. You can have sublime moments, but they will never point the way to lasting higher values, only to more despair.

The political dimension of Žižek's analysis comes out strongly in these studies. It is a form of downbeat realism. A series of sources of value, moral laws and sublime experiences are brought down; first, by reversing Kantian arguments and, second, by removing all transitions to values outside a miserable world. The realism is in constantly showing the evil underside to supposedly elevating experiences and ideas. There can still be joy and humour in this downward spiral, perhaps felt most strongly in Žižek's interpretations of a great range of film and literature, with no care for distinctions between high and low art. Yet these positive moments are not staging posts on the way towards settled and reliable laws and practices. The sublime cannot save us.

The most despairing and shocking version of this relentless negation comes in Žižek's refusal of any form of reconciliation after the Holocaust – not reconciliation between peoples so much as reconciliation with horror and cruelty as things that can be overcome, not repeated. Instead of redemption, he only finds more despair in perverse comedy: 'laughter that is not done from the position of reconciliation, laughing at the vanity of the conflicts that persist, but a laughter through which the subject's total capitulation and disorientation transpires'.[93] The comedy is a palliative for complete abandonment and confusion; it is nihilism as cynical humour.

Žižek's critical approach is a demonstration through repeated negations, putting other definitions of the sublime through a series of reversals and leaving them without valid appeal to value. In our diagram of the sublime this is reflected by cycles rather than simple movements:

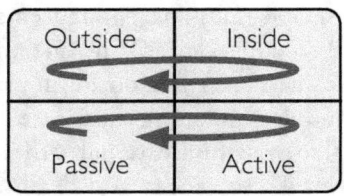

First, the experience of the sublime is drawn into subjectivity, but this positive move for Kant is negated by a further move to the outside, where law becomes an evil imposition. Second, the paradoxical and yet positive Kantian idea of the free selection of governing laws, balancing activity and passivity, is turned into violently thwarted activity, where a deep and inescapable passivity becomes the core of being: outside negated to inside, inside negated to outside, in an endless spiral.

This spiral pattern is a constant in Žižek's work. It is much harder to determine the dynamic effects of his critical philosophy for collectives, multiplicities, classifications and individuals. Though the philosophy works against collectives and classifications, where these are based on sublime values, leaving them with no foundations or aims to base their unity upon, this is not counterbalanced by a move to individuals, if individuals themselves require sublime values for their identity. This is where the destructive and downbeat cynicism of Žižek's method and style come into play at an individual level, since no individual existential value is left untouched and unbroken.

It could perhaps be claimed that the centre of gravity of the cyclical movement of the critical work is multiplicity, in the sense that all values and things are disintegrated into multiple parts through successive negations. This would be consistent with a critical emancipation in misery with no values other than the freedom afforded by critique: we are freed from values and identities. The sense of multiplicity has to be defined cautiously here, since it is neither a multiplicity of many new values, nor a stable multiplicity determinable according to components, directions or features. Žižek gives us multiple comic renditions of the futility of holding on to sublime values:

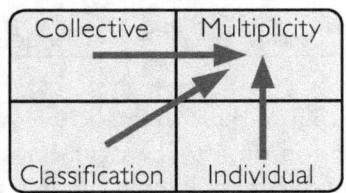

However, this conclusion about the direction of Žižek's analyses of the sublime concedes too much to the structure of his argument and does not pay enough attention to his rhetoric and its effects. The manner in which definitions of the sublime are given is important in assessing their effects. Although a definition can involve specific arguments and concepts, the way these are developed has its own legacies, through style, examples, references, figures, paradigms, vocabulary, themes, connections to major and minor historical movements and ideas, to promises and images, to media, arts, sciences and technologies. This is where Žižek's philosophy is deceptive. On the one hand, it has a deep commitment to a critical attitude and path, drawing spontaneity, repression and manufacture towards critique:

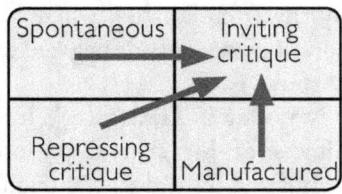

On the other hand, Žižek's rhetoric is restrictive and manipulating, due to its uncritical dependence on the philosophical presuppositions of its references (Lacan and Hegel), its examples (from art and society), its cynical and mocking tones and styles (in form and content), its weary (yet amused) despair, and its disingenuous juxtaposition of claims to social commitment with the destruction of extant values. This means that the frame of Žižek's argument is contradicted by its manner, smothering critique in its allegiances to Hegel and Lacan, restricting multiple and individual values in broad social and aesthetic images and interpretations, and removing all sense from critique in the manufacture of a world-weary cynical nihilism mitigated by fleeting social and critical comical postures:

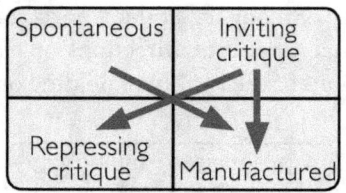

There's no easy way out of these contradictions at the heart of Žižek's work, since the manner is intrinsic to the argument, as shown by the importance of the empirical and aesthetic interpretations for the demonstration of the falsity of historical appeals to value, by the key roles played by Hegelian and Lacanian arguments and ideas, and by the dependence on a large-scale vision for understanding social and political problems. Despite his concern for misery in the sublime, Žižek's philosophy remains a reductive and broad-brush view of society and value.

Any promised emancipation through cynical critique comes laden with generalisations and simplifications. Though Žižek seeks to undermine the sublime as source of value, his philosophy does nothing to open the way to new values and new directions, because its attraction to large-scale and single-track analysis works against finding value in individual and multiple ways. In contrast to Nietzsche's sublime and untimely individuals, Žižek curtails time in a doomed descent, only funny for those who have the luxury to stand outside it and mock it, if only for a moment.

The abject and egalitarian sublime

Breadth and large-scale vision, leading to generalisation, are the source of Žižek's failure to draw out a new sublime. His approach does not overcome ideas of the sublime as universal experience, even as he severs the link between the sublime and value. So while he moves to misery, in the sense of minute and fragile manifestations of the sublime, he only does so as a shadow of historically imposed and general ideas of what sublime values should be. We are therefore left between a deflation of values and the remnants of universal ideas; oscillating miserably between them, or wallowing in cynical humour with few opportunities for renewal and redress.

In *Disparities*, Žižek discusses a thinker who has come closer to a multiple, miserable and yet affirmative sublime, but he curtails her work by blocking it in its negative, historical and political aspects.[94] Julia Kristeva's essay on the abject – as that which we reject as disgusting and horrifying, yet also feel attracted to and cannot rid ourselves of – has strong affinities with the sublime. Close to Burke, she defines the abject in terms of attraction and repulsion: 'Tirelessly, like a boomerang that cannot be tamed, a pole of attraction and repulsion pulls those who are inhabited by it literally out of themselves.'[95] By describing the abject in terms of a spinning pole, alternating between pull and push, and by insisting on the way it expels subjects from their own identities, opening up new potential, Kristeva puts an end to the spectator-based empirical definitions of the sublime. The sublime is a form of perpetual self-alienation and artistic creativity.

Like the dynamic sublime in Kant, the abject is not rejected as an understood or represented object, it is instead sensed as inner disruption: 'When I am taken over by abjection, the twist of affects and of thoughts I thereby name, has strictly speaking no definable *object*.'[96] Yet, closer to the sublime in Nietzsche, and with some more distant and problematic connections to Kant's work on genius, the abject is also where culture and art are generated: 'at the edge of inexistence and hallucination, of a reality that will annihilate me if I acknowledge it. The abject and abjection are my safeguards [*garde-fous*]. They are primers for my culture.'[97] With Kristeva, the sublime is on a creative borderline between social reality and individual survival. Value becomes something created in an ambiguous situation of construction and destruction, emergence and rejection.

Through mortality, violence and conflicts, and our fragility, reality is a threat to the self. It induces the confusion and incapacity of delirium; its powers are signs of annihilation. The abject helps us to turn away from these threats by safeguarding reality through proxy-defences and repulsions. In our denial of the abject, and in being ourselves taken as abject, ordered and stable forms of reality can be defined. Yet both of these rejections are ways into a creative relation to culture, preparing us to sense it and make it differently, because the determination of the abject is itself creative; we define the abject and are ourselves determined in relation to it.

So while Kristeva shares the psychoanalytic frame for reflecting on the abject and on the sublime, she asks different questions to the idealist tradition Žižek follows and curtails in its progressive aims. Instead of asking what the sublime signifies and which values it amplifies, she seeks out its sources and pays close attention to its effects and their creative potential. The difference is between an ideal logical analysis, allied to generalising empirical observations that provide a basis for negative judgements about value, and a genealogical study of a physical and psychic manifestation, in a literary setting, leading to a greater attention to symptoms and causes, and to their potential for creativity in situations of stress and menace.

This sense of collective origins and detailed individual effects gives Kristeva's theory of the sublime five important features for egalitarianism. First, unlike Nietzsche, sublime creativity is not restricted to a special few but is rather part of a collective deep memory, a potential for all. Second, unlike Kant, Schopenhauer and Žižek (in their different ways), Kristeva does not seek a single and pure moral or political outcome for the sublime, whether good or bad. Instead, positive and negative effects of the sublime and the abject remain within it even in its creative effects.

These points then combine into a third. Unlike the tendency to identify chosen groups or the universal, Kristeva's abject sublime is multiple, in the sense of varying in value and location across different individuals without excluding any or reducing all of them to a single type. This last point is the most fragile, however, since some aspects of her method contradict the multiplicity it arrives at. The greatest danger here comes from psychoanalytic language and divisions, since they perpetuate restrictive models for existence; for instance, in Freudian analyses of the incest taboo as implying a triangular relation with the mother and father.[98] Kristeva skirts this danger by taking the abject as prior to any such model, in the sense of coming before and taking priority over it. Instead of placing the origin of the abject and the sublime in Freudian or Lacanian theory, she explains these theories alongside many other literary sources where all contribute to a more nuanced understanding of the processes of abjection.

The fourth point expands on the third by situating the sublime and the abject in historical, biological and geographical processes. Shared across minds, bodies, spaces and times, yet also necessarily individual, the sublime becomes a true multiplicity, rather than a collection of separate units or a uniform group. These processes are revealed by literature as driven by and testifying to the abject and hence to the sublime. On the one hand, there are somatic symptoms, beyond language and disturbing for it, that writing seeks out but can never capture. On the other hand, writing sublimates the abject, naming it and elevating it to a sublime value: 'The abject is bordered by the sublime.'[99] Memory is the reason why the sublime and literature are individual in this pursuit, since they only emerge thanks to a recalled and transformed past.

Finally, the fifth point is about the internal and reflexive – self-critical and self-destructive – instability of the abject sublime. It is not a simple process of construction through positive values, but rather an ongoing process of creation and then dismantling of the identity emerging with that creation. This is because the abject not only drives the creativity but also inhabits it, leading to a constant repulsion of the abject within, in relation to how it also becomes abject for others. This a difficult but crucial point, explaining the acuity of Kristeva's study of the process of writing, as a constant and deep dissatisfaction, a rejection of valued past work and its sublimation into new creativity.

When the sublime object is lost and melts into the self, it disappears into memory: 'The sublime "objet" is dissolved in the transports of bottomless memory.'[100] However, this memory is radically individual, attached to particular bodies and events: 'from station to station, memory to memory, love to love, transferring that object to the luminous point where I become lost to it'.[101] This individual process of loss makes memory infinite: 'Not within words and perception but always with and through them, the sublime is a *something more* that swells within us, exceeding us and making us *here*, and throwing us *there*, as other and brilliant.'[102] This infinity keeps the excess of the sublime over our faculties, but only through a dependence upon language and sensation as actively searching for, rejecting, and rejected by the sublime.

So there is a double process of situation in Kristeva's definition. An identity is made in place and forced elsewhere. These twin processes recast the value of the sublime as intensification ('brilliant') but only on condition of becoming other and different: a creative transformation. The value of the sublime is not in the here and now, or in any set of norms, objects, identities, acts, measures, ideals, goals or behaviours, but rather in taking a burgeoning individual identity into the unknown through a recreation of difficult memories.

In our diagrams of the sublime, Kristeva's abject sublime is neither passive nor active, neither inside nor outside. Instead, they depend on one another in relation to individuating creativity:

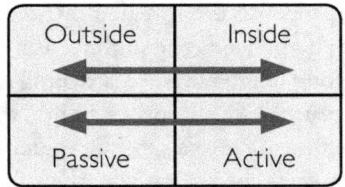

Why individuating rather than individual? Because the process does not make a self or subject, but is rather a transformation that determines a way through infinite memories towards the new and the different; a pattern is individuated but no finished individual emerges.

There are many such paths, and, so long as we accept that the abject and the sublime come before and cannot be subjected to psychoanalytic categories, the model Kristeva offers us is radically multiple, requiring many studies, like her work on literature, rather than one programmatic or paradigmatic one:

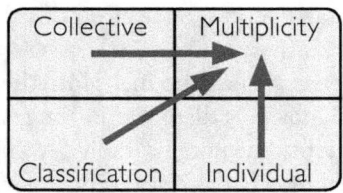

However, this does not mean that the outcome is some form of atomisation into individual subjects. To avoid this, Kristeva appeals to two types of infinity and excess. First, each individuation depends on an infinite and shared past; not shared as the same, but rather connected to a common reserve taken differently each time. Second, towards otherness, each individuation works with a shared language and common perceptions to create an infinite variety of potential directions.

Kristeva ends her section on the abject as stand-in (or lining, *doublure*) for the sublime with the following description: 'Swerve [écart], impossible closure, missed Whole, joy: fascination.'[103] It's a very different definition to those coming before it, but it rethinks the sublime as a jolt and departure, a difficult and endless opening, involving thwarted desires of identity and finality, accompanied nonetheless by joy and an enthralling experience of new departures.[104] Is it critical, though? Or does the abject sublime, with its reliance on individuating processes and multiplicity, represent the high point of an uncritical multiplication of inconsistent values? Does it point away from critique, thereby inviting the violence and disasters of fake, subjective and irresponsible values?

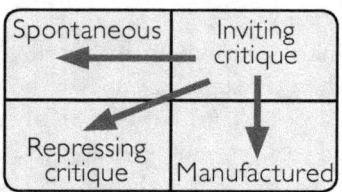

This accusation of a fall into multiple and equivalent values misses the point of why Kristeva renders the sublime as abject. First, the move from the sublime to the abject – from pure heights to misery and repulsion – comes out of critical reflection on rejection, repression and otherness. Second, the divided and equivocal nature of the abject sublime as positive and negative, and as source of values and rejection of them, means that this critical moment is carried through to the abject sublime. It can never be taken as pure higher value and is instead always on the verge of infamy and self-destruction and doubt.

Kristeva's feminism runs parallel to these novel critical ways of addressing the sublime. Historically, definitions of the sublime have either excluded women or forced them into a male ideal and image. The abject sublime can be read in this way too, as Kristeva shows in her reading of the influential and controversial French novelist Louis-Ferdinand Céline,[105] through his idealisation of woman as a loved yet chaste muse, and rejection of her as a suffering and 'masochist' mother.[106] For Céline, woman inspires male creativity but only if she stays away from it. Yet she also holds it back, as a reminder of the suffering and baseness of life. This duality is where Kristeva reverses the tradition, showing how Céline's writing depends on the feminine as abject.

Creativity does not come from ideal purity and high sublimity, but from failure under the challenge of the abject portrayed by the male writer as homicidal and obsessive: 'Nevertheless, the pathetic power of the feminine, as drive or murder, is only in fact unleashed at the cost of male degradation and collapse – collapse of the father and of virile authority.'[107] Though the feminine is driven away from sublime inspiration, it returns as a threat and power impossible to shake off. The abject haunts the male sublime and brings it down.

Yet this collapse is the true source of literary creativity and value. By being possessed and driven by a horror it cannot escape, literature achieves true inspiration: 'Is this the feminine that writing shies away from? Or, if you will, is it by this feminine, defined as the other of the subliming air, that writing is, in a more ambiguous way, inspired.'[108] This ambiguity goes beyond the opposition of male and female, of high and low, of pure and tainted. Instead, each instance of sublime creativity in literature has its abject source, a mixture of minds, places, bodies, cultures and languages driven by something it cannot objectify and simply reject. The abject sublime is a miserable and mixed origin of the highest values.

By rejecting the binary divisions or universal claims for the sublime, Kristeva demonstrates how the superior values of the sublime, for instance in literary creativity, intellectual sensitivity, or bodily receptivity and power, should not be restricted to a type and even less to a sex or gender. Sublime creativity and sublime experience are there for all, and always as mixes of positive and negative effects, with an internal and truly valuable propensity for self-critical transformation.

Chapter 6

Defining the Egalitarian Sublime

The sublime and egalitarian politics

In working through the history of the sublime, the guiding questions for the egalitarian sublime are not the longstanding questions of political theory about the possibility and desirability of equal justice, wealth, health and opportunity. They are more limited but also more disruptive for ideas of equality following from sublimity. Can there be a definition of the sublime with egalitarian effects? How has the sublime been defined such that its effects are unequal?

This shift from wider questions about egalitarian principles, political systems and acts to questions about the effects of the sublime has far-reaching consequences for the reach of this study. First, it implies that, as far as this essay is concerned, the sublime is subservient to and should not be assumed to determine political equality as it applies to systems. Irrespective of whether the sublime is equal for all or not, there is a further task of ensuring that societies are egalitarian. This political equality will set down the conditions necessary for acting upon ideas of an egalitarian sublime and acting against those that are not egalitarian, but this will be secondary to ensuring equality and freedom independent of any consideration of the sublime.

Second, the shift draws attention to the relation of the sublime to an egalitarianism. Are the values transmitted with the sublime significant for an egalitarian politics? Are those values consistent with them? According to Article 1 of the Declaration of the Rights of Man from 1789, 'Men are born and remain free and equal in rights. Social distinctions may be founded only upon the general good.'[1] If the sublime is taken as secondary to freedom and equality, and if we take the Declaration as the keystone for those ideas, then they should apply to the pursuit of the sublime, within the constraints of the general good. An egalitarian sublime falling short of or contradicting the Declaration ought not to be adopted as the basis for an egalitarian society.

Furthermore, sublime experiences and the values flowing from them can fail as egalitarian even on their own terms, thereby running counter to freedom and to equality. As an event or series of objects taking us over, the sublime implies lack of freedom and inequality – at the basic level of striking some but not all of us as passive recipients, impacted in different ways. Some philosophers, but far from all, subsequently attempt to return to the general good and to activity, by adding moral and rational conditions and consequences to the sublime. Others turn against the sublime as negative or unpromising when taken as the basis for political values, organisation and action.

Historically, the values of the sublime are divided and highly variable, as shown by the great number of definitions that clash with each other in terms of what they call sublime, why they call it sublime, how they think the sublime works, and how we should react to it, create it, or even supress it. To make judgements between them, and assess them in egalitarian terms, it has been necessary to develop a system of criteria for judging their effects on groups and individuals and for analysing how the sublime is constructed and applied.

At a more fundamental level than the Declaration of Rights, but still in line with the traditional debate about political and legal equality and freedom, the sublime challenges ideas of a single and consistent human nature, as expressed in the statement 'born and remain free and equal'. If the sublime distinguishes between us, or is reserved for some but not all, then human nature is divided in and through it, leading to sublime leaders and lesser followers, or a sublime race and a lowly one, or a sublime future for only a small portion of humanity.

Even when it is put in the service of a 'general good', as in the technological and Kantian sublimes, the general good produced by the sublime is fragile and can be shown to be self-contradictory or divisive. For example, if a technological or natural sublime depends on ideas of a destiny according to the beliefs and types of some humans and not others, as has often been the case, then we are not dealing with a general good, but rather with the frequently violent imposition of a tendentious good – a Western, or Northern, or Kingly, or Male, or Christian sublime, for instance.

Even the egalitarian sublime (as multiple, open, sceptical and self-destructive), argued for at the end of the last chapter, is ill-suited to building and justifying large-scale egalitarian political systems, where equality before the law, within economic systems and in terms of educational and other types of opportunity is the aim. The egalitarian sublime depends on these systemic forms of equality, in the sense that they ensure the conditions are right for encouraging an egalitarian sublime, but its form means it is not a direct basis for those other kinds of equality. So though there is an indirect argument for political equality as a condition for the sublime, as there is from freedom to equality under law, this argument involves compromises and a secondary position for the egalitarian sublime.

For example, it might well be the case that in order to encourage a multiplicity of sublime experiences there has to be a uniform and standard legal and political system, where all are treated as equals. Similarly, a minimum floor for living standards might limit certain kinds of sublime experience and creativity but nonetheless be a necessary condition for supporting multiple and different sublimes for all. If there are to be egalitarian societies, one of their achievements will be to encourage and protect a multiplicity of sublime experiences and creations, but this will always involve give-and-take between political and economic systems and different ways into sublimity and individual and group values.

I have phrased these points tentatively and conditionally because it is also beyond the scope of this study to decide upon political economy. However, in broad terms, there are some general principles to be garnered from the search for an egalitarian sublime. These principles are from the point of view of the sublime and should not be seen a supplanting other arguments for egalitarian politics and economics; they are a starting point for negotiating the to-and-fro between the sublime and the systems it depends upon and more loosely influences.

First, if the tendencies of the sublime towards inequality are to be resisted, the legal system must be equal for all, in the strong sense of also righting earlier iniquities, applying fair laws equally and according to equal principles, and submitting laws and norms to review, constantly responding to new forms of iniquity. Second, since the sublime will be greatly limited for lives under duress and stress, economic and political systems setting minimal standards for health, housing, food, land and energy are necessary to spread the potential for the sublime widely. Third, since the sublime depends on estrangement, displacement, differences in the intensity of experiences, and encounters with novel experiences and ideas, the system should, at the very least, make these possible for all and, ideally, try to find ways of encouraging them, within education and culture made equally available for all.

Fourth, given the range and variety of sublimes, they will give rise to conflicts with no overarching value system. As such, forms of democracy maximising representation, openness and differences are best-suited to providing a frame for this multiplicity of sublime experiences, creations and values. Fifth, against this commitment to democracy – defined very loosely as a system giving voice to as many claims in society as possible and resolving their differences through some form of collective decision making (and not necessarily one depending on simple majorities or on direct democracy) – the multiple sublime adds a chaos condition, whereby any stable democratic system ought to invite destructive and confounding movements and events into it. This condition is there to ensure that opportunities for new values and experiences are given, and that the system monitors the potential and benefits of that openness as well as its own tendencies to ossify and to reject challenges.

This gives us a picture of the egalitarian sublime within a wider system, also egalitarian, with tensions between the anarchic nature of the sublime taken as multiplicity, without scale, proper object and final definition, and an ordered democratic system. The order supports but also limits and represses the sublime.

For instance, to take an extreme case, extreme experiences in sexuality, at the borderlines of survival, or in artistic creativity, can combine the intensity, attraction and repulsion, and creative moments characteristic of the sublime, but an egalitarian democratic state might well discourage them for wider reasons of equality and justice, if they bring harm to others or if their wider implications involve unequal values.

Similarly, certain landscapes and experiences might be taken to be the most elevating forms of the sublime, but if maintaining them comes at the cost of unequal consequences elsewhere, such as need for land, then sublimity should give way to political equality. Strictly taken, from the point of the view of the sublime, this will be a repressive moment, but one nonetheless justified by a wider egalitarian context.

The multiple sublime will therefore be caught in the tensions and debates around what Étienne Balibar has named equaliberty (*égaliberté*). Equality and liberty are co-dependent but also give rise to contradictions that need to be overcome by an egalitarian politics. For Balibar, this unity and tension between equality and liberty is always historical: 'The history of equaliberty, the struggles against the separation of equality, is the history of the way the various tensions of this relation is worked out and displaced through multiple identities and institutions.'[2] The political goals of equality and liberty lead to, and must be thought within, accompanying antinomies of citizenship:

> It would be essentially constructed as a double unity of opposites: a unity (even an identity of *goal*) of *man* and *citizen*, which would from then on appear as correlative despite all the practical restrictions on the distribution of rights and power; and a unity (even an identity of *reference*) of the concepts of *freedom* and *equality*, perceived as two faces of a single 'constituent of power,' despite the constant tendency of bourgeois political ideologies (what we would generically call 'liberalism') to give the former an epistemological and even ontological priority by making it the natural right par excellence (to which the inverse socialist tendency to privilege equality responds).[3]

However, when freedom is replaced by sublime value or openness to a multiplicity of sublime values, the problems arising from the historical lack of any such unity grow more severe, given the many different values held by humanity at odds with equal citizenship, and given the contradictions and conflicts implied by this divergence of value and equality.

Firstly, human and citizen are not terms consistent with the sublime; they can arise out of it, but they do so as unequal. Secondly, the power of the sublime, though political, is not consistent with the idea of freedom and equality as constituents of a politically equal and free society. On the contrary, with its close association with propaganda in its construction through manipulation and deception – even if well intended – the sublime has served and will serve powers seeking unequal societies; for instance, types of totalitarian rule, but also the liberal and socialist tendencies described by Balibar when they seek an aesthetic and emotional foundation for their values.

Does this mean we should eliminate the sublime from all politics and, to go further, from all aesthetics in so far as they are political? Stephen Zepke considers this question through the work of Jacques Rancière, positioning him as a stern opponent of the sublime on the grounds of politics and aesthetics: 'The work of Jacques Rancière is concerned with the sublime, but in a negative sense. He hates it.'[4] Zepke stages this rejection of the sublime through Rancière's criticisms of Lyotard and Deleuze. The simple version of the argument is that Rancière opposes the barriers presented by the sublime to reason, to communal understanding, and to means to arrive at more equal societies.

In more complex terms, the concern is that the sublime leads to a split between the ethical and the political on the grounds of aesthetics. The ethical is then taken over by the limits and shocks to the human typical of the sublime. When brought together these points disengage art from the political and conclude with a turn away from politics as communal and equal: 'when the difference between aesthetics and politics disappears in the ethical necessity of "justice" of the sublime disruption of the human, aesthetics can get no further than a continual re-enactment of the art-work's de-figuration of the human and the "interminable postponement or deferral of the promised fraternity"'.[5] The halting effect on those who experience the sublime hinders political action and understanding.

Rancière's 'dissensus', or the bringing to light of a deep lack of sense and understanding in the political sphere, requires news ways of communicating and resolving disagreement within a changing democratic system: 'Dissensus is not a confrontation between interests or opinions. It is the demonstration (*manifestation*) of a gap in the sensible world. Political demonstration makes visible that which had no reason to be seen; it places one world in another.'[6]

The important difference here is in this last expression 'places one world in another'. For Rancière, this manifestation is what aesthetics and political action should do. However, in his interpretation of the sublime in Lyotard and Deleuze, they are seen as placing one world against another. If that's right then a democratic society where it is possible to manifest dissensus is on the way to equality in a manner impossible for the sublime.

The problem is that this reading of the sublime is exceptionally narrow, reflecting little of the history of the sublime other than a limited interpretation of Kant. It focuses on one aspect of sublime effects, separating it from wider contexts, whether in Lyotard or any other thinker of the sublime. As we have seen throughout this essay, the sublime is never simply a break or barrier; firstly, because it is internally complex, combining pleasure and pain, attraction and repulsion; secondly, because it is situated within extended systems of values and concepts such that it is always accompanied by wider processes following on from it and including it.

It is absurd to claim, as Rancière does, that Lyotard's use of the sublime is 'a way of blocking the originary path from aesthetics to politics, of imposing at the same crossroad a one-way detour leading from aesthetics to ethics'.[7] This is a heavy-handed misreading because Rancière is simply ignoring the fact that Lyotard (and Deleuze) spend large parts of their wider philosophies describing and tracking all the different ways in which art and aesthetics have been political and will continue to be, including through the sublime.

Furthermore, they both give accounts of how art shifts in its political position over cycles where the sublime avant-garde can recede into political authority and institutions. In missing this, Rancière is deflecting their arguments as they could apply to the plausibility and ethical value of his own ideas of dissensus and consensus. He detracts from the critical potential of these arguments by setting up a false dichotomy: either aesthetics and ethics as detached, divisive and sublime; or aesthetics and politics as a demonstration and ongoing attempt at community and equality.

This dichotomy has never been the difficulty for the sublime, including when it is defined by Lyotard or Deleuze. The problem is rather about the effects of the sublime in a continuous and entangled world of politics, ethics and aesthetics. So though it might be right to reject the sublime due to its effects on this world, the reasons Rancière gives for doing so are themselves distortions of the sublime, with their own negative results in missing what it can teach us about the dangerous effects of aesthetic and other founding ideas, including dissensus and consensus, when they are taken as the basis for values.

Unequal by definition

Aside from the primacy of political equality over an egalitarian sublime, questions about equality and the sublime are odd because they enquire about the egalitarian nature of definitions, rather than a state, a legal system, an economy, a political theory, or social practices. Definitions aren't concrete systems or realised acts. They aren't even goals or ideals. Why would they be considered to be egalitarian, or not? The reason is in the effects. Definitions of the sublime are statements about our highest values. These statements do not directly change material or ideal situations, but they set the scene for how we think about values and pursue them. This combination of definition and value is at the heart of the problem of equality in the sublime, because definitions lead to identities and distinctions. Values are then assigned around them; we feel, think and act according to those values.

For example, if humans and animals are defined as different, if those categories are given different values, and if the values can be associated with specific features to be acted upon, then conditions are in place for inequality and unequal treatment. The interaction between humans and animals has been blighted and characterised by violence, partly due to definitions of animals as unfeeling or incapable of the kinds of suffering dependent on memory and anticipation that humans undergo. We now know these definitions were wrong, but we still live with their deep consequences and effects, not only for animals but also for humans.

Lack of understanding of pain in animals, allied to the separation of humans and animals, contributed to the development of experiments and tests on animals that are now recognised as causing significant pain and suffering, including affects such as anxiety and foreboding, once thought to apply only to humans. Taking account of more recent research, new guidelines are being brought in to alleviate pain in laboratory animals: 'Current scientific evidence strongly suggests that mammals, including rodents (the most commonly used laboratory animals), are able to experience pain. Researchers, veterinarians, animal care personnel, and IACUC members should heed the 4th Government Principle and use professional judgment and best practices to avoid or minimize unnecessary pain.'[8] The parallel with the sublime is that if distinctions stemming from a contingent, or false, account of a sensation or experience are reinforced by categories of value, as they are in the sublime, then a misleading set of definitions can become widely applied principles for an unequal treatment.

Though partly misrepresented, a famous instance of this entailment is ascribed to Descartes and, more so, to his intellectual legacy. He draws a distinction between humans and animals around the idea that animals cannot think. This does not imply that they cannot feel like humans can, but rather that some kinds of feeling associated with reflection (such as anxiety and dread) cannot be experienced by them. Janice Thomas sums up the more subtle version in this way:

> Descartes never denies organism consciousness, perceptual consciousness, access consciousness or phenomenal consciousness to non-human animals. The consciousness Descartes does deny to them is merely (not that this is a small thing) the capacity for self-conscious reflective receipt or awareness of one's inner states which he believes belongs uniquely to those fortunate (and immortal) animals endowed with rational souls.[9]

One of the reasons this denial by definition is no small thing is in the treatment of animals by humans. When added to the claim that reflection increases pain for humans, it leads to the conclusion that, in some situations, animals feel less or no pain when compared to humans, so there can be some cases where positive benefits for human welfare outweigh concerns for the welfare of animals.

Though it has not yet been a central concern in this essay, the question of whether animals experience the sublime is an important one for ensuring that the egalitarian is understood in the widest possible sense. Many of the definitions of the sublime considered here implicitly bar animals from the sublime by relying on traits and faculties usually reserved for humans, such as higher forms of creativity and moral reflection. At its worst, and granting a tentative exception to Nietzsche, this tendency sees humans in their animal form as being furthest from the sublime; for instance, when in the grips of external causation, or when acting on instinct, or when under the impulse of will defined as drive or desire. The same is true for sublime objects and landscapes, where those emptied of animals or least suited to them are seen as most sublime. The traditional sublimities of high mountains, empty deserts and stormy seas are not only represented as inhospitable for humans but also as devoid of animals.

Lars Spuybroek counters this erasure of animals from the sublime by making a feature of human entwinement with nature, and everything in it. This resists the tendency of the sublime to privilege emptiness and lone humanity, replacing it with a nature of processes and interdependent feelings: 'Feelings create entangled webs, and webs can only emerge through felt relations.'[10] This entanglement is a long way away from the environmental sublime proposed by Emily Brady, since Spuybroek's sublime defends an aesthetic combination of technology and nature: 'A "politics of nature" will never suffice: if we want to find a way to live (and to survive) we need a wholesale construction of nature, not merely on technical and physiological grounds but on aesthetic grounds.'[11] A lot turns here on the 'we'. There is still a human-centred monism in this position if this one world of many things privileges human emotions and constructs, even if they are then entangled with nature, as Ruskin's Gothic stones are. That's why I would claim that a full egalitarian sublime can only be multiple, resisting the idea of a single sublime in favour of many sublimes and many values, not necessarily entangled, and perhaps more often at odds with one another.

Though Nietzsche's sublime aims at a future for humanity through creative individuals, the way to the sublime in *Thus Spoke Zarathustra* is always accompanied by animals: 'And Zarathustra said again: "I love you, my animals!" But the eagle and the serpent pressed around him when he said these words, and looked up at him. All three stood silently together in this attitude, and sniffed and breathed in the good air together. For the air here outside was better than with the Higher men.'[12] This does not mean animals are sublime, but rather that man, the sickly animal, needs the company of other animals – fire hounds, spiders, lion, serpent – to teach him the sublime way.[13]

One of the main fields for the critique of effects of the sublime set out in my analysis is revealed in this banishment of animals. The sublime has shown itself to be the construction of an illusory spontaneity – a kind of naturalness and immediacy – while the sublime event is manufactured. The immediacy is fake and repressive of critique, including of any critical unmasking of its production. We like to imagine ourselves alone, or in small groups, in the face of a sublime naturally and directly addressed to us and to us alone – the sublime trail of mountaineers, of fragile ships, of explorers of jungles and wastelands, of cinemagoers transfixed by special effects, game players moving through sublime digital recreations of the Far West, and dreamers contemplating new images of the cosmos. This imagination is complicit with the systems and interests manufacturing the sublime.

Joseph Addison gives an early version of the natural sublime, with its emphasis on immensity and suspended danger for an isolated human. It has the traditional sublime hallmarks of nigh impossibility of representation, identification of the highest values, tension between terror and delight as conduits for reflection on the infinite, and a transfer from an overloaded imagination to understanding and reason:

> I cannot see the heavings of this prodigious bulk of waters, even in a calm, without a very pleasing astonishment; but when it is worked up in a tempest, so that the horizon on every side is nothing but foaming billows and floating mountains; it is impossible to describe the agreeable horror that rises from such a prospect. A troubled ocean to a man who sails upon it, is, I think, the biggest object that he can see in motion, and, consequently, gives his

imagination one of the highest kinds of pleasure that can arise from greatness... The imagination prompts the understanding; and, by the greatness of the sensible object, produces in it the idea of a Being who is neither circumscribed by time nor space.[14]

Beyond these familiar characteristics, the dynamics of this construction of the sublime are telling. Addison encircles the human, making it the centre and focus of a natural process rather than a mere part, or participatory process. He divides motion between external physical upheaval and internal stress, thereby providing a basis for the distinction between human centre and natural environment.

Finally, for Addison, there is a transfer and sublimation of value, in the sense of a transformation to a higher kind of value, from natural chaos to human ideas and then upwards to God: 'Were we only to consider the sublime in this piece of poetry, what can be nobler than the idea it gives of the Supreme Being thus raising a tumult among the elements, and recovering them out of their confusion, thus troubling and becalming nature.'[15] The highest value will be humanity touched by infinity, as salvation from nature in the ordering of the disarray it brings upon the senses.

Addison's remarks were published in the earliest incarnation of *The Spectator* with a style imitating observations and reports on coffee-house conversations.[16] This sublime is for onlookers and listeners, with the time and luxury to watch and experience rather than do. It is a sublime of the leisured traveller, painter or writer, observing from a distance. According to an apocryphal story, Turner was lashed to a mast while preparing his sublime painted whirls of disaster at sea. This is a story of heroic artistic commitment to experience but, against appearances and Turner's early lack of wealth, it is a privileged kind of experience and immersion. Rather than struggling at the pumps or trying to free a rope in the rigging, the artist absorbs the storm and this absorption is an abstraction from many other activities it depends upon. As such, this spectating sublime will always be a matter of class, where leisure, money and preparation for special kinds of moral and theoretical reflection count for more than location, endeavour, practical involvement, and the sheer struggle for survival. Furthermore, it is a preselection of the sublime, concentrating value on special kinds of experience, rather than allowing for sublime values to be present in many different experiences and practices.

The paradigmatic version of the sublime division into classes is given by Kant, commenting on the difference between the scientist and explorer, Horace-Bénédict de Saussure, and a Savoyard peasant: 'Thus (as Mr de Saussure relates) the good and otherwise sensible Savoyard peasant did not hesitate to call anyone a fool who fancies glaciered mountains.'[17] The peasant fails to be sensible by lacking comprehension of Saussure's lofty intentions and, more importantly, of the gain in understanding and moral development afforded by the sublime: 'In fact, however, [Saussure's] intention was to instruct mankind, and that excellent man got, in addition, the soul stirring sensation and gave it into the bargain to the readers of his travels.'[18] Kant's lack of empathy, imagination and analysis is jarring here. Those who warn of us of the folly of an act, on the basis of greater familiarity with an environment or task, do so because they have experience of dangers and threats. They have come close to disaster and their practical wisdom is hard won.

For an egalitarian sublime, those who are not seeking the sublime as adventurers should neither be closed off from experiencing the sublime in their most familiar surroundings, nor be classed as lacking in understanding of them. A 'peasant' will have experienced the life-giving trickle of water at the edge of receding ice, the imperceptible shift from winter to spring in organic scents carried by shifts in the wind, the terror of cracking sounds from overstressed woodwork or ice sheets in an Alpine storm, and the risks of births and futility of deaths in remote mountains. The critical difference is a matter of ease, belief and purpose, not learning and imagination. Guides, pilots, Sherpas, porters, drivers – and all those left working or not, far away from sublime vistas – can and do experience the sublime, even if they lack the funds, reasons, or opportunity to experience those of more fortunate classes.

We have a modern parallel to Kant's distinction between the peasant and de Saussure in the Alps, in space and space travel. The combination of scale, danger, science and moral inspiration in the possibility of exploring space is a new version of the sublime of extremes and infinity; it is reflected in the success of a number of films about space and human survival brought out in recent years.[19] Novels and films come with the new moral question of a future for humanity away from a dying earth. If the fortunate and no doubt wealthy few escaping to new planets are to be our new chosen ones for this new sublime, as others die out, then the lack of equality in this type of grandiose sublimity will have reached its summit.

Kant's error is to set a rare kind of aesthetic, moral, philosophical and scientific culture as a condition for the sublime: 'It is a fact that what is called sublime by us, having been prepared through culture, comes across as merely repellent to a person who is uncultured and lacking in the development of moral ideas.'[20] The problem isn't just that these conditions are ideological, in the sense of imposing a particular political ideology through aesthetic categories, but also that the definition of the sublime is falsely restrictive on its own grounds. It shows a further lack of imagination and awareness of the different forms and scales of sublime experience brought about by a narrow definition, focused on significant grandeur and dutiful self-command, and their moral and religious motivations.

For Terry Eagleton, the ideological imposition consequent to these restrictions is an advocacy for a covert puritanism around moral disinterestedness. The sublime turns out to have remained interested in some experiences, but for concealed reasons. Eagleton makes his point about ideological puritanism in a critique of Stanley Fish, developed through references to Kant and Aristotle: 'It is worth adding that Fish's assumption that in order to criticize my beliefs and desires I must stand entirely to one side of them is a hangover from Kantian puritanism. For Kant, moral self-reflection or practical reason must be wholly independent of interest and inclination; for Aristotle, by contrast, a certain critical reflection of one's desire is actually a potential within it.'[21] This ideological skew is damaging for a Kantian egalitarian project, since its claim to universality founders on the restricted nature of its ideological foundation, but more harm is done earlier, as soon as the highest values are set down narrowly; only for some, not all.

Kantian progressives might object that the social and cultural distinctions are not immutable. Given the right cultural preparation all humans should be able to experience the sublime. In addition to the dangerous assumption that everyone should want to ascribe to this culture and abandon their own, or even be able to do so, this is also to miss the necessity of distance and ease for Kant's definition.

So long as there is some kind of toil or attention or reason, drawn to something other than the effect of a rare and special kind of aesthetic experience on the right kind of moral being, there will be no Kantian sublime moment or lesson. If there is to be a Kantian sublime education, it will still be divisive, not only in type of sublime experience, but also in who will have the opportunity to experience it, who will do the teaching, what they will teach, where the teaching comes from, and how it is imposed and instilled.

Together with these separations between humans, the sublime continues to divide nature and animals. As we have seen with Schopenhauer, the sublime not only applies to wild and mountainous scenes but also to places deemed uninhabited, wasted, infertile and desolate, so they might imbue us with terror at the possibility of annihilation. The image of an empty nature when at its most sublime is an example of these effects at their strongest. But this void is false and manufactured: mountains, seas and deserts are full of animal and plant life, much more so than human life:

> Deserts have a reputation for supporting very little animal life, but in reality they often have high biodiversity, represented by mammals (Camel, Jackrabbit, Pronghorn), birds (Roadrunner, Lappet-Faced Vulture, Ostrich), reptiles (Sidewinder, Horned Lizard), amphibians (Sonoran Desert Toad), arthropods (Bark Scorpion, Black Widow). The Australian desert fauna is

marked by a very high diversity of reptiles in comparison with other regions, and fewer mammals, a situation shared in some degree with the South American deserts.[22]

This fauna and flora has at times been managed, at other times removed, or imported, or hunted to extinction, destroyed by the results of human interventions on landscapes and climate – whether planned or (at first) unwitting. If the sublime is to exclude animals (and most plants), both as objects of the sublime and as capable of sublime experiences, then it will contribute to our uncritical and devastating relation to animals and nature.

When reinforced by political ideologies built on the sublime, these divisions have long-lasting and terrible consequences. In her critique of the Kantian and Nietzschean sublimes, Christine Battersby shows how their legacy around race and gender is not simply ideal and intellectual, but is written on bodies and in language: 'As such, the female and raced sublime is not simply ineffable, and is also more material and more historically specific than it might be supposed.'[23] Against this violence, she advocates a feminine sublime in art, acting as a form of resistance: 'For me, it is the most interesting women artists and writers who manage both to confront and convey the dangers of these fleshy and spatial, temporal, human and female antinomies in what they create. And the female sublime is, above all, a site in which the dislocations of the female subject positions are explored and made visible.'[24] For the project of an egalitarian sublime, the female sublime is an historically necessary sublime, contributing to a multiplicity of different critical responses to earlier reductive forms of the sublime through the creation of many, if always transitory, new values.

We are still suffering from the wounds of reductive and yet general definitions separating humans into groups of differing value, in particular around migration and immigration, exploited by 'nationalist populist ideologies' worldwide. '[There are] ascendant nationalist populist ideologies and strategies that pose a sobering threat to racial equality by fuelling discrimination, intolerance and the creation of institutions and structures that will have enduring legacies of racial exclusion.'[25] There are legacies from earlier definitions of the sublime in these modern horrors; for instance, in Kant's racism and ignorance in his *Observations on the Feeling of the Beautiful and the Sublime*: 'So essential is the difference between these two human kinds, and it seems to be just as great with regard to the capacities of the mind as it is with respect to colour', he says in his anthropological remarks, thereby committing the twofold error of elevating the most casual pseudo-empirical observation into timeless and vicious dogma.[26]

The fourth section of Kant's early work on the sublime is dominated by distinctions of this kind, between men and women, between nations, peoples, creeds and characters. This connects to his later work, not only in the continued division between the beautiful and the sublime, always defined through place and situation in the earlier works, but in his identification of the sublime with rapture and thoughtfulness, again only for some not all.

For the sublime, the aesthetic limitations of Kant's critical work are inherited from his dissection of nations and peoples in the early part-empirical and part-dogmatic work: 'among the peoples of our part of the world the Italians and the French are, in my opinion, those who most distinguish themselves in the feeling of the beautiful, but the Germans, the English, and the Spaniards those who are most distinguished from all others in the feeling of the sublime. Holland can be regarded as the land where this finer taste is fairly unnoticeable.'[27] Little travelled compared to Rousseau or Voltaire, Kant never went to England, Spain, France, The Netherlands or Italy, yet repeats platitudes about them throughout his observations.

Kant regularly misses the possibility of rapture and of the highest values in objects and experiences lacking in his particular conceptions of scale and grandeur. He condemns the Dutch to mere decoration, despite their artistic and economic golden age known throughout Europe in prints, texts and collections at the time: 'The taste of the Dutch nation for a painstaking order and decorousness that leads to worry and embarrassment also leaves little feeling for the unaffected and free movements of genius, the beauty of which would only be disfigured by the anxious avoidance of errors.'[28] If we have to select a single cause, the Dutch 'embarrassment of riches' came from a conflicted moral concern for sublime excess and its dubious economic and social sources, rather than any taste for tidiness and decorum. Simon Schama observes that 'Our "burgher of Delft" . . . responds to the embarrassment of his riches – of house, daughter, rich apparel – by being a judge in the sight (literally) of the church, an arbiter of the deserving poor, the figure for whom they may stand at the gate.'[29] Kant cannot correct the direction of causation, reversing the direction of order to embarrassment, without having to find another deeper cause of embarrassment. He would thereby have to acknowledge its sublime beginnings and extend his definition of the highest and most excessive taste, its experience and its effects.

John R. J. Eyck counters Kant's argument with a response in tune with the multiplicity of scales and types of sublime defended here. He still retains the moral frame for the argument, but shows how modesty can itself lead to sublime results and effects:

> In the wake of prevailing (post-) Kantian paradigms, the Dutch alternative outlined here – filtered through a moral inclination towards modesty before the omnipotent – offers a counterpoint to predominant cultural tendencies,

casting those notions of the sublime into relief... grandeur on a smaller scale can be as great: not so much an antisublime, perhaps, as a semi, quasi-, or minisublime.[30]

In answer to Kant's crude anthropology, Eyck calls for a subtler sublime, multiplying degrees and types of the sublime by changing relations and scales. This is an important move towards a more egalitarian sublime, because it opens up the possibility of many different sublime experiences and forms of creativity.

There is a not only a connection of moral character with aesthetic feeling in Kant's judgements about nations, but also with geography, language, history, food, art and architecture. In his long-running lectures on anthropology, Kant returns to the sublime and nationality: 'The Italian unites French vivacity (gaiety) with Spanish seriousness (tenacity), and his aesthetic character is a taste that is linked with affect; just as the view from his Alps down into the charming valleys presents matter for courage on the one hand and quiet enjoyment on the other.'[31] There are many superficial resemblances to Nietzsche on similar themes and the sublime artist here: 'Germans want to achieve, through the artist, a kind of imaginary, longed-for passion; Italians want through him to take a rest from their real passions; the French want from him the chance to display their judgment and occasions to speak. Let us therefore be fair!'[32] This is only a surface likeness. The early Kant lacks Nietzsche's irony and wariness of national types. The late Kant's cosmopolitanism misses Nietzsche's awareness of the pervasive tenacity of location and rootedness, such that Nietzsche still speaks of the 'soul' of Europe for New Europeans and 'great discoverers in the realm of the sublime', whereas Kant's universalism should – but cannot – shake off its European past.[33]

For Kant, the connection between geography and sublimity is made through the effects of landscape on feelings, and the way those effects shape ('tune') character: 'Temperament here is neither mixed nor unsteady..., rather it is a tuning of sensibility toward the feeling of the sublime, in so far as it is also compatible with the feeling of the beautiful.'[34] There is a missed opportunity in this idea of fine-tuning for the sublime, since nothing prevents multiple directions and outcomes for sensibility, following from the multiplicity of ways to shape temperament according to place, culture, bodies, feelings, languages, history, desires and chance. Kant's wish for one outcome according to reason takes him away from the multiple possibilities of his early insights and even his misrepresentations.

Barbara Claire Freeman shows how Kant's search for a moral outcome for the sublime leads to domination not only over the sublime object itself, but also over all life-forms deemed to fall short of moral sublimation:

> Thus, the central moment of the sublime marks the self's newly enhanced sense of identity; a will to power drives its style, a mode that establishes and maintains the self's domination over its object of rapture... rather than represent the object of rapture as a way of incorporating it, as the traditional sublime of domination does, the feminine sublime does not attempt to master its objects of rapture.[35]

Like Battersby's, Freeman's feminine sublime is a move towards a more egalitarian sublime, since its aim is not the domination of an experience or encounter. Furthermore, the feminine sublime seeks to avoid the role of 'spectatorship' in the sublime, replacing it with social construction, avoiding binary distinctions and resisting mastery.[36]

The harshest version of this criticism of Kant's sublime comes from Adorno's *Aesthetic Theory*. His interpretation of Kant prefigures similar arguments made by Žižek and situates the Kantian sublime at the beginning of a process where all later adoptions of the sublime become complicit in a founding negativity, including modern art – perhaps above all. Adorno begins by drawing a connection between the scale of the Kantian sublime and its deceitful support for unequal power relations: 'by situating the sublime in overpowering grandeur and setting up the antithesis of power and powerlessness, Kant directly affirmed his unquestioning complicity with domination'.[37]

This is not to connive with any particular power, but rather to plot to support a disjunction between nature and what Adorno calls spirit and Kant calls reason: 'With profound justification [Kant] defined the concept of the sublime by resistance of spirit to the overpowering.'[38] Grandeur induces the subject to resist the power of nature with freedom and moral choice, 'a space liberated from fetters and strictures, a liberation in which it is possible to participate'.[39] Why wouldn't this liberation be viewed as valuable, as a discovery of a general human capacity to overcome natural limits and build a better moral world based on universal values?

Dependence on negation is the reason the sublime does not lead to an overcoming of power. This negativity is built into the structure of Kant's sublime: 'The legacy of the sublime is unassuaged negativity, as stark and illusionless as was once promised by the semblance of the sublime.'[40] The free rational subject is a form of negativity liberated from constraints in nature and within itself. It is negative because its freedom comes from an opposition to nature, from an individualism that negates other individuals and social groups, and from a resistance to internal restraints such as conscience and instinct. Furthermore, on Kant's account, negation is supposed to return to this subject in the form of freely chosen universal law.

Nature as limit is negated by the excess of the sublime object. However, this object is only an appearance of grandeur; it is not grandeur as such – another denial. The true sublime is within the grasp of the subject, opposing that outer appearance through inner will and reason. Free subjects are themselves contradicted in freely giving up their autonomy by submitting to moral law. This moral law is an added negation (as we also saw in Žižek) because it leads to domination by a superior order: the established social, economic, religious and cultural powers.

When it comes to concealing the power of a dominant class and order behind the universals of the sublime, Kant's harshest critic is Pierre Bourdieu. His analysis of Kant's *Critique of Judgment* is different from the strictly formal philosophical points made by Adorno. It rests instead on the traces of the influence of class and political order in Kant's aesthetics. Bourdieu's argument falls mid-way between form and hidden content. This explains why he uses a language of veils and traces, rather than directly accusing Kant of social and cultural prejudice. Instead, Bourdieu detects a type of sublimation in Kant's critical work: 'The *social categories of aesthetic judgement* can only function for Kant himself and for his readers in the form of highly sublimated categories, such as oppositions between beauty and attraction, pleasure and enjoyment [*jouissance*] or culture and civilisation.'[41]

The idea of sublimation is not about the elevation of the sublime but rather indicates how cultural and social values are purified yet also remain in Kant's distinctions as 'sorts of euphemisms that, outside any conscious intention to dissimulate, still allow social oppositions to be expressed and felt in a form according with a specific field'.[42] These are two key points for a critical reading of Kant on the basis of the egalitarian sublime. First, intention is not necessary for the dissimulation and manipulation of unequal values in the sublime. These distortions occur because of the effects of the definition of the sublime and do not depend on what an original author may or may not have intended.

Second, social oppositions and their inscription into an unequal form of society and culture do not have to be actual cases of discrimination and division, in order to offer powerful support to such cases and to lead to them. For example, an actual case could be a decision to fund a single opera house attended by a cosmopolitan elite, rather than theatre lessons in schools throughout a country. While distant from this direct division into classes, the sublimated formal support for the decision could come from a distinction drawn between sublime art, achieved only by very few creators and enjoyed only after years of cultural preparation, and popular art, seen as derivative, falling short of the standards achieved by genius, and as enjoyed only because superior education is as yet lacking. The fundamental problem is at the level of the distinctions and evaluations in the definitions of the sublime; these prepare for the more visible but in fact secondary divisions. That's why Adorno's focus on negation is the basis for the most far-reaching criticism of Kant's sublime.

For Adorno, it isn't that the problems with the sublime end with Kant. They start with him. When art seeks to go beyond Kant and replace the natural sublime with tragic and comic sublimes, it can only prolong his submission to power, shoring up 'established domination': 'Tragedy and comedy perish in modern art and preserve themselves on this perishing.'[43] Art continues to seek the sublime, in mockery of our diminishment and of the insignificance of grandeur – 'the comedy of the tragic' – but leaves the latter intact, unjust and in power, in a 'neutralization of truth'.

Negative distinctions supporting a dominant order – around sex and gender, colour, lightness and darkness of skin, continents, landscapes, religions, cultures, nations and lands – are a recurring theme for definitions of the sublime from Burke onwards. As Meg Armstrong shows, these definitions are part of a language constructing subjects as divided by marks of identity taken from the sublime: 'aesthetic discourse at least since Burke and Kant locates this subject [the subject constructed by the ideology of the aesthetic] within a global network of "bodies" (sensual signs of the sublime) whose gendered, national, and racial markings are integral to that subject's self-identification (if not also its unspoken or illegitimate desires)'.[44] The violence and repression of this process come from the combination of the necessity of the sublime, its claim to the highest values, and the division of people and places according to marks of identity. The necessity assigns permanence to the division and attributes unshakable values to the identities – to the point where these become factors of self-identification. Value and identity are inscribed into flesh, written on the body by the sublime.

Against Locke's greater empiricism about darkness, where he denies the necessity of its association with terror because it varies according to experience and causes, Burke appeals to physiological and psychological arguments where darkness necessarily brings about terror because of a privation of our senses and terror of the unknown, 'all is dark, uncertain, confused, terrible, and sublime to the last degree'.[45] Earlier than Kant, but with similarities in making assumptions about the fixed nature of sensibility and psychology, Burke makes a necessary connection between darkness and terror, thereby missing, for instance, the terror induced by pitiless light, and the ethical turn-around of exchanging positions and empathising with, or imagining, the terror that whiteness can bring. Instead, for Burke, 'black has always something melancholy in it'.[46] Again, the 'always' does the most damage, moving from flawed empiricism to necessity, then onwards to an irreversible inequality of values, all through sublime aesthetics.

Not after the sublime

In studying both historical and more recent definitions of the sublime, the method of micro dialectics has been used here to uncover their negative effects. This close-up work has then been given continuity and connections in suggesting patterns of effects. Some of the strongest of these were distinctions around activity and passivity; differences between internal and external sources of value; the formation of groups, classes, individuals and multiplicities; and the operation of dissimulation and critique. The next problem for the egalitarian sublime is how to connect these effects to the idea of equality. What definition of egalitarian is appropriate to investigate that problem?

This is again an odd question. Shouldn't we start with a definition of equality, thereafter assessing the possibility and desirability of applying it, prior to any reflection on the egalitarian nature of definitions of the sublime? The method of microcritique involves a combination of long views and detailed analysis. It assumes immersion into an ever-changing and complex scene, as well as the necessary transformation of this scene by the enquiry and its presuppositions. For microcritique, the effects of any move, such as a new definition, should be taken as dynamic transformations through existing scenes. Taken together, these assumptions mean that starting with a concept of equality or even aiming for it cannot be adequate to the problem, because we always have to start in the middle of a complex situation and we can only make tentative moves to transform it.

Instead, a more vague and changeable idea of equality emerges with the enquiry. This does not imply a lack of importance for it. Such a conclusion would follow from comparisons with an absolute and unchanging concept of equality, or from the idea that change and differences in degree and practical consequences are too relative to be effective or respected. Against both of those positions, this study has instead tried to map the ways in which definitions of the sublime lead to inequality. But doesn't this negative sense presuppose knowledge of positive equality?

On the contrary, it is pragmatically easier to detect an inequality than equality itself. Equality vanishes; whenever we are supposed to find it, closer inspection comes across differences amounting to significant imbalances and causes of negative consequences – like the differences between two 'same' rocks under a microscope, or two adjacent gardens on the contours of a slope, or two patches of skin under a stark sun, two ligaments or chains of molecules put under intolerable stress. This does not mean we shouldn't aim for equality. It means we should do so by tackling inequality.

Where definitions of terms such as the sublime and value are concerned, at the very least this implies learning from the ways in which earlier attempts have failed and led to ingrained injustice. In this sense, inequality is not lack of equality and not judged according to a standard of equality. Rather, inequality is a persisting and damaging imposition of distinctions and associated unequal values. These distinctions can be familiar ones from egalitarian debates: differences in opportunities, material conditions, legal status, education, availability of health, representation and wealth. They can also be deeper and more pervasive definitions based on identity or position: race, gender, sex, sexuality, creed, culture, place and provenance.

This reflection on consequent inequalities is more modest than egalitarian political projects and theories. It is in no way designed to supplant them or deny their importance. The microcritique of the sublime and its many definitions is designed to show and then learn from some effects around inequality. The point isn't to arrive at a final definition or practice, but rather to offer a mapping of how defining the sublime and determining values sets down patterns for inequality and hence offers guidance – only guidance – for thinking about how we define our highest experiences, objects, natural and built environments, aesthetic encounters and the values flowing from them.

'Sublime' can be said of an inner state or process, or of an external object or source. It can be an inner experience or an outer cause. Irrespective of whether these statements are correct, the distinction between inner and outer has consequences for the egalitarian nature of the sublime. This is not a question of whether these inner and outer manifestations are the same for all, but rather whether the sources of value are within us or outside us, and whether these internal or external events leave us in a state of passivity or follow from activity.

In turn, this has consequences for how and whether we should seek to rectify injustice and unfairness. Freedom and liberty as conditions for equality are at stake in these distinctions. Those stakes increase or decrease dependent on the equality of any given world and on the values ascribed to different processes and powers.

The expression 'after the sublime' recurs in Genevieve Lloyd's recent book *Reclaiming Wonder: After the Sublime*, where she argues for wonder as a replacement for the sublime: 'Perhaps, after the sublime, wonder can come to represent the acceptance of a world without the Absolute, in which the startled recognition of difference can give rise to both challenge and shared delight.'[47] We can go beyond the sublime and yet retain some of its positive values if we abandon our search for the absolute and the universal.

Yet earlier definitions of the sublime were already attempts to avoid universals: Burke's many sublimes, opposed to one absolute experience or type; Nietzsche's sublime individuals, rising above the masses' desire for knowledge of unchanging absolutes and universals; the feminine sublime as resistance to the absolutes of gendered divisions; Žižek's interpretation of

Hegel's sublime as remnant of the absolute; and Kristeva's abject sublime, internally divided and ephemeral.

The use of 'after' is an internal contradiction. Lloyd describes many contemporary sublime experiences and manifestations, from religious enthusiasm to the experience of war. They persist and grow in a time of wonder, when enthusiasm follows from a wondrous experience, a reaction to wonder, rather than simple opposition to it.

The desire to come after the sublime defines wonder as absolved of the sublime, but it makes more sense to define wonder as a species of the sublime. The idea of being startled by difference in wonder is consistent with sublime experience. When we are startled we are threatened, shaken, challenged and discomfited in ways close to terror in the sublime. Wonder is then a combination of terror and delight, more than a simple attraction and amazement. The questions 'How can that be?', 'How do they do that?' and 'Isn't this extraordinary?' are misread if shorn of elements of mistrust and fear. They are double-edged questions, teetering on the border of rejection and repulsion even as they express wonder.

Wonder is a fragile and dangerous form of innocence, denying its historical setting and environments, as well as the threats accompanying anything worthy of wonder, such as a new life, or barren and lifeless expanses, or new and potentially terrible discoveries. Lloyd doesn't think wonder has quite arrived yet, as a replacement for the sublime ('*Perhaps*, after the sublime, wonder *can come* . . .'). The reason it hasn't come yet is that the world is still made according to values inherited from historical definitions of the sublime and still constructed from new definitions of the sublime: from the technological sublime, the environmental sublime, or the anti-sublime of the attempt to break the connection between the sublime and value.

If we are to pass beyond the sublime taken as absolute, as we should in the search for a more egalitarian society, two alternative moves are necessary. First, there must be a continuing critique of all the ways in which sublime experiences, events and objects lead to inequality. Second, the general and universal ambitions of the sublime and the inevitable search for value and meaning should be replaced by an anarchic multiplicity of sublimes, with inbuilt limits, self-destruction and self-criticism. Wonder, as defined by Lloyd, can be one strand of this multiplicity.

As such, wonder will not replace the sublime but rather add to a coexistence of different sublime experiences and values. Lloyd's description of wonder is a definition of a self-overcoming sublime. She recognises its inner faults; for instance, being prone to stupidity ('intermingled with the numbing effects of stupidity').[48] Wonder is also self-destructive, in the sense of transitory: 'a condition which, of its nature, cannot be sustained for everything all of the time'.[49]

If that's the case, then wonder should always be accompanied by critical attention to its tendency to stupidity, to failure and to misuse. Above all, though, as an instance of the sublime, wonder should not be defined as coming after the sublime, but rather as taking its place among many other variations, such as enthusiasm, fanaticism, extreme creativity, abjectness and absorption in processes of mutation through encounters with other lives or objects. These variations must remain secondary to an egalitarian political system, rather than rule over it.

Finally, wonder is still a deeply unequal affect, channelling the sublime distinction between those who experience it and those who don't through the incomprehension that accompanies an encounter with those who do not share our wonder. *How could you not wonder at a new life, or at the 'immensity of the universe'?*[50] *What's wrong with you?* Lloyd's definition of wonder divides between those attuned to the fragility of life and reason when confronted by immensity, and those whose values make them perhaps overconfident in their power, or closed to the immensities of their surroundings, or drawn to the miserable, or to baseness, or to minute endeavours. There is nothing intrinsically wrong with any of these, when compared to wonder; their value will depend on practical situations and particular cases. There is worth in a sublime combination of humility and awe, but it is not shared equally by all, nor should it be.

Chapter 7

Conclusion: The Sublime as Crisis

One of the common factors running through this essay has been that the sublime is a crisis: a time of threat and danger, but also a time of decision and change. For the sublime, danger is always held off in some way, in order to introduce the inner complexity of the sublime as going beyond immediate fear and perishing into kinds of pleasure and attraction, or at least relief. But that is also a feature of crisis, since under threat there is still an opportunity to respond and to act; at the crisis point of an illness, for example.

As crisis, we could assume the sublime is a pure experience, something terrible and yet also promising that happens to us. This is a mistake. The most important lesson learned here is how the sublime is made as crisis, even if it is then also felt and undergone. It is constructed in two ways and the coexistence of these ways is what makes the idea of the sublime powerful and interesting. The sublime is made by something or someone: an artist, gods, an orator, technologies, many different kinds of nature, an economy, a political system, history, built spaces, wars and revolutions, collapse and decline. All have been identified as agents of sublime crisis.

The sublime is also made by writers reflecting on the meaning of the sublime. It is defined by them. They do not make it out of nothing, but instead inherit it as a source of the highest values they want to change. When the sublime is experienced, we inherit the results of earlier definitions; for instance when the sublime has been defined as a style, or as a goal, or as something to be created, or as the future of humanity, or as the fruit of new technologies, or as caring for, or despoiling, natural and now virtual environments.

My aim was to consider whether the sublime has been egalitarian and whether it could be reconstructed as egalitarian. This wish turned out to be far too optimistic: both of the ways the sublime has been made have led to deep inequalities. The sublime divides. Even when this propensity is known, when philosophers such as Kant have sought to turn it into a source of universal equality, their efforts have bequeathed further division.

This doom-laden history of increasingly refined ways of balancing the divisiveness of the sublime with its recuperation as a source of superior community has culminated in a negation of the sublime as a sign of value. 'Let's forget about the sublime' is the new cry, or let's finally replace it with something better, or with nothing at all. This reaction cannot shake off the sublime or go beyond its unequal implications.

The sublime is a crisis, but it is also a response to crisis. In times of strife we search for the right values to carry us through. A crisis is a threat to old values and hence to older versions of the sublime, since for there to be a crisis they must have failed in some way; but it is also a severe test calling for new values and hence for a new version of the sublime.

Every new definition of the sublime has been a response to crisis and an attempt to connect the sublime to values adequate to the nature of a novel threat. In rhetoric, the turn to the sublime is a response to a crisis in truth, seeking to define how speech can carry truth unmistakably – as when we seek a sublime and truthful journalism, rising above the fray of politics. As style, sublimity is appealed to when the old is challenged by the new, where the sublime is something we have lost but need to recapture, or where it is the mark of our modernity, against the decay of old style. When applied to nature, the idea of the sublime can be a response to a crisis in the beautiful, where artistic beauty is seen as falling away into decoration, becoming mere amusement; but it can also be a response to a natural crisis, when nature is defined as sublime to justify its preservation or elevation, or to lament its loss.

We have seen the sublime applied to political crises, not only when used to describe revolution, for good and bad, but also when used in propaganda, to associate the highest values with often the lowest and most violent forms of political leadership and repression; or when the sublime responds to corruption and decay, either in a nostalgia for past glories, or in a search for renewed hope, in art or improving emotions such as delight or wonder. This political employment of the sublime is also moral, where moral improvement and sublimity are given the task of providing guidance for political salvation.

Philosophically, the sublime is a formal response to a crisis of powers. Capacities, abilities, practices and knowledge that ought to see us through experiences and challenges fall short. When they fail in this way, the breakdown not only causes sublimity, in the experience of reaching a limit against a superior power, it is also an opportunity to rely on the sublime to help us through the crisis and teach us new capacities. This combination of negation and overcoming reaches its final point when the negation is seen as terminal, such that there is no way beyond the sublime as limitation, leading to the conclusion that it cannot be the way to new and better values.

The most telling recent return to the sublime is in technology. It shows the adaptability of the concept, transferring from its roots in nature to a technological effect. Here the crisis can either come from technology itself, in its destructiveness and the awe around new inventions, or from a wider social and political collapse, to which technology is supposed to respond with sublime and transforming power – in new ideas about money or computing power, for example.

There is also the production of the sublime by technology, through the invention of sublime virtual worlds, mimicking and improving upon natural ones, or in avant-garde arts, where the sublime power of the emotions is triggered and exploited in new and disconcerting ways. Much of the history of the sublime is replicated in this contrast between the sublime as pleasing effect of amazement, in the entertainment of computer games for example, and as the painful interruption of life, by experiences that are terrible and yet significant.

The technological turn reinforces the argument against the sublime as egalitarian. Not only is it made, but it is manufactured according to the aims of makers and with the potential – or even the incentive – to deceive those experiencing the sublime. This is the deepest inequality of the sublime, whether as defined or as experienced. It always divides between those who produce the sublime or its theory, and those who consume it and are subjected to it. In that sense, it is an unequal instrument of control. It always has been.

Nonetheless, over the course of this essay I have avoided the most obvious deduction: abandon the sublime. There are different reasons for this and none of them can be definitive. First, if the sublime is discarded, but we retain the universal aims it led to, then we are still dealing with legacies from the sublime. It is still with us as a remnant, in our images of universal values and their sublime justifications, whether religious, or from Enlightenment enthusiasm, or both – few political rallies are free from the sublime, or its simulation, now more than ever.

Second, if the sublime is abandoned for aimlessness – in the sense of an absence of higher values – then older and more sinister versions of the sublime will fill the gap created by this absence and by a continued desire for the certainties of superior values. Or else the threat of nihilism will increase, as it always does in times of seemingly unavoidable crisis. Another of the worrying signs coming out of this study of the sublime follows from the collapse of each urgent attempt at the sublime, because their failure leaves a void, such as the obliteration of the natural sublime, or the fearsome perversion of technological sublimity into atomic warfare, or images of technological sublimity shorn of all humans, or where humans are lesser beings in a world in which technology has outrun the human – as we are already seeing in new modes of warfare.

Third, if we hold on to lower degrees of aesthetic experiences, expecting them to be free of the flaws of the sublime, we miss the continuum from the beautiful to the sublime. Though the beautiful can fulfil the role of guiding us towards higher values, it is not free of the flaws revealed by the sublime. The most sensitive thinkers of the sublime, such as Schopenhauer and Burke, realise that it is not simply opposed to the beautiful. There are instead different degrees of the sublime and the beautiful, positioning them on a spectrum, rather than in logical opposition to one another.

Fourth, if we reinvent the sublime, giving it a different name, and claiming to have broken with its legacies and effects, we only repeat its deceptions and its propensity for inequality, in new and supposedly pure emotions, experiences and values. There has always been a trick of terminology latent in using the idea of the sublime, since the word stands in for the highest and best, while concealing the complexity of the theories and manipulations justifying this exceptional elevation. The trick is easily unmasked if the new term behaves like the sublime, providing superior values through a tension between attraction and repulsion, and an extreme experience such as awe, allied to a rational thread leading to a better world, such as an explanation of how wonderment can lead to positive types of respect.

For these reasons I have proposed an alternative, anarchist version of the sublime, counter to its tendencies to inequality. The sublime should be multiple, in the strong sense of there being many different sublimes, each one understood as a source of a different and transformative value, stemming from a tension between attraction and repulsion. This anarchist sublime should also be critical, not only of other versions of the sublime with their unequal, repressive and violent tendencies, but also self-critical, seeking out those same negative aspects within itself. This goes further, however, since each sublime should be self-destructive, only a passing transformation, rather than the foundation for eternal values and permanence.

When this new definition and the critique of other definitions are combined, the search for an egalitarian sublime comes to an end as a political dream. The sublime must be secondary to political and social equality, understood as the aim of making societies equal in rights, freedom and opportunity. Equality is a condition for the sublime and not the other way round. Egalitarian philosophies should always be wary of the sublime. It will always undo their aims by introducing new kinds of division and distinction.

Notes

Chapter 2

1. Brady, *The Sublime in Modern Philosophy*, p. 1.
2. Heath, 'Longinus and the Ancient Sublime', p. 12.
3. Warnick, *Fénelon's Letter to the French Academy*, p. 4.
4. Boileau, *Satires*, p. 107, my translation.
5. Levine, *Between the Ancients and the Moderns*, p. 200.
6. Adamson, *Classical Philosophy: A History of Philosophy without Any Gaps*, p. xii.
7. Doran, *The Theory of the Sublime from Longinus to Kant*, p. 43.
8. Ibid., p. 3.
9. Chignell and Halteman, 'Religion and the Sublime', pp. 184ff.
10. Ibid., p. 199.
11. Monk, *The Sublime*, p. 233.
12. Santayana, *The Life of Reason or the Phases of Human Progress, Volume 1*, p. 284.
13. Suzman, *Affluence without Abundance*, 452/738.
14. Beattie and Geiger, *Frozen in Time: The Fate of the Franklin Expedition*, p. 2.
15. Ibid., pp. 48–9.
16. Suzman, *Affluence without Abundance*, 434/738.
17. *Oxford English Dictionary*, Second Edition, Oxford: Clarendon, 1989.
18. Iggers, 'Foreword', p. vii.
19. Breisach, *Historiography: Ancient, Medieval & Modern*, p. 4.
20. Halverson, *Historiography and Fiction*, pp. 1–10.
21. Saltzman, 'Reading Anselm Kiefer's Book *Die Himmelspaläste*: *Merkaba*', p. 18.
22. Sloterdijk 'Works and Nights: On Art after Modernism', p. 48.
23. Hoerschelmann, 'Ways of Worldly Wisdom: The Battle of Hermann', pp. 73–4.
24. Sloterdijk, 'Works and Nights: On Art after Modernism', p. 48.
25. See Chatzantonis, *Deleuze and Mereology: Multiplicity Structure and Composition*.
26. Ginzburg, 'Microhistory', pp. 10–35.
27. *Die Alexanderschlacht* (1529). Altdorfer painted the Battle of Issus in 1529, when Ottoman armies besieged Vienna, thereby providing historical resonances with the 333 BCE battle between Alexander and Darius III. Krichbaum, *Albrecht Altdorfer*, pp. 143–50.
28. Wood, *Albrecht Altdorfer and the Origins of Landscape*, p. 22.
29. Ibid.
30. Ginzburg, 'Microhistory', p. 26.

31. Ibid.
32. Wood, *Albrecht Altdorfer and the Origins of Landscape*, p. 22. Like stage left and stage right, the left to right flow should be understood from the perspective of the painting looking out, rather than the viewer looking in. Wood is therefore referring to a thwarted movement from East to West.
33. Ginzburg, 'Microhistory', p. 26.
34. By 'the mid-1980s, the US and other Western countries were openly siding with Iraq and providing economic and military aid'. Dannreuther, 'The Gulf Conflict', p. 164. See also Gordon, 'The Last War Syndrome', p. 118.
35. Ginzburg, *History, Rhetoric and Proof*, p. 25.
36. Ibid.
37. Ginzburg, 'The Conversion of the Jews of Minorca (A.D. 417–418)', in *Threads and Traces*, pp. 25–33.
38. Ginzburg, *Threads and Traces*, p. 164.
39. Ibid., p. 67.
40. Ibid., p. 57.
41. Davis, *The Return of Martin Guerre*, p. 3.
42. Ibid., p. 5.
43. Ginzburg, *Threads and Traces*, p. 57.
44. Magnússon and Szijártó, *What is Microhistory?*, p. 15.
45. Patton, 'Introduction', in Baudrillard, *The Gulf War Did Not Take Place*, p. 11. Patton is arguing against Christopher Norris and his inability to distinguish between arguing for the role of virtual images in the constitution of reality and arguing for the negation of 'all distinctions between truth and falsehood'. (Norris, *The Truth about Postmodernism*, p. 6.) One does not follow from the other and there is plenty of evidence that Baudrillard makes truth claims, including when he is arguing for hyperreality.
46. Norris, *The Truth about Postmodernism*, p. 6.
47. Allison, *Destructive Sublime*, p. 187.
48. Norris, *Reclaiming Truth*, p. 183.
49. Baudrillard, *The Gulf War Did Not Take Place*, p. 85.
50. Ginzburg, 'Microhistory', p. 27.
51. Ibid.
52. Ibid.
53. Ginzburg, 'Microhistory', p. 33.
54. Ibid.
55. Ibid.
56. Ibid.
57. Ibid.
58. Ginzburg, 'The Bitter Truth: Stendhal's Challenge to Historians', in *Threads and Traces*, p. 150.
59. Ibid., p. 146.
60. Ginzburg, 'Following in the Tracks of Israël Bertuccio', in *Threads and Traces*, pp. 135–6.
61. Magnússon and Szijártó, *What is Microhistory?*, p. 4.
62. Ginzburg, 'Montaigne, Cannibals and Grottoes', in *Threads and Traces*, p. 52.
63. Ginzburg, 'Microhistory', p. 34.
64. Petrella, 'Mater Materia Prima', p. 58; Golding, *Boccioni*, p. 27.
65. Boccioni, 'Futurist Painting', p. 238.
66. Golding, *Boccioni*, p. 27.
67. Ginzburg, 'Microhistory', p. 34.
68. Ibid.
69. Kracauer, *History: The Last Things Before the Last*, pp. 124–7.
70. Nye, *American Technological Sublime*, pp. 171–2.

Chapter 3

1. Nye, *American Technological Sublime*, p. 29. Nye is commenting on the nineteenth century and Kant, but the male-dominated aspects of sublime imagery continue through the following century, for instance, in the sublime and male-oriented iconography of heavy industry and space exploration.
2. Letter to Scott, 10 July 1802, Seward, *Letters of Anna Seward*, Vol. VI, p. 39; see also her letter to Whalley, 7 October 1799, for a reference to the sublimity of mountain views. Seward, *Letters of Anna Seward*, Vol. V, p. 251.
3. Letter to Thomas Park, 27 September 1802, Seward, *Letters of Anna Seward*, Vol. VI, p. 46.
4. Letter to Rev H. F. Cary, 7 August 1806, ibid., pp. 302–3.
5. Letter to Park, 25 September 1800, Seward, *Letters of Anna Seward*, Vol. V, p. 324. There's an in-depth discussion of Seward and Romantic women writers on the sublime in Monk, *The Sublime*. For an introduction to Seward's life see Seward, *Anna Seward's Life of Erasmus Darwin*, pp. 10–17, and Sir Walter Scott's appreciation in Seward, *The Poetical Works of Anna Seward*. Among recent critical work on the feminine and feminist sublime, books by Barbara Claire Freeman and Christine Battersby stand out. See Freeman, *The Feminine Sublime*, and Battersby, *The Sublime, Terror and Human Difference*.
6. Burke, *A Philosophical Enquiry into the Origin of our Ideas of the Sublime and Beautiful*, p. 129.
7. Ibid.
8. Ibid.
9. Ibid., p. 32.
10. Ibid.
11. Ibid., pp. 52–3.
12. Ibid., p. 7.
13. Ibid., p. 57.
14. Elkins, 'Against the Sublime', pp. 88–9.
15. In his renewal of the historical argument for land tax, Todd S. Mei claims land cannot be seen as any individual's or group's property by natural right. Land is given to all as natural excess and taken by a few as economic means. See Mei, *Land and the Given Economy*.
16. Tàpies, 'The Tattoo and the Body', pp. 133–4.
17. Penrose, *Tàpies*, p. 108. My interest in drawing a parallel between effects in painting and in descriptive diagrams should not be read as a claim about the ultimate significance of Tapiès. He has been read as metaphysical and symbolist by Penrose, but there are different interpretations explicitly inimical to that earlier position: 'Tàpies would have no doubt been horrified to be described as a conceptual artist, but in fact at times he made work as if he were one.' Godfrey, 'Was Tàpies a Conceptual Artist After All?', p. 37. Matter painting is also a reductive label for an artist whose works range widely in inspiration from the Spanish Civil War to Buddhism, twentieth-century literature and philosophy, and the very different styles of many of his contemporaries. I would apply ideas about the sign from my earlier book *A Process Philosophy of Signs* to Tapiès and make the conjecture that even in his most 'symbolic' works such as Calligraphy (1958) there has to be an open and dynamic effect of signs on a wider material *before* there can be any settled signification. See *Tàpies: The Complete Works, Volume 1: 1943–1960*, p. 337.
18. Penrose, *Tàpies*, p. 180.
19. Antoni Tàpies, quoted in ibid., p. 173.
20. Newman, 'The Sublime is Now', p. 27.
21. Ibid.

22. Ibid.
23. Ibid.
24. Ibid.
25. There's a connection between Newman's abstraction and Burke's much earlier remarks on grandeur and his critique of the form of the cross and its dependence on 'a broken unconnected figure'. Burke, *A Philosophical Enquiry*, p. 57.
26. Ibid., p. 100.
27. Ibid., p. 143.
28. Kant, *Observations on the Feeling of the Beautiful and the Sublime*, p. 58.
29. Nietzsche, 'On the Uses and Disadvantages of History for Life', p. 78.
30. Ibid.
31. Ibid.
32. Ibid.
33. Ibid.
34. Lyotard, *The Differend*, p. 75.
35. 'Expressed morally: you are no longer capable of holding on to the sublime, your deeds are shortlived explosions, not rolling thunder.' Ibid., p. 83.
36. Burke, *A Philosophical Enquiry*, p. 129.
37. Ibid.
38. O'Brien, *The Suspecting Glance*, 153.9/173.
39. Nietzsche, 'On the Uses and Disadvantages of History for Life', p. 120.
40. Ibid., p. 121.
41. Ibid.
42. Ibid.
43. Ibid., p. 118.
44. Burke, *A Philosophical Enquiry*, p. 21.
45. Suleri, *The Rhetoric of English India*, p. 37.
46. Gibbons, *Edmund Burke and Ireland*, p. xiii.
47. Ibid.
48. Paulson, *Representations of Revolutions*, p. 67.
49. Burke, *A Philosophical Enquiry*, p. 26.
50. Ibid., p. 29.
51. Ibid., p. 27.
52. Ibid.
53. Ibid., p. 30.
54. Nietzsche, 'On the Uses and Disadvantages of History for Life', p. 111.
55. Tim Cloudsley argues for a connection between shamanism, the sublime and Nietzsche in a 'wild aesthetic vision'. Cloudsley, *Shamanism and the Sublime*, p. 17.
56. Matthew Rampley argues that the function of the sublime in Nietzsche is to 'dispel the aura of representation'. This applies all the more strongly to a represented end, where that aura gains greater strength in the privileged position of the end goal. Rampley, *Nietzsche, Aesthetics and Modernity*, p. 91.
57. Burke, *A Philosophical Enquiry*, p. 61.
58. For a discussion of the similarities and differences between Burke and Nietzsche on the sublime, see Paul Guyer's 'Introduction' in *Edmund Burke, a Philosophical Enquiry into the Sublime and the Beautiful*, pp. vi–xxxvii.
59. Battersby, *The Sublime, Terror and Human Difference*, p. 189.
60. Ibid.
61. Ricoeur, *Time and Narrative*, Vol. 1, p. 41.
62. Rehding, *Music and Monumentality*, p. 15ff
63. Nietzsche, 'On the Uses and Disadvantages of History for Life', p. 67ff.
64. Ibid., p. 76.
65. Ibid., p. 75.
66. Nietzsche, *Thus Spoke Zarathustra*, p. 177.

67. Ibid., p. 179.
68. Ibid., p. 180.
69. Klossowski, *Nietzsche and the Vicious Circle*, p. 153.
70. Nietzsche, 'On the Uses and Disadvantages of History for Life', p. 93.
71. Ibid.
72. Ibid., p. 94.
73. Ibid.
74. Ansell Pearson demonstrates the importance of the sublime despite the relative scarcity of both German adjectives for sublime in Nietzsche's text ('erhaben' and 'sublim'). Battersby explains how the adjectives connect in an overall account of the sublime: 'English translators of Nietzsche are faced with a dilemma; Nietzsche loves to play with the figurative language of height, but when he uses the language of the "erhaben" – 28 times in the *Birth of Tragedy* – we certainly need to read these references in terms of the aesthetic debates concerning the sublime. Later, Nietzsche would sometimes use the much less common German word "sublim".' Battersby, *The Sublime, Terror and Human Difference*, p. 161.
75. Ansell Pearson, '"Holding on to the Sublime"', p. 769.
76. Ibid., pp. 774ff.
77. Ibid., p. 776.
78. Ibid., p. 780.
79. Nietzsche, 'On the Uses and Disadvantages of History for Life', p. 97.
80. Ansell Pearson, '"Holding on to the Sublime"', p. 782.
81. Richardson, *Nietzsche's New Darwinism*, p. 8.
82. Ibid., p. 262.
83. For an account of Nietzsche's critical stance on Darwin, see Johnson, *Nietzsche's anti-Darwinism*, p. 79ff.
84. Ryle and Soper, *To Relish the Sublime*, p. 2.
85. Ibid., p. 65.
86. Guyer, 'The German Sublime After Kant', pp. 102–3.
87. Ibid.
88. Nietzsche, 'On the Uses and Disadvantages of History for Life', p. 113.
89. Burke, *A Philosophical Enquiry*, p. 38.
90. Ibid., p. 32.
91. Nietzsche, 'On the Uses and Disadvantages of History for Life', p. 120.
92. Church, *Nietzsche's Culture of Humanity*, p. 79.
93. Ibid.
94. Ibid.
95. Nietzsche, 'On the Uses and Disadvantages of History for Life', p. 106.
96. Ansell Pearson, '"Holding on to the Sublime"', p. 784.
97. Nietzsche, 'On the Uses and Disadvantages of History for Life', p. 106.
98. Ansell Pearson, '"Holding on to the Sublime"', p. 785.
99. Gorichanaz, 'Beautiful and Sublime', p. 376.
100. Ansell Pearson, '"Holding on to the Sublime"', p. 782.
101. Ibid.

Chapter 4

1. Carter, *Dietrich's Ghosts*, p. 210.
2. Ibid.
3. Amundsen, *Performing Ideology*, p. 307.
4. In recent work the point about misplaced enthusiasm has been put with most verve by James Elkins, with his accusations of a turn away from the real world through sublime elitism, distance and nostalgia. He stresses the irresponsibility, ideological nature,

distance from modern philosophy and avoidance of difficult judgements in the sublime. Ironically, just as Elkins was proposing a moratorium on the use of the sublime, the term went through its strongest resurgence for over a century. See Elkins, 'Against the Sublime'.
5. Litman, *Le sublime en France*, p. 132, my translation.
6. Ibid., p. 139.
7. Ibid.
8. Johnson, 'The Postmodern Sublime', p. 126.
9. Gasché, '. . . And the Beautiful?', pp. 28–9.
10. Ibid.
11. Ibid.
12. Derrida, *La vérité en peinture*, p. 157, my translation.
13. Ibid., p. 153.
14. Hegel, *Aesthetics: Lectures on Fine Art*, p. 363.
15. Ibid.
16. Costelloe, 'The Sublime', pp. 1–7.
17. Nietzsche, *Dawn*, p. 270.
18. Ibid., p. 220.
19. Nye, *American Technological Sublime*, p. 17.
20. Ibid.
21. Ibid., p. 37.
22. Ibid., p. 255.
23. Ray, *Terror and the Sublime in Art and Critical Theory*, p. 7.
24. Nye, *American Technological Sublime*, p. 296.
25. Ibid., p. xiii.
26. Ibid., p. 29.
27. Ibid., p. xiii.
28. Ibid., p. 43.
29. Kessler, *Picturing the Cosmos*, p. 231. Note that the critical point is about the sublimity of the images achieved by manipulation, irrespective of the original intention which may be more strictly scientific, for instance when adding artificial colours to pick out relevant features.
30. Ibid.
31. Ibid.
32. Nye, *American Technological Sublime*, p. 108.
33. Ibid., p. 43.
34. Ibid., p. 35.
35. Ibid., p. 255.
36. Ibid., p. 296.
37. Brady, *The Sublime in Modern Philosophy*, p. 114.
38. See Stafford, *The Sublime Savage*.
39. Kirwan, *Sublimity*, p. 2.
40. Brady, *The Sublime in Modern Philosophy*, p. 206.
41. Ibid., p. 153.
42. Ibid., pp. 119–20.
43. Zepke, *Sublime Art*, p. 99.

Chapter 5

1. See Ray, *Terror and the Sublime in Art and Critical Theory*, p. 6.
2. Ibid.
3. Kearney, 'Terror, Philosophy and the Sublime', p. 43.
4. Ibid.

5. Lyotard, 'The Sublime and the Avant-Garde', p. 103.
6. Ibid.
7. This shift from Kant to Adorno in Lyotard's writing is tracked by Matthew R. McLennan in his *Philosophy, Sophistry, Antiphilosophy*, pp. 26–7. Ashley Woodward explains how this change in the sublime also underpins the rich new work on art in Lyotard's philosophy, in surprising and productive directions such that 'the aesthetic of the sublime seems to be possible in relation to art made with new technologies in spite of – or even because of – the factors which rule out an aesthetic of the beautiful'. Woodward, *Lyotard and the Inhuman Condition*, p. 145.
8. Blakemore, *Burke and the Fall of Language*, p. 61.
9. Furniss, *Edmund Burke's Aesthetic Ideology*, p. 117.
10. Devetak, 'The Gothic Scene of International Relations', p. 630.
11. Kant, *The Metaphysics of Morals*, p. 175.
12. Kant, 'An Answer to the Question "What is Enlightenment?"', p. 55.
13. Kant, *The Metaphysics of Morals*, p. 175.
14. Kant, *Critique of Judgment*, p. 123.
15. Ibid.
16. Ibid.
17. Kant, 'The Contest of Faculties', p. 188.
18. '[Kantian philosophy is] the most plausible guideline when the question is for justice of the institutional make-up of the UN.' Rauber, 'The United Nations – a Kantian Dream Come True?', pp. 49–50.
19. Kant, 'The Contest of Faculties', p. 182.
20. Burke, *Reflections on the Revolution in France*, p. 6.
21. Lyotard *The Differend*, pp. 161–71, and Lyotard, *L'enthousiasme*, pp. 45–77.
22. Lyotard, *Leçons sur l'analytique du sublime*, p. 286, my translation.
23. Acharya, 'Multilateralism and the Changing World Order', p. 793.
24. Schopenhauer, *The World as Will and Representation, Volume I*, p. 532.
25. Ibid.
26. Shapshay, 'Schopenhauer's Transformation of the Kantian Sublime', p. 497.
27. Ibid.
28. Schopenhauer, *The World as Will and Representation, Volume I*, p. 200.
29. Crowther, *The Kantian Sublime*, pp. 173–3.
30. Ibid.
31. Schopenhauer, *The World as Will and Representation, Volume I*, p. 201.
32. Janaway, *Schopenhauer*, p. 95.
33. Schopenhauer, *The World as Will and Representation, Volume I*, p. 200.
34. Ibid., p. 202.
35. Neill, 'Schopenhauer on Tragedy and the Sublime', p. 209.
36. Ibid.
37. Ibid., p. 205.
38. Mishra, *Devotional Poetics and the Indian Sublime*, p. 28.
39. Ibid., p. 16.
40. Ibid.
41. Nicholls, 'The Influence of Eastern Thought on Schopenhauer's Doctrine of the Thing in Itself', p. 197.
42. Schopenhauer, *The World as Will and Representation, Volume I*, p. 202.
43. Ibid.
44. Ibid., p. 203.
45. Ibid., p. 202.
46. Ibid., p. 203.
47. Spuybroek, *The Sympathy of Things*, p. 176.
48. Ibid.
49. Ibid., p. 255.

50. Schopenhauer, *The World as Will and Representation, Volume I*, p. 203.
51. Ibid.
52. Ibid., p. 205.
53. Ibid.
54. Jacquette, *The Philosophy of Schopenhauer*, p. 162.
55. Schopenhauer, *The World as Will and Representation, Volume I*, p. 412.
56. Martin, 'The "Prehistory" of the Sublime in Early Modern France', p. 101.
57. 'Certainty, joy, certainty, emotion, sight, joy'. Pascal, *Pensées and other Writings*, p. 178.
58. Vandenabeele, *The Sublime in Schopenhauer's Philosophy*, p. 175.
59. Vasalou, *Schopenhauer and the Aesthetic Standpoint*, p. 102.
60. Egyed, 'Spinoza, Schopenhauer and the Standpoint of Affirmation', p. 126.
61. Nietzsche, *Writings from the Late Notebooks*, p. 259.
62. Ibid., p. 240.
63. Ibid.
64. Rampley, *Nietzsche, Aesthetics and Modernity*, pp. 87–8.
65. Ansell Pearson, '"Holding on to the Sublime"', p. 773.
66. Žižek, *The Sublime Object of Ideology*, p. 71.
67. Ibid., pp. 18–19.
68. Ibid., p. 207.
69. Žižek, *Disparities*, p. 385.
70. Buttler, *Slavoj Žižek: Live Theory*, p. 122.
71. Žižek, *Tarrying with the Negative*, p. 46.
72. Burnham, *Kant's Philosophies of Judgement*, p. 203.
73. Žižek, *Tarrying with the Negative*, p. 46.
74. Rutherford, *Leibniz and the Rational Order of Nature*, p. 14.
75. Žižek, *The Universal Exception*, p. 314.
76. Žižek, *The Sublime Object of Ideology*, p. 207.
77. Žižek, *Organs without Bodies*, p. 48.
78. Žižek, *The Sublime Object of Ideology*, p. 207.
79. Žižek, *On Belief*, pp. 89–90.
80. Žižek, *Tarrying with the Negative*, p. 47. This passage is replicated word for word in *Interrogating the Real*, p. 146, but with an added distinction drawn in Lacan between two types of law, as moral and pacifying, and as irrational pressure. This distinction would make the argument invalid by supplying a form of law consistent with sublimation were it not for an extra step whereby the irrational law is given as sublime and superior to the moral law.
81. Žižek, *Tarrying with the Negative*, p. 47.
82. Ibid.
83. Žižek, *Disparities*, p. 160.
84. Gardner, *Kant and the Critique of Pure Reason*, p. 326.
85. Žižek, *The Sublime Object of Ideology*, p. 194.
86. Žižek, *Tarrying with the Negative*, p. 48.
87. Ibid., p. 49.
88. Ibid., p. 50.
89. Žižek, *The Sublime Object of Ideology*, p. 204.
90. Žižek, *Tarrying with the Negative*, p. 50.
91. Ibid.
92. Ibid., p. 51.
93. Žižek, *Disparities*, p. 166.
94. Ibid., p. 210.
95. Kristeva, *Pouvoirs de l'horreur*, p. 9, my translation.
96. Ibid.
97. Ibid., p. 10.

98. Ibid., pp. 76–8.
99. Ibid., p. 19.
100. Ibid.
101. Ibid.
102. Ibid.
103. Ibid.
104. David B. Johnson describes Kristeva's abject as a perversion of the sublime, but this supposes that the sublime is well-defined enough to be perverted in the first place. My view is that the sublime has always been a flexible term to the point where its history is one of successive 'perversions' to the point where we should view these rather as connected transformations. See Johnson, 'The Postmodern Sublime', p. 125ff.
105. An influential modernist, Céline was also a supporter of the Third Reich and the author of notorious anti-Semitic pamphlets. Their republication was opposed and then abandoned in France in 2018. 'Gallimard suspend son projet de réédition des pamphlets antisémites de Céline', *Le Monde*, 11 January 2018, www.lemonde.fr.
106. Kristeva, *Pouvoirs de l'horreur*, p. 186.
107. Ibid., p. 198.
108. Ibid.

Chapter 6

1. Declaration of the Rights of Man, 1789, http://avalon.law.yale.edu/18th_century/rightsof.asp.
2. Read, 'The "Other Scene" of Political Anthropology', pp. 120–1.
3. Balibar, *Equaliberty: Political Essays*, p. 4.
4. Zepke, *Sublime Art*, p. 202.
5. Ibid., p. 231.
6. Rancière, *Dissensus*, p. 46.
7. Ibid., p. 139.
8. *Recognition and Alleviation of Pain in Laboratory Animals*, p. 4.
9. Thomas, 'Does Descartes Deny Consciousness to Animals?', p. 363.
10. Spuybroek, *The Sympathy of Things*, p. 253.
11. Ibid.
12. Nietzsche, *Thus Spoke Zarathustra*, p. 307.
13. Joseph p. Vincenzo offers a comprehensive account of these interdependencies, including discussion of the wider literature and, notably, Heidegger's interpretation of Nietzsche on animals; see Vicenzo, 'Nietzsche's Animal Menagerie', pp. 61–76.
14. Addison, 'On the Wonders of the Deep', in *Addison's Essays from the Spectator*, pp. 459–60.
15. Ibid., p. 461.
16. *Encyclopaedia Britannica*, 'The Spectator, British Periodical 1711–1712', www.britannica.com/topic/The-Spectator-British-periodical-1711-1712.
17. Kant, *Critique of Judgment*, pp. 124–5.
18. Ibid.
19. For popular post-war films about survival and death, combining sublime imagery with moral lessons about Earth and space, we could begin with *2001: A Space Odyssey* (Stanley Kubric, Metro-Goldwyn-Mayer 1968) then *Star Wars* (George Lucas, 20th Century Fox, 1977), the *Star Trek* franchise (for instance, *Star Trek II: The Wrath of Khan*, Nicholas Meyer, Paramount Pictures, 1982) and *The Fifth Element* (Luc Besson, Gaumont Buena Vista International, 1997).
20. Kant, *Critique of Judgment*, pp. 124–5.
21. Eagleton, *The Ideology of the Aesthetic*, p. 172.
22. Sivaperuman et al. (eds), *Deserts: Fauna, Flora, and Environment*, p. viii.

23. Battersby, *The Sublime, Terror and Human Difference*, p. 189.
24. Ibid., p. 156.
25. 'Report of the Special Rapporteur on contemporary forms of racism, racial discrimination, xenophobia and related intolerance', United Nations General Assembly, Seventy-Third Session, 6 August 2018, http://undocs.org/en/A/73/305.
26. Kant, *Observations on the Feeling of the Beautiful and the Sublime*, p. 59.
27. Ibid., p. 50.
28. Ibid., p. 51.
29. Schama, *The Embarrassment of Riches*, p. 575.
30. Eyck, 'The "Subtler" Sublime in Modern Dutch Aesthetics', p. 146.
31. Kant, *Anthropology from a Pragmatic Point of View*, p. 219.
32. Nietzsche, *Dawn*, p. 163.
33. Nietzsche, *Beyond Good and Evil*, pp. 148–9.
34. Kant, *Anthropology from a Pragmatic Point of View*, p. 219.
35. Freeman, *The Feminine Sublime*, p. 3.
36. Ibid., p. 5.
37. Adorno, *Aesthetic Theory*, p. 199.
38. Ibid.
39. Ibid.
40. Ibid.
41. Bourdieu, *La distinction*, p. 578.
42. Ibid.
43. Adorno, *Aesthetic Theory*, p. 199.
44. Armstrong, '"The Effects of Blackness"', p. 214.
45. Burke, *A Philosophical Enquiry*, pp. 141–2.
46. Ibid., p. 148.
47. Lloyd, *Reclaiming Wonder*, p. 203.
48. Ibid., p. 219.
49. Ibid.
50. Ibid., p. 218.

Bibliography

Acharya, Amitav, 'Multilateralism and the Changing World Order', in Thomas G. Weiss and Sam Daws (eds), *The Oxford Handbook on the United Nations*, Oxford: Oxford, University Press, 2018, pp. 781–96.
Adamson, Peter, *Classical Philosophy: A History of Philosophy Without Any Gaps*, Oxford: Oxford University Press, 2014.
Addison, Joseph, *Addison's Essays from the Spectator, with Explanatory Notes*, London: Ward, Lock and Co., 1882.
Adorno, Theodor, *Aesthetic Theory*, trans. Robert Hullot-Kentor, London: Athlone, 1999.
Allison, Tanine, *Destructive Sublime: World War II in American Film and Media*, New Brunswick: Rutgers University Press, 2018.
Amundsen, Julie Rongved, *Performing Ideology: Theatricality and Ideology in Mass Performance*, PhD Thesis, University of Oslo, 2013, at https://julierongvedamundsen.files.wordpress.com/2016/01/avhandling260313.pdf.
Ansell Pearson, Keith, '"Holding on to the Sublime": Nietzsche on Philosophy's Perception and Search for Greatness', in *Nietzsche, Power and Politics: Rethinking Nietzsche's Legacy for Political Thought*, ed. Herman W. Siemans and Vasti Roodt, Berlin: Walter de Gruyter, 2008, pp. 767–800.
Armstrong, Meg, '"The Effects of Blackness": Gender, Race and the Sublime in Aesthetic Theories of Burke and Kant', *The Journal of Aesthetics and Art Criticism*, 54:3 (1996), pp. 213–36.
Balibar, Étienne, *Equaliberty: Political Essays*, Durham NC: Duke University Press, 2014.
Battersby, Christine, *The Sublime, Terror and Human Difference*, London: Routledge, 2007.
Baudrillard, Jean, *The Gulf War Did Not Take Place*, trans. Paul Patton, Sydney: Power Publications, 1995.
Beattie, Owen and John Geiger, *Frozen in Time: The Fate of the Franklin Expedition*, London: Bloomsbury, 1987.
Blakemore, Steven, *Burke and the Fall of Language: The French Revolution as a Linguistic Event*, London: University Press of New England, 1988.
Boileau, *Satires*, Paris: Librairie de la Bibliothèque Nationale, 1884.
Bourdieu, Pierre, *La distinction: critique sociale du jugement*, Paris: Minuit, 1979.
Brady, Emily, *The Sublime in Modern Philosophy: Aesthetics, Ethics and Nature*, Cambridge: Cambridge University Press, 2013.
Breisach, Ernst, *Historiography: Ancient, Medieval and Modern*, 2nd edition, Chicago: University of Chicago Press, 1994.

Burke, Edmund, *A Philosophical Enquiry into the Origin of our Ideas of the Sublime and Beautiful*, London: R. and J. Dodsley, 1757.
Burke, Edmund, *Reflections on the Revolution in France*, London: J. Parsons, 1793.
Burnham, Douglas, *Kant's Philosophies of Judgement*, Edinburgh: Edinburgh University Press, 2004.
Buttler, Rex, *Slavoj Žižek: Live Theory*, London: Continuum, 2005.
Carter, Erica, *Dietrich's Ghosts: The Sublime and the Beautiful in Third Reich Film*, London: British Film Institute, 2004.
Chatzantonis, Yannis, *Deleuze and Mereology: Multiplicity Structure and Composition*, PhD Thesis, University of Dundee, 2010, at https://discovery.dundee.ac.uk/ws/portalfiles/portal/1298074/Chatzantonis_phd_2010.pdf.
Chignell, Andrew and Matthew C. Halteman, 'Religion and the Sublime', in Timothy M. Costelloe (ed.), *The Sublime: From Antiquity to the Present*, Cambridge: Cambridge University Press, 2012, pp. 183–20.
Church, Jeffrey, *Nietzsche's Culture of Humanity: Beyond Aristocracy and Democracy in the Early Period*, Cambridge: Cambridge University Press, 2015.
Cloudsley, Tim, *Shamanism and the Sublime*, Glasgow: Tim Cloudsley, 2000.
Costelloe, Timothy M., 'The Sublime: A Short Introduction to a Long History', in Timothy M. Costelloe (ed.), *The Sublime: From Antiquity to the Present*, Cambridge: Cambridge University Press, 2012, pp. 1–7.
Courtine, Jean-François, Michel Deguy and Jean-François Lyotard, *Du sublime*, Paris: Belin, 2009.
Crowther, Paul, *The Kantian Sublime: From Morality to Art*, Oxford: Clarendon, 1989.
Dannreuther, Roland, 'The Gulf Conflict: A Political and Strategic Analysis', in *The Iran-Iraq War and the First Gulf War*, London: Routledge, 2006, pp. 153–242.
Davis, Natalie Zemon, *The Return of Martin Guerre*, Cambridge MA: Harvard University Press, 1983.
Derrida, Jacques, *La vérité en peinture*, Paris: Flammarion, 1978.
Devetak, Richard, 'The Gothic Scene of International Relations: Ghosts, Monsters, Terror and the Sublime after September 11', *Review of International Studies*, 31:4 (2005), pp. 621–43.
Doran, Robert, *The Theory of the Sublime from Longinus to Kant*, Cambridge: Cambridge University Press, 2015.
Eagleton, Terry, *The Ideology of the Aesthetic*, Oxford: Blackwell, 1990.
Egyed, Bela, 'Spinoza, Schopenhauer and the Standpoint of Affirmation', *Phænex: journal of existential and phenomenological theory and culture*, 2:1 (2007), pp. 110–31.
Elkins, James, 'Against the Sublime', in Roald Hoffmann and Iain Boyd Whyte (eds), *Beyond the Finite: The Sublime in Art and Science*, Oxford: Oxford University Press, 2011, pp. 75–90.
Eyck, John R. J., 'The "Subtler" Sublime in Modern Dutch Aesthetics', in Timothy M. Costelloe (ed.), *The Sublime: From Antiquity to the Present*, Cambridge: Cambridge University Press, 2012, pp. 135–46.
Freeman, Barbara Claire, *The Feminine Sublime*, Berkeley: University of California Press, 1996.
Furniss, Tom, *Edmund Burke's Aesthetic Ideology: Language, Gender, and Political Economy in Revolution*, Cambridge: Cambridge University Press, 1993.
Gardner, Sebastian, *Kant and the Critique of Pure Reason*, London: Routledge, 1999.
Gasché, Rodolph, '. . . And the Beautiful?', in Timothy M. Costelloe (ed.), *The Sublime: From Antiquity to the Present*, Cambridge: Cambridge University Press, 2012, pp. 24–36.
Gibbons, Luke, *Edmund Burke and Ireland: Aesthetics, Politics and the Colonial Sublime*, Cambridge: Cambridge University Press, 2003.
Ginzburg, Carlo, *The Cheese and the Worms*, trans. John Tedeschi and Anne C. Tedeschi, London: Routledge, 1980.

Ginzburg, Carlo, 'Microhistory: Two or Three Things that I Know about It', trans. John Tedeschi and Anne C. Tedeschi, *Critical Inquiry*, 20:1 (1993), pp. 10–35.

Ginzburg, Carlo, *History, Rhetoric and Proof: The Menahem Stern Jerusalem Lectures*, Hanover: Brandeis University Press/Historical Society of Israel, 1999.

Ginzburg, Carlo, *Threads and Traces: True, False, Fictive*, trans. Anne C. Tedeschi and John Tedeschi, Berkeley: University of California Press, 2012.

Godfrey, Tony, 'Was Tàpies a Conceptual Artist After All?', in Àlvaro Rodríguez Fominaya, *Antoni Tàpies: From Object to Sculpture (1964–2009)*, Bilbao: Guggenheim Museum, 2014, pp. 31–8.

Golding, John, *Boccioni: Unique Forms of Continuity in Space*, London: The Tate Gallery, 1985.

Gordon, Michael R., 'The Last War Syndrome: How the United States and Iraq Learned the Wrong Lessons from Desert Storm', in Jeffrey A. Engel (ed.), *Into the Desert: Reflections on the Gulf War*, Oxford: Oxford University Press, 2013, pp. 112–47.

Gorichanaz, Tim, 'Beautiful and Sublime: The Aesthetics of Running in a Commodified World,' *Journal of the Philosophy of Sport*, 43:3 (2016), pp. 365–79.

Gray, Noel, 'Geometry and the Sublime: Imagination and the Closure of Creativity', in David Jarrett (ed.), *The Most Sublime Act: Essays on the Sublime*, London: University of North London Press, 1996, pp. 1–11.

Guyer, Paul, 'The German Sublime After Kant', in Timothy M. Costelloe (ed.), *The Sublime: From Antiquity to the Present*, Cambridge: Cambridge University Press, 2012, pp. 102–17.

Guyer, Paul, 'Introduction', in Edmund Burke, *A Philosophical Enquiry into the Sublime and the Beautiful*, Oxford: Oxford University Press, 2015.

Halverson, Rachel J., *Historiography and Fiction: Sigfried Lenz and the 'Historikerstreit'*, New York: Peter Lang, 1990.

Heath, Malcolm, 'Longinus and the Ancient Sublime', in Timothy M. Costelloe (ed.), *The Sublime: From Antiquity to the Present*, Cambridge: Cambridge University Press, 2012, pp. 11–23.

Hegel, G. W. F., *Aesthetics: Lectures on Fine Art*, trans. T. M. Knox, Oxford: Clarendon, 1975.

Hoerschelmann, Antonia, 'Ways of Worldly Wisdom: The Battle of Hermann', in Antonia Hoerschelmann (ed.), *Anselm Kiefer: The Woodcuts*, Ostfildern: Hatje Cantz Verlag, 2016, pp. 73–4.

Hoffmann, Roald and Iain Boyd Whyte (eds), *Beyond the Finite: The Sublime in Art and Science*, Oxford: Oxford University Press, 2011.

Iggers, George G., 'Foreword', *Historiography: An Annotated Bibliography of Journal Articles, Books, and Dissertations, Volume I*, ed. Susan K. Kinnell, Santa Barbara: ABC-CLIO, 1987.

Jacquette, Dale, *The Philosophy of Schopenhauer*, Chesham: Acumen, 2005.

Janaway, Christopher, *Schopenhauer*, Oxford: Oxford University Press, 1994.

Jarrett, David (ed.), *The Most Sublime Act: Essays on the Sublime*, London: University of North London Press, 1996.

Johnson, David B., 'The Postmodern Sublime', in Timothy M. Costelloe (ed.), *The Sublime: From Antiquity to the Present*, Cambridge: Cambridge University Press, 2012, pp. 118–31.

Johnson, Dirk, *Nietzsche's Anti-Darwinism*, Cambridge: Cambridge University Press, 2010.

Kant, Immanuel, *Critique of Judgment*, trans. Werner S. Pluhar, Cambridge: Hackett, 1987.

Kant, Immanuel, 'An Answer to the Question "What is Enlightenment?"', in *Political Writings*, ed. Hans Reiss, Cambridge: Cambridge University Press, 1991, pp. 54–60.

Kant, Immanuel, 'The Contest of Faculties', in *Political Writings*, ed. Hans Reiss, Cambridge: Cambridge University Press, 1991, pp. 176–90.

Kant, Immanuel, *The Metaphysics of Morals*, in *Political Writings*, ed. Hans Reiss, Cambridge: Cambridge University Press, 1991, pp. 131–75.

Kant, Immanuel, *Anthropology from a Pragmatic Point of View*, trans. Robert B. Louden, Cambridge: Cambridge University Press, 2006.

Kant, Immanuel, *Observations on the Feeling of the Beautiful and the Sublime and other Writings*, Cambridge: Cambridge University Press, 2011.

Kearney, Richard, 'Terror, Philosophy and the Sublime: Some Philosophical Reflections on 11 September,' *Philosophy and Social Criticism*, 29:1 (2003), pp. 23–51.
Kessler, Elizabeth A., *Picturing the Cosmos: Hubble Space Telescope Images and the Astronomical Sublime*, Minneapolis: University of Minnesota Press, 2012.
Kirwan, James, *Sublimity: The Non-Rational and the Irrational in the History of Aesthetics*, London: Routledge, 2005.
Klossowski, Pierre, *Nietzsche and the Vicious Circle*, trans. Daniel W. Smith, London: Athlone, 1997.
Kracauer, Siegfried, *History: The Last Things Before the Last*, New York: Oxford University Press, 1969.
Krichbaum, Jörg, *Albrecht Altdorfer: Meister der Alexanderschlacht*, Cologne: DuMont Buchverlag, 1978.
Kristeva, Julia, *Pouvoirs de l'horreur: essai sur l'abjection*, Paris: Seuil, 1980.
Levine, Joseph M., *Between the Ancients and the Moderns: Baroque Culture in Restoration England*, New Haven: Yale University Press, 1999.
Litman, Théodore A., *Le sublime en France*, Paris: Nizet, 1971.
Lloyd, Genevieve, *Reclaiming Wonder: After the Sublime*, Edinburgh: Edinburgh University Press, 2018.
Lyotard, Jean-François, *L'enthousiasme: la critique kantienne de l'histoire*, Paris: Galilée, 1986.
Lyotard, Jean-François, *The Differend: Phrases in Dispute*, trans. Georges Van Den Abbeele, Manchester: Manchester University Press, 1988.
Lyotard, Jean-François, *Leçons sur l'analytique du sublime*, Paris: Galilée, 1991.
Lyotard, Jean-François, 'The Sublime and the Avant-Garde', in *The Inhuman*, trans. Geoffrey Bennington and Rachel Bowlby, Cambridge: Polity Press, 1991, pp. 89–107.
McLennan, Matthew R., *Philosophy, Sophistry, Antiphilosophy: Badiou's Dispute with Lyotard*, London: Bloomsbury, 2015.
Magnússon, Sigurður Gilfi and István M. Szijártó *What is Microhistory? Theory and Practice*, London: Routledge, 2013.
Martin, Éva Madeleine, 'The "Prehistory" of the Sublime in Early Modern France: An Interdisciplinary Perspective', in Timothy M. Costelloe (ed.), *The Sublime: From Antiquity to the Present*, Cambridge: Cambridge University Press, 2012, pp. 77–101.
Mei, Todd S., *Land and the Given Economy: The Hermeneutics and Phenomenology of Dwelling*, Evanston: Northwestern University Press, 2017.
Mishra, Vijay, *Devotional Poetics and the Indian Sublime*, Albany: SUNY, 1998.
Monk, Samuel H., *The Sublime*, Ann Arbor: University of Michigan Press, 1960.
Morley, Simon, *The Sublime*, Cambridge MA: MIT Press, 2010.
Neill, Alex, 'Schopenhauer on Tragedy and the Sublime', in Bart Vandenabeele (ed.), *A Companion to Schopenhauer*, Oxford: Blackwell, 2012, pp. 206–18.
Newman, Barnett, 'The Sublime is Now', in Simon Morley, *The Sublime*, Cambridge MA: MIT Press, 2010, pp. 25–7.
Nicholls, Moira, 'The Influence of Eastern Thought on Schopenhauer's Doctrine of the Thing in Itself', in Christopher Janaway (ed.), *The Cambridge Companion to Schopenhauer*, Cambridge: Cambridge University Press, 1999, pp. 171–212.
Nietzsche, Friedrich, *Thus Spoke Zarathustra*, trans. R. J. Hollingdale, London: Penguin, 1969.
Nietzsche, Friedrich, 'On the Uses and Disadvantages of History for Life', in *Untimely Meditations*, trans. R. J. Hollingdale, Cambridge: Cambridge University Press, 1983, pp. 57–124.
Nietzsche, Friedrich, *Beyond Good and Evil: Prelude to a Philosophy of the Future*, trans. Judith Norman, Cambridge: Cambridge University Press, 2002.
Nietzsche, Friedrich, *Writings from the Late Notebooks*, ed. Rüdiger Bittner, Cambridge: Cambridge University Press, 2003.
Nietzsche, Friedrich, *Dawn: Thoughts on the Presumptions of Morality*, trans. Brittain Smith, Stanford: Stanford University Press, 2011.
Norris, Christopher, *The Truth about Postmodernism*, Oxford: Blackwell, 1993.

Norris, Christopher, *Reclaiming Truth: Contribution to a Critique of Cultural Relativism*, London: Lawrence and Wishart, 1996.
Nye, David E., *American Technological Sublime*, Cambridge MA: MIT, 1994.
O'Brien, Conor Cruise, *The Suspecting Glance*, London: Faber, 2015.
Pascal, Blaise, *Pensées and other Writings*, trans. Honor Levi, Oxford: Oxford University Press, 1995.
Patton, Paul, 'Introduction', in Jean Baudrillard, *The Gulf War Did Not Take Place*, trans. Paul Patton, Sydney: Power Publications, 1995, pp. 1–22.
Paulson, Ronauld, *Representations of Revolutions (1789–1820)*, New Haven: Yale University Press, 1983.
Penrose, Roland, *Tàpies*, London: Thames and Hudson, 1978.
Petrella, Fausto, 'Mater Materia Prima: Clinical and Critical Remarks', trans. Stephen Sartarelli, in *Boccioni's Materia: A Futurist Masterpiece and the Avant-Garde in Milan and Paris*, New York: Guggenheim Museum, 2004, pp. 55–61.
Rampley, Matthew, *Nietzsche, Aesthetics and Modernity*, Cambridge: Cambridge University Press, 2000.
Rancière, Jacques, *Dissensus: On Politics and Aesthetics*, trans. Steven Corcoran, London: Bloomsbury, 2010.
Rauber, Jochen, 'The United Nations – a Kantian Dream Come True? Philosophical Perspectives on the Constitutional Legitimacy of the World Organisation', *Hanse Law Review*, 5:1 (2009), pp. 49–76.
Ray, Gene, *Terror and the Sublime in Art and Critical Theory: From Auschwitz to Hiroshima to September 11 and Beyond*, New York: Palgrave Macmillan, 2005.
Read, Jason, 'The "Other Scene" of Political Anthropology: Between Transindividuality and Equaliberty', in Warren Montag and Hanan Elsayed (eds), *Balibar and the Citizen Subject*, Edinburgh: Edinburgh University Press, 2017, pp. 111–31.
Recognition and Alleviation of Pain in Laboratory Animals, Washington DC: National Academies Press, 2009.
Rehding, Alexander, *Music and Monumentality: Commemoration and Wonderment in Nineteenth-Century Germany*, Oxford: Oxford University Press, 2009.
Richardson, John, *Nietzsche's New Darwinism*, Oxford: Oxford University Press, 2004.
Ricoeur, Paul, *Time and Narrative, Volume 1*, trans. Kathleen McLaughlin and David Pellauer, Chicago: University of Chicago Press, 1984.
Rutherford, Donald, *Leibniz and the Rational Order of Nature*, Cambridge: Cambridge University Press, 1995.
Ryle, Martin and Kate Soper, *To Relish the Sublime: Culture and Self-Realisation in Postmodern Times*, London: Verso, 2002.
Saltzman, Lisa, 'Reading Anselm Kiefer's Book *Die Himmelspaläste: Merkaba*', in Peter Nisbet (ed.), *Anselm Kiefer, the Heavenly Palaces: Merkaba*, New Haven: Yale University Press, 2003, pp. 13–18.
Santayana, George, *The Life of Reason or the Phases of Human Progress, Volume 1, Reason in Common Sense*, New York: Charles Scribner's Sons, 1920.
Schama, Simon, *The Embarrassment of Riches: An Interpretation of Dutch Culture in the Golden Age*, New York: Alfred A. Knopf, 1988.
Schopenhauer, Arthur, *The World as Will and Representation, Volume I*, trans. E. F. J. Payne, New York: Dover, 1969.
Seward, Anna, *The Poetical Works of Anna Seward with Extracts from her Literary Correspondence*, ed. Walter Scott, Edinburgh: John Ballantyne and Co., 1810.
Seward, Anna, *Letters of Anna Seward, Written between the Years 1784 and 1807*, ed. Walter Scott, Edinburgh: Archibald Constable and Co., 1811.
Seward, Anna, *Anna Seward's Life of Erasmus Darwin*, ed. Philip K. Wilson, Studley: Brewin Books, 2010.
Shapshay, Sandra, 'Schopenhauer's Transformation of the Kantian Sublime', *Kantian Review*, 17:3 (2012), pp. 479–511.

Sivaperuman, C., Grunwaldt, E. G. and Guevara, J. C. (eds), *Deserts: Fauna, Flora, and Environment*, Hauppauge: Nova Science Publishers, 2012.
Sloterdijk, Peter, 'Works and Nights: On Art after Modernism', in Antonia Hoerschelmann (ed.), *Anselm Kiefer: The Woodcuts*, Ostfildern: Hatje Cantz Verlag, 2016, pp. 33–52.
Spuybroek, Lars, *The Sympathy of Things: Ruskin and the Ecology of Design*, London: Bloomsbury, 2016.
Stafford, Fiona J., *The Sublime Savage: A Study of James MacPherson and the Poems of Ossian*, Edinburgh: Edinburgh University Press, 1988.
Suleri, Sara, *The Rhetoric of English India*, Chicago: University of Chicago Press, 1992.
Suzman, James, *Affluence without Abundance: The Disappearing World of the Bushmen*, London: Bloomsbury, 2017.
Tàpies, Antoni, *Tàpies: The Complete Works, Volume 1: 1943–1960*, complied by Anna Agustí, Barcelona: Edicions Polígrafa, 1988.
Tàpies, Antoni, 'The Tattoo and the Body (1997): Conversation with Manuel Borja-Villel', in Youssef Ishaghpour, *Antoni Tàpies: Works, Writings, Interviews*, Barcelona: Ediciones Polígrafa, 2007, pp. 133–50.
Thomas, Janice, 'Does Descartes Deny Consciousness to Animals?', *Ratio* (new series), XIX (2006), pp. 336–63.
Vandenabeele, Bart, *The Sublime in Schopenhauer's Philosophy*, Houndmills: Palgrave Macmillan, 2015.
Vasalou, Sophia, *Schopenhauer and the Aesthetic Standpoint: Philosophy as a Practice of the Sublime*, Cambridge: Cambridge University Press, 2013.
Vicenzo, Joseph P., 'Nietzsche's Animal Menagerie: Lessons in Deep Ecology,' *Mosaic: an Interdisciplinary Critical Journal*, 39:4 (2006), pp. 61–76.
Warnick, Barbara, *Fénelon's Letter to the French Academy*, Lanham MD: University Press of America, 1984.
Williams, James, *A Process Philosophy of Signs*, Edinburgh: Edinburgh University Press, 2016.
Wood, Christopher S., *Albrecht Altdorfer and the Origins of Landscape*, London: Reaktion Books, 1993.
Woodward, Ashley, *Lyotard and the Inhuman Condition: Reflections on Nihilism, Information, and Art*, Edinburgh: Edinburgh University Press, 2016.
Zepke, Stephen, *Sublime Art: Towards an Aesthetics of the Future*, Edinburgh: Edinburgh University Press, 2017.
Žižek, Slavoj, *The Sublime Object of Ideology*, London: Verso, 1989.
Žižek, Slavoj, *Tarrying with the Negative: Kant, Hegel and the Critique of Ideology*, Durham NC: Duke University Press, 1993.
Žižek, Slavoj, *On Belief*, London: Routledge, 2001.
Žižek, Slavoj, *Organs without Bodies: Deleuze and Consequences*, Abingdon: Routledge, 2004.
Žižek, Slavoj, *The Universal Exception*, London: Continuum, 2006.
Žižek, Slavoj, *Interrogating the Real*, London: Bloomsbury, 2013.
Žižek, Slavoj, *Disparities*, London: Bloomsbury, 2016.

Index

Acharya, 119, 126
activity *see* passivity
Adami, 82
Adamson, 10
Addison, 37, 129, 163–4
Adorno, 7, 112, 170–4
Allison, 22
Altdorfer, 17–19
Altman, 33
Amundsen, 76
anarchism, 1, 7, 158, 175, 180
animals, 3, 6, 70, 161–2, 166–7
Ansell Pearson, 62–4, 69–72, 185
Anthropocene, 5
Aristotle, 59, 166
Armstrong, 172
Arnauld, 130
art, 16–19, 42–6, 55, 57, 62–3,
    67–8, 71, 81–2, 101–4, 170–2
Avila, 130

Bacon, 81
Balibar, 158–60
Battersby, 57–8, 167, 170, 183, 185
Baudrillard, 21–2
Bergson, 64
Blake, 50

Blakemore, 113
Boccioni, 29–30
Boileau, 9, 11, 79–80
Bourdieu, 170–1
Brady, 5, 8, 98–107, 162
Breisach, 15
Burke, 1, 10, 37–40, 45, 49–57,
    67–8, 81–2, 99, 112–15, 125,
    127, 149, 172, 174, 180
Burnham, 136
Buttler, 136

Carter, 76
catastrophe, 4, 96–7, 105–6, 120
Céline, 153, 189
Chignell, 12
Church, 68–9
Cloudsley, 184
colonialism, 54
cosmopolitanism, 118–21, 141–2,
    169, 171
Costelloe, 83
Courtine, 84
Crowther, 123

Dante, 37
Darwin, 64

Davis, 21, 33
deception, 44, 46, 80, 104, 107, 120–1, 159, 180
Declaration of the Rights of Man, 155–8
Deguy, 84
Deleuze, 64, 81, 138, 160
delight, 10, 37–8, 49, 53–5, 79–82, 100, 137, 175, 178
democracy, 56, 76, 89–90, 95, 109, 157–8
Derrida, 82–3
Descartes, 64, 161–2
Devetak, 114
diagram, 4, 18, 23, 27, 34, 40–4, 51, 73–5, 90–8, 104–6, 117, 120–1, 130–1, 146–7, 152–3
Doran, 11–12

Eagleton, 166
education, 46, 65, 70, 89, 93–4, 156–7, 166, 171, 174
egalitarianism, 1, 4–6, 11, 14–15, 17, 22, 24, 34–5, 36, 39–40, 45–6, 56, 59–75, 83, 90, 97–8, 104, 114–21, 123, 132–3, 149–53, 155–72
Egyed, 132
Elkins, 39, 185
enlightenment, 54, 66–7, 76, 115, 119, 136
enthusiasm, 58, 76–7, 89, 91, 95, 118, 176, 185
environment *see* nature
ethics, 24, 83, 100–3, 108, 116–17, 123–4, 140–7, 165–6
exclusion, 26–7
Eyck, 168–9

Fénelon, 9
Fish, 166
Franklin, 13

Freeman, 169–70, 183
Freud, 150
Furniss, 113

Gasché, 81
Gerard, 99
Gibbons, 54
Ginzburg, 15–35
Giorgione, 104
Godfrey, 183
Goethe, 47
Golding, 30
Gorichanaz, 72
Goya, 82
Gray, 84
Guyer, 66, 114–15, 184

Halteman, 12
Hartmann, 47
Haydn, 37
Hearst, 88
Hegel, 6, 63, 77, 82, 126, 133, 137–40, 144–5, 175
Heidegger, 49, 82, 189
Historikerstreit, 15–16
history, 3, 8–15, 23, 25–32, 47–8, 56, 59, 62, 85–6
Hoffmann, 83
Holocaust, 16, 146
Hughes, 88
humanity, 3, 5, 28–9, 32–5, 46, 51, 53, 56–7, 61–75, 89, 100, 116–17, 123–4, 177, 179

Iggers, 15
imagination, 4, 18, 38, 62, 78, 92–3, 102–4, 114, 122, 127, 144, 163–5
infinity, 38, 44, 72, 151–2, 164–5
Inuit, 13–14

Jacquette, 129

Janaway, 125
Jarrett, 83
Johnson, 81, 185, 189

Kant, 1, 4–7, 11, 22, 38, 40, 45, 49, 58, 64, 66, 72, 75, 82–4, 95, 98, 100–1, 104, 114–27, 133–4, 136–47, 149–50, 156, 160, 164–72, 178
Kearney, 111–13
Kessler, 92–3, 186
Kiefer, 16
Kinnell, 15
Kirwan, 99
Klossowski, 61
knowledge, 48–50, 52, 64, 72, 125, 129–33, 178
Kracauer, 24, 31
Kristeva, 6, 29, 112, 133, 149–54, 175, 189

La Bruyère, 79–80
Lacan, 77, 137, 139–42, 150, 188
Le Roy Ladurie, 21
Leander, 76
Leibniz, 137
life *see* nature
Litman, 80
Lloyd, 132, 174–6
Locke, 172
Longinus, 9, 11, 79
Lorrain, 55
Lyotard, 49, 81, 84, 103, 118–19, 126, 160

Machiavelli, 50, 144
McLennan, 187
MacPherson, 98–9
McTaggart, 138
Magnússon, 21
manifest destiny, 95–6, 101
Martin, 130–1

Mei, 183
memory, 13, 16, 43, 47, 59–60, 69, 71, 128, 151, 161
method, 4, 14–15, 17, 23–7
microcritique, 23–8, 32–5, 40–2, 173–4
microhistory, 3, 15–17, 23–8, 32–5, 101
Milton, 37
Mishra, 126
Monk, 12, 183
morals *see* ethics
Morley, 83
multiplicity, 2, 17, 27, 29, 33, 73–5, 92, 105, 120, 128, 131, 147, 150, 152, 175, 180

narrative, 20–1, 26–7, 32–3, 59, 112–13
nature, 4, 6, 36–8, 52, 57, 60, 63–5, 67–71, 89, 97, 98–107, 109, 116–17, 120, 123, 128, 162–4
negation, 21–2, 49–50, 72, 109, 130, 134–45, 170–1, 178
Neill, 125
Newman, 42–6, 56
Nietzsche, 1, 5, 36, 46–75, 84, 115, 123, 133, 138, 149–50, 162–3, 167, 169, 174, 185, 189
Norris, 22
Nye, 5, 85–98, 106

object, 2
O'Brien, 50–1

pain, 37–8, 49–50, 53, 79–80, 108–9, 124
Pascal, 130
passivity, 2, 50–1, 55–6, 62, 79, 91, 105, 118, 130–1
Patton, 21

Paulson, 54
Penrose, 183
Perrault, 9
Plato, 63, 123, 133, 138
pleasure *see* pain
politics, 6, 23–4, 37–9, 50–1, 56, 84–5, 93–5, 103, 115–16, 133–4, 146–7, 155–72
postmodernism, 19, 39–40

Rampley, 133
Rancière, 159–60
Rauber, 187
Ray, 87, 110
reason, 13, 47, 53, 65–7, 76–7, 82, 87, 115–19, 120–6, 137, 139–40, 142, 144–5, 159, 163, 166, 170–1, 176
Rehding, 59
Rembrandt, 104
revolution, 37, 51, 56, 113–15, 118, 178
rhetoric, 9, 20, 95, 98, 109, 121, 147–8, 178
Richardson, 64
Ricoeur, 59
Riefenstahl, 58
Rousseau, 168
Ruskin, 127–8, 163
Ryle, 65

Santayana, 12–14
Saussure, 164–5
Schama, 168
Schopenhauer, 1, 6, 47, 63, 121–33, 135, 138, 150, 180
science, 34, 48, 51–3, 68, 72, 77–8
Scott, 36
Seward, 36
Shapshay, 122
sign, 2, 32, 34, 37, 39, 43, 67, 100, 118, 145, 150, 178

Sloterdijk, 16–17
Soper, 65
Spinoza, 132
sport, 37, 55, 71–2
Spuybroek, 127–8, 162–3
Stefansson, 13
sublime
    abject, 6, 29, 149–54
    anarchism, 1
    beautiful, 36, 79, 81–3, 122, 126–8, 140, 178
    Buddhism, 126–7, 130, 133
    classical and modern, 9, 16, 70, 79–80
    contemplation, 37
    cosmos *see* space
    creativity, 37, 51, 53, 56, 60, 62–7, 71–2
    crisis, 177–80
    critique, 11–12, 14, 62, 77–8, 93, 106, 109, 120–1, 148, 152–3
    definition, 1, 8–13, 22, 40–2, 83–4, 86–7, 161–2, 173
    digital, 10–11
    feminine, 36, 153, 167, 170, 174
    gothic, 38, 44, 114, 128
    grandeur, 8, 16, 39, 57, 99, 130, 137, 165, 168, 170–2
    Hinduism, 126–7
    India, 126
    individuals, 46–9, 51–2, 57–68, 71–5, 84–5, 122, 125, 131, 147, 152
    inequality, 1–2, 5
    misery, 6
    nihilism, 3
    propaganda, 7, 16, 19, 58, 76–7, 92
    racism, 7, 45, 92, 167, 172–3

religion, 12, 17, 89, 104, 110, 116–17, 126, 133, 135, 137–9, 144–6
romanticism, 11–12, 55, 87–9, 93, 97, 101
space, 88, 92–4, 186, 189
universality, 1, 56, 83, 115–21, 129, 140, 176
war, 21–2 37–8, 76, 94
Suleri, 54
Suzman, 13–14
sympathy, 50–1, 53–5, 68
Szijártó, 21

Tàpies, 42–3
technology, 1, 5–6, 21–2, 32–3, 53, 72, 77, 85–98, 103, 179
terror, 10, 22, 37, 49, 53–5, 78–80, 81–2, 100, 108–13, 124, 175
terrorism, 110–14
Thomas, 162
time, 33, 47, 58–63, 65–6, 138, 151
eternal return, 56, 61
Titus-Carmel, 82
truth, 3, 12, 19, 21–5, 62, 68, 104, 135, 178
Turner, 55, 164

unconscious, 80–1, 108–10, 112–14, 133
United Nations, 83, 118–19, 187
untimely, 5, 46, 56, 58–62, 65

value, 1–3, 5–6, 9, 23–4, 42, 52–3, 58–63, 67, 72–5, 78–9, 84–6, 108, 122, 135, 153–4, 164, 172–3
Vandenabeele, 131
Vasalou, 131
Vicenzo, 189
Voltaire, 168

Warnick, 9
Whyte, 83
woman, 9, 36, 45, 153–4, 167
wonder, 86, 174–6, 178
Wood, 18
Woodward, 187
Wren, 9

Yeats, 50

Zepke, 103, 159
Žižek, 1, 6, 51, 77, 82, 112, 133–49, 150, 159, 170, 174, 188

EU representative:
Easy Access System Europe
Mustamäe tee 50, 10621 Tallinn, Estonia
Gpsr.requests@easproject.com

www.ingramcontent.com/pod-product-compliance
Lightning Source LLC
Chambersburg PA
CBHW070357240426
43671CB00013BA/2534